Global Governance and the Quest for Justice

Volume IV: Human Rights

This book — one in the four-volume set, Global Governance and the Quest for Justice — focuses on human rights in the context of 'globalisation' together with the principle of 'respect for human rights and human dignity' viewed as one of the foundational commitments of a legitimate scheme of global governance. The first part of the book deals with the ways in which 'globalisation' impacts on established commitments to respect human rights. When human rights are set against, or alongside, potentially competing priorities such as 'security' or 'economy', how well do they fare? Does it make any difference whether human rights commitments are expressed in dedicated free-standing instruments or incorporated as side-constraints (or 'collaterally') in larger multi-functional instruments? In this light, does it make sense to view a trade-centred community such as the EU as a prospective regional model for human rights? The second part of the book debates the coherence of a global order committed to respect for human rights and human dignity as one of its founding principles.

If 'globalisation' aspires to export and spread respect for human rights, the thrust of the papers in this volume is that it could do better, that legitimate global governance demands that it does a great deal better, and that lawyers face a considerable challenge in developing a coherent jurisprudence of fundamental values as the basis for a just global order.

Global Governance and the Quest for Justice

Volume 1: International and Regional Organisations
Edited by Douglas Lewis

Volume 2: Corporate Governance
Edited by Sorcha Macleod and John Parkinson

Volume 3: Civil Society
Edited by Peter O'Dell and Chris Willett

Volume 4: Human Rights
Edited by Roger Brownsword

Global Governance and the Quest for Justice

Volume IV: Human Rights

Edited by

ROGER BROWNSWORD

School of Law, King's College, London
Honorary Professor of Law, University of Sheffield

·HART·
PUBLISHING

OXFORD AND PORTLAND OREGON
2004

Published in North America (US and Canada) by
Hart Publishing
c/o International Specialized Book Services
5804 NE Hassalo Street
Portland, Oregon
97213-3644
USA

Hart Publishing is a specialist legal publisher based in Oxford, England.
To order further copies of this book or to request a list of other
publications please write to:

Hart Publishing, Salters Boatyard, Folly Bridge, Abingdon Rd,
Oxford, OX1 4LB Telephone: +44 (0)1865 245533
Fax: +44 (0)1865 794882
email: mail@hartpub.co.uk
WEBSITE: http//:www.hartpub.co.uk

British Library Cataloguing in Publication Data
Data Available

ISBN 1-84113-409-0 (paperback)

Typeset by Olympus Infotech Pvt Ltd, India, in Palatino 10/12 pt
Printed and bound in Great Britain by
Lightning Source UK Ltd

Preface

Law, as Lon Fuller famously remarked, orders social life by 'subjecting human conduct to the governance of rules';[1] but, as he also remarked, law is not just about *order*, it is about the establishment of a *just* order.[2] Law, formal as well as informal, hard or soft, high or low, purports to set (just) standards and to provide the framework for the (fair) resolution of disputes. Legal rules, of course, are not the only mechanisms for channelling behaviour — market prices, for example, may be as prohibitive as the rules of the criminal code — but it is a truism that it is society's need for effective and legitimate governance that offers the raison d'etre for law.

Fifty years ago, the legal imagination centred on governance within and by the nation state. The municipal legal system was the paradigm; its architecture (especially its division of the public from the private) clean-lined; its organisation hierarchical; its *modus operandi* (even if Austin had over-stated the coercive character of law) largely one of command and control; and its authority unquestioned.[3] Beyond the boundaries of local legal systems, the first seeds of regional and global governance had been sown but it was to be some time before they would begin to flower. If anyone ruled the world, it was the governments of nation states.

Fifty years on, the landscape of legal governance looks very different. To be sure, the municipal legal system remains an important landmark. However, governance within the nation state no longer respects a simple division of the public and the private; in many cases, hierarchical organisation has given way to more complex regulatory networks; each particular regulatory space is characterised by its own distinctive regime of governance and stakeholding; command and control is no longer viewed as the principal regulatory response; and, confronted with various crises of legitimacy, nation states have sought to retain public confidence by aspiring to more responsive forms of governance.[4]

At the same time that local governance has grown more complex and difficult to map, the world beyond the nation state has moved on. Not

[1] LL Fuller, *The Morality of Law* (New Haven, Yale University Press, 1969) at 96.

[2] LL Fuller, 'Positivism and Fidelity to Law — A Reply to Professor Hart' (1957–58) 71 *Harvard Law Review* 630.

[3] HLA Hart, *The Concept of Law* (Oxford, Clarendon Press, 1961).

[4] See, eg, J Black, 'De-centring Regulation: Understanding the Role of Regulation and Self-Regulation in a "Post-Regulatory" World' (2001) 54 *Current Legal Problems* 103; N D Lewis, *Choice and the Legal Order: Rising Above Politics* (London, Butterworths, 1996); P Nonet and P Selznick, *Law and Society in Transition: Toward Responsive Law* (New York, Harper & Row, 1978); and G Teubner, 'Substantive and Reflexive Elements in Modern Law' (1983) 17 *Law and Society Review* 239, and 'After Legal Instrumentalism? Strategic Models of Post-Regulatory Law' in G Teubner (ed), *Dilemmas of Law in the Welfare State* (Berlin, Walter de Gruyter, 1986) 299.

only has regional governance developed rapidly (in Europe, to the point at which a Constitution for the enlarged Union is under debate), but manifold international agencies whose brief is global governance are now operating to regulate fields that are, in some cases, narrow and specialised but, in other cases, broad and general. If mapping municipal law has become more challenging, this applies *a fortiori* to governance at the regional or global level where the regulatory players and processes may be considerably less transparent. Moreover, these zones of governance — the local, the regional, and the global — do not operate independently of one another. Accordingly, any account of governance in the Twenty-First Century must be in some sense an account of global governance because the activities of global regulators impinge on the activities of those who purport to govern in both local and regional zones.

To a considerable extent, global governance has grown alongside the activities of organisations whose predominant concerns have been international security and the promotion of respect for human rights. However, it has been the push towards a globalised economy that has perhaps exerted the greater influence — that is to say, 'globalisation' has served to accelerate both the actuality, and our perception, of global governance. With the lowering of barriers to trade and the making of new markets (traditional as well as electronic), the processes of integration and harmonisation have been set in motion and the governance activities of bodies such as the IMF, the World Bank and the WTO have assumed a much higher profile.[5] If nation states still rule the world, their grip on the reins of governance seems much less secure.[6]

Against this background, *Global Governance and the Quest for Justice* is a four-volume set addressing the legal and ethical deficits associated with the current round of 'globalisation' and discussing the building blocks for modes of global governance that respect the demands of legality and justice. To put this another way, this set explores the tension between the order that is being instated by the governance that comes with globalisation (the reality, as it were, of globalised governance) and the aspiration of a just world order represented by the ideal of global governance.[7]

Each volume focuses on one of four key concerns arising from globalised governance, namely: whether the leading international and regional organisations are sufficiently constitutionalised,[8] whether transnational

[5] See eg, J Stiglitz, *Globalization and its Discontents* (London, Penguin, Allen Lane, 2002). For an account that is less focused on the economy, see B de Sousa Santos, *Toward a New Legal Common Sense* 2nd ed (London, Butterworths, 2002).

[6] Compare the analysis in B Edgeworth, *Law, Modernity, Postmodernity* (Aldershot, Ashgate, 2003). According to Edgeworth, governance in the 'postmodernized' environment is characterised by the decline of the monocentric national legal system.

[7] Compare the central themes of G Monbiot, *The Age of Consent* (London, Flamingo, 2003).

[8] D Lewis (ed), *International and Regional Organisations.* (Oxford, Hart Publishing, forthcoming 2005).

corporations are sufficiently accountable,[9] whether the distinctive interests of civil society are sufficiently represented and respected[10] and whether human rights are given due weight and protection.[11] If the pathology of globalised governance involves a lack of institutional transparency and accountability, the ability of the more powerful players to act outside the rules and to immunise themselves against responsibility, a yawning democratic deficit, and a neglect of human rights, environmental integrity and cultural identity, then this might be a new world order but it falls a long way short of the ideal of global governance.

In the opening years of the twenty-first century, the prospects for legitimate and effective governance — that is to say, for lawful governance — are not overwhelmingly good. Local governance, even in the best-run regimes, has its own problems with regard to the effectiveness and legitimacy of its regulatory measures; regionalisation does not always ease these difficulties; and globalised governance accentuates the contrast between the power of those who are unaccountable and the relative powerlessness of those who are accountable. Yet, in every sense, global governance surely is *the* project for the coming generation of lawyers.[12] If the papers in these volumes set in train a sustained, focused and forward-looking debate about the co-ordination of governance in pursuit of our best conception of an ordered and just global community, then they will have served their purpose — and, if law plays its part in setting the framework for the elaboration and application of such global governance, then its purpose, too, will have been fulfilled.

Roger Brownsword and Douglas Lewis
Sheffield, February 2004

[9] S Macleod and J Parkinson (eds), *Corporate Governance* (Oxford, Hart Publishing, forthcoming 2005).
[10] P Odell and C Willett (eds), *Civil Society* (Oxford, Hart Publishing, forthcoming 2005).
[11] R Brownsword (ed), *Human Rights* (Oxford, Hart Publishing, 2004).
[12] See D Lewis, 'Law and Globalisation: An Opportunity for Europe and its Partners and Their Legal Scholars', (2002) 8 *European Public Law* 219.

Contents

List of Contributors

Elspeth Berry, Senior Lecturer in Law, Nottingham Law School, Nottingham Trent University

Professor Deryck Beyleveld, Law Department, University of Sheffield

Professor Roger Brownsword, School of Law, King's College London, and Honorary Professor of Law, University of Sheffield

Dr Beverley Clucas, School of Law, University of Hull

Professor Scott Davidson, Pro-Vice-Chancellor, University of Canterbury, New Zealand

Dr Duncan French, Law Department, University of Sheffield

Chris Gallavin, School of Law, University of Hull

Michael Head, Senior Lecturer in Law, University of Western Sydney

Professor Sheldon Leader, Law Department, University of Essex

Dr Sabine Michalowski, Law Department, University of Essex

Dr Shaun D Pattinson, Law Department, University of Sheffield

Dr Chandra Sriram, School of International Relations, University of St Andrews

Professor Laura Westra, Professor Emerita, University of Windsor

Andrew Williams, School of Law, University of Warwick

1

Introduction: Global Governance and Human Rights

ROGER BROWNSWORD

EACH YEAR, THOUSANDS of statutory instruments pass into law. In the year 2001, SI No 3644 was one such. This, however, was no routine statutory instrument. For, this was the Human Rights Act 1998 (Designated Derogation) Order in which the Home Secretary announced that provisions in what would become the Anti-Terrorism, Crime and Security Act 2001 would require there to be a derogation from Article 5 of the European Convention on Human Rights (ECHR). In plain English, the Government was to change the law so that persons could be lawfully detained in circumstances that, it openly accepted, might not be fully consistent with respect for the right to liberty and security of the person as enshrined in Article 5 of the ECHR. Or, in even plainer English, the Government proposed to sacrifice the liberty and security of one group of persons (thus far, the 14 or so foreign nationals resident in the United Kingdom so detained)[1] for the sake of the liberty and security of another group of persons (those many millions of persons in the United Kingdom not so detained).

Why should the Government enact such an extraordinary measure? Quite simply, these were no ordinary times. In the wake of the tragic events of September 11, 2001 — the most violent backlash yet against American global influence — the United States and her allies needed to take measures for their own protection. This was an emergency with a capital E; all systems needed to be put on the highest alert. Anyone

[1] Under the 2001 Act, 16 suspects have been detained; two of them were freed to go to countries (France and Morocco) that were prepared to accept them; and 13 have appealed to the Special Immigration Appeals Commission (SIAC), but only one (a Libyan man known simply as M) has been successful. In M's case, SIAC, presided over by Mr Justice Collins, ruled that the evidence did not justify M's detention. On appeal by the Home Secretary, the Court of Appeal, upheld SIAC's ruling: see A Gillan, 'Defeat for Blunkett as Judges Free Detainee' *The Guardian*, March 19, 2004, p 2. And, see note 8 below.

doubting that terrorism was a clear and present danger (a threat both without and within) need only contemplate the rubble that once was the Twin Towers; and, whilst bringing rights home in a more civilised time was all very well, in the troubled world of post 9/11 the exigencies of survival and security took priority.

This particular episode in the local governance of the United Kingdom (like the dramatic detention of large numbers of persons by the United States in Camp Delta at Guantánamo Bay[2]) points to an important issue about the level of commitment to human rights. Whether, at one end of the scale, governments derogate from human rights after the most careful consideration of the arguments (and within a legal framework that expressly permits derogation in exceptional circumstances), or at the other end of the scale, human rights are simply ignored or set aside whenever it is convenient or expedient to do so, the fact is that human rights are displaced — they are not treated as the first priority. In a context of emerging global governance (as the general editors sketch in their Preface) one suspects that, while the pressure to sign up to human rights will increase, the reasons for displacing human rights will become more varied and pressing. Paradoxically, then, the more that governance seems to be committed to human rights, the less it actually is.[3]

These reflections lead directly to the first of two general questions that underlie the contributions to this volume. Indeed, the first question (which is addressed by the papers in the first half of the collection) focuses precisely on the level of respect that is given to human rights when they are in competition with other priorities for governance. This is not simply a matter of whether human rights have any chance when they are in competition with considerations of exceptional emergency (threats to national security and the like) but also of how well they fare when they are woven routinely into the groundrules for global trade. In a world of globalised governance, are human rights destined to take second place?

Taking up this question, Michael Head and Sabine Michalowski critically review the brute displacement of human rights by, respectively, the Australian and the Argentinian governments in the face of recent 'emergencies'. Whereas, broadly speaking, the Australian emergency provisions reflect concerns about security, the measures taken in Argentina were in response to an economic crisis and in compliance

[2] In June 2004, by a 6–3 majority, the US Supreme Court ruled that US domestic courts have jurisdiction to hear challenges to the legality of detention at Guantánamo Bay. See, Julian Borger and Vikram Dodd, 'Supreme Court Blow for Bush on Guantánamo', *The Guardian*, June 29, 2004, p 13.

[3] As would seem to be the case if the provisions of the Anti-Terrorism Crime and Security Act 2001 were to be copied across to cover security threats presented by British *citizens*. See G Peirce, 'This Covert Experiment in Injustice' *The Guardian*, February 4, 2004, p 22.

with the conditions dictated by the IMF. There is a double message to the legal community in these papers: first, that a hard look should be taken at so-called emergencies to ensure that they are not being cited as a pretext by governments minded to increase police power at the expense of civil liberties; and, secondly, that judicial deference to the executive branch should not involve the suspension of legal judgment as to the necessity, proportionality, and unavoidability of whatever exceptional measures are taken.

Sheldon Leader, too, addresses the displacement of human rights. However, he detects and characterises a more subtle displacement in the work of the burgeoning international agencies (particularly those agencies whose function is to promote trade or commerce). 'Collateralism', as Leader terms it, captures a culture that tends towards specialised institutional interests being given a disproportionate weight where decisions calling for a balancing of considerations fall to be made. This is not to say that human rights are not taken seriously by such institutions — far from it, some rights might even be treated as having fundamental importance. However, the effect of policy informed by the collateralist mind-set is that adjustments and balances tend to favour those rights that run with the grain of the institutional goals. What makes this process so insidious is that, from the agency's perspective, it is perfectly natural to be guided by precisely those considerations that give the body its specialised governance function and its distinctive identity.

The focus of the papers by Andrew Williams and Elspeth Deards moves to the European Union. From its modest beginnings as a relatively small trade association, the community has grown into a major articulation of regional governance, cultivating a single market and now seeking to integrate respect for human rights into its (essentially economic) constitutive objects. Will this work? The discussions by Williams and Deards prompt doubts on at least two scores. First, even if the Union is granted an explicit human rights competence as a matter of law, in practice can it succeed in synthesising European commercial imperatives (its traditional mission) with a European culture of human rights? Secondly, so long as the Union treats its larger international function as the representation of *regional* interests, can it do justice to the *universality* of human rights? In both cases, the Union would need to transform its understanding of its distinctive governance role otherwise human rights, if not marginalized, would be vulnerable to collateralism.

These papers are complemented by Laura Westra's powerful caution that we 'collateralise' environmental considerations at our peril. According to Westra, because the integrity of the environment is presupposed by the enjoyment of any kind of human right (including the right to life) and the pursuit of any kind of human activity (including commercial and economic activities), we should treat the right to a sustainable environment as fundamental — if there is to be a war on terror, it should encompass a war on those who would despoil the environment.

The papers by Duncan French and Chris Gallavin offer a bridge into the second half of the collection. They reflect on the distance between international aspiration and international *realpolitik*, between the idealistic rhetoric of the many declarations on matters of social welfare adopted by the international community and the actual agenda of signatories, and between the retributive victim-orientated purity of the framework set out in the Rome Statute founding the International Criminal Court and the realities of international politics. For French, the lesson is that, in act and deed, international governance must start to match its fine words — the real must start to live up to the ideal; while, for Gallavin, the lesson is that, in an imperfect world, some degree of flexibility is required if things are to move forward — the ideal must at least be situated within the real.

In contrast with a setting of globalised governance, where human rights are in competition with a range of rival governance imperatives and where the commitment of governments to human rights is less than complete, imagine a more congenial setting. Imagine that global governance enjoyed the luxury of a one-dimensional concern with respect for human rights and the justice of the global order. Imagine, in other words, that governance was guided exclusively by moral reason. Under such improved conditions, how straightforward would it be to advance the project of *just* global governance? This is the second of the two general questions that inform the contributions to this volume.

Clearly, other things being equal, the prospects of just governance are better where it is accepted that the guiding principle is that the 'moral' thing should be done. However, in a global context of competing moral viewpoints, the essays in the second part of the collection highlight that competing moral views can be almost as problematic as competition between moral and non-moral priorities.

Sometimes, we seem to start in much the same place, but we understand our commitments in rather different ways. Thus, as Bev Clucas and Scott Davidson demonstrate, the problem can be that particular human rights, even rights (such as the right to life) that are agreed to be fundamental or axiomatic, are interpreted by different judges in different contexts in different ways; similarly, the various ways in which judicial interpreters respond to clear gaps and omissions in human rights regimes reflect important differences of adjudicative ideology.

Sometimes, the problem runs deeper. For, as Chandra Sriram highlights in her paper, we do not always start in the same place. So, for instance, even if it is agreed that a human rights atrocity has occurred and that there needs to be a legal response, there may be very different views — generated by radically competing conceptions of international criminal justice — as to who should respond, as to where the response should be (whether the court or commission should be internal or external), and as to the nature of the response (echoing Gallavin, is retributivism or regeneration, recrimination or reconciliation the appropriate objective?).

Still in the deep waters of moral pluralism, Deryck Beyleveld and Shaun Pattinson reflect on the fundamentally different viewpoints in Europe concerning the moral status (and dignity) of the human embryo, views that have generated a patchwork of local regulatory positions with regard to the use of human embryos for research and that have recently frustrated the articulation of an agreed regional position covering stem cell research. Famously, similar differences almost blocked the adoption of Directive 98/44/EC on the Legal Protection of Biotechnological Inventions (where the focal concern was the patentability of human gene sequences) — and, no doubt, if it were to be proposed that a common position should be agreed in Europe with regard to the regulation of abortion, the same value disagreements would be rehearsed; and regulators would find themselves in the same deep water. Nevertheless, as Beyleveld and Pattinson observe, the currents of globalisation tend to flow towards more permissive positions making it difficult for the more restrictive regimes to hold their lines or, at any rate, to sustain a practice that is fully consistent with declared principle.

Finally, in closing the volume, my own paper points to the development of new technology as another shifting feature of the global context that sets the frame for the aspiration to just governance. If we agree that the benefits of such technologies should be exploited provided that this is consistent with respect for human rights and human dignity, regulators face the kind of interpretive challenges indicated by fellow contributors in this second part of the book; human rights and, especially, human dignity cover a multitude of moral differences. Moreover, reverting to the themes of the first part of the book, if regulators find that they are unable to secure regimes of governance that are either just or effective, we might find a wholesale turn to technology as an instrument of regulation. In which case, in addition to renewed concerns for the prospects of human rights, the spread of technology-reliant governance will concentrate the mind on the meaning of human dignity.

If 'globalisation' aspires to export and spread respect for human rights, the thrust of the papers in this volume is that it could do better, that legitimate global governance demands that it does a great deal better, that lawyers face a considerable challenge in developing a coherent jurisprudence of fundamental values as the basis for a just global order and that, as ever, the tension between effective governance and legitimate governance — between mere order and *just* order — threatens to frustrate our best efforts.

Should we, then, look forward to the coming century of governance with confidence and in a spirit of optimism? Writing (pre 9/11) in the

Millennium year, Anne-Marie Slaughter aptly remarked that '[t]he compression of distance and the dissolution of borders that drives globalization has proved far more efficient at producing global markets than global justice.'[4] Nevertheless, she saw encouraging signs in the willingness of national judges to learn from the human rights expertise available worldwide. Post 9/11 should we be so sanguine? Are things destined to improve? Will the inadequate world of globalised governance yield to more adequate regimes of legitimate global governance?

In the short run, we can surely expect no dramatic transformation. The global context in which local governance now self-consciously operates makes it too easy for the pursuit of sectional interest to be wrapped up in the rhetoric of the public interest — the pressures of 'globalisation' are too easily a pretext or an excuse for weak governance.[5] Moreover, the cause of global governance is not assisted if those who most loudly proclaim the virtues of human rights and the Rule of Law feel able to opt out when they perceive the circumstances as so demanding. As Helena Kennedy has recently written:

> The nature of a government's response to terrorism within its borders will depend on the type of violence, its history and roots, its seriousness, the extent to which it has community support and the effect on the international community's respect for human rights. Sensitive political judgements have to be made. The way in which mature legal systems deal with subversion or attack has global implications: toleration of infringements of civil liberties gives poor signals to those nations which are struggling to establish democracies. It also gives succour to tyrants who have little interest in the rule of law or the pursuit of justice.[6]

In this light, and specifically with reference to the detention policies adopted on both sides of the Atlantic post 9/11, those who allege that 'the example being set by the US and the UK is being used to legitimise repression internationally on an ever-increasing scale'[7] would seem to have a point.

In the medium term, the attempt to harmonise commercial and cultural values in an enlarged European zone of regional governance, like the attempts to invest trade agencies with missions that incorporate human rights, will tell us whether it is possible for human rights to be seamlessly integrated in this way. It may be that we come to understand that respect

[4] A M Slaughter, 'Judicial Globalization' (2000) 40 *Virginia Journal of International Law* 1103, at 1103.
[5] See, eg, Jim Wurst, 'Counterterrorism to Blame for Erosion of Rights, Expert Says' UN Wire <http://www.ishr.ch> (January 11, 2004).
[6] H Kennedy, *Just Law* (London, Chatto and Windus, 2004) at 61.
[7] L Christian, 'Guantánamo Bay: A Global Experiment in Inhumanity' *The Guardian*, January 10, 2004, p 24 — concerns echoed, too, by the Joint Committee on Human Rights; see Alan Travis, 'Blunkett Faces Revolt on Internment', *The Guardian*, August 5, 2004, p 5.

for human rights will never be effectively achieved by 'bolt-ons' or 'balances' or by way of 'side-constraints' or similar mechanisms. To counteract collateralism, perhaps we must follow the example of Article 1 of the Basic Law in Germany and make human rights and human dignity the most fundamental values, our first and paramount legal priorities, in any constitution of governance.

In the longer run, the sustainability of the environment will be a cause for continuing concern; and, whilst technology will serve to lower the barriers to communication, it will also offer opportunities for the powerful to enhance their positions and increase the gap between the 'haves' and the 'have-nots' in the global village. If there is to be any prospect of legitimate global governance, lawyers have a special responsibility to place themselves in the vanguard of the quest for justice. It is not enough to argue against lawlessness, nor even to encourage dialogue that builds on a shared sense of justice while seeking to address fundamental differences of value; and neither is it enough to accept paper commitments to human rights. Just order, to be sure, is a tall order. However, if (legitimate) global governance is to have any chance in the twenty-first century, the commitment to human rights must be real, the vision of a just order clear, and the resolution of the legal community unshakeable.[8]

[8] As we go to press, challenges both to the legality of SI 2001/3644 and to a number of certificates issued under the 2001 Act have been raised and largely rejected. In *A & Others v Secretary of State for the Home Department* [2004] QB 335, the Court of Appeal held that derogation was lawful; but the decision is under appeal to the House of Lords. And, in *A & Others v Secretary of State for the Home Department* [2004] EWCA Civ 1123, the Court (by a majority) ruled that, where the Secretary of State certifies that he reasonably believes that a person's presence in the UK is a risk to national security and that he reasonably suspects that the said person is a terrorist (or, similarly, where SIAC so holds), then such an assessment is not invalidated by dint of reliance on evidence that has been obtained by torture — at any rate, provided that UK agents are not responsible for such acts or complicit in their commission. Neuberger LJ's dissent (leaning heavily on the fair trial requirement in Article 6 of the ECHR) takes a stronger stand against abuse of process and in support of the Rule of Law; however, the reality is captured better by Laws LJ's concluding remarks to the effect that, while the reconciliation of competing constitutional fundamentals may not have been perfect, there is no reason to think that the government 'has at all lost sight of those constitutional principles which it is the court's special duty to protect: the rule of law and the avoidance of arbitrary power' (at para 282).

Part I: Competing Priorities — Are Human Rights Destined to be Second-Best?

2

The Global 'War on Terrorism': Democratic Rights Under Attack

MICHAEL HEAD*

INTRODUCTION

ONE OF THE most striking challenges for global governance in the 21st century is the protection of democratic rights. In the opening years of the new century, numbers of governments have used the threat of terrorism as a pretext to erode such vital principles as free speech, freedom of political association, prevention of arbitrary detention, and the right to seek asylum.

In Australia (and there are parallels elsewhere, notably in the United States and Britain), the dawn of the century saw three fundamental shifts in the state machinery — legislation in 2000 to permit the calling out of the military against civilian unrest; in 2001 to authorise the forcible turning away of refugee boats; and in 2002 to grant detention and proscription powers, as well as expanded surveillance powers, to the government and its security and intelligence agencies. These measures have profound implications for civil liberties, as well as for the future of international covenants, such as the Refugee Convention and the International Covenant on Civil and Political Rights (ICCPR). These global human rights instruments have proved largely irrelevant in curbing such powers.

The Howard government in Australia followed the lead of the Bush administration in the United States and the Blair government in Britain by declaring that the 11 September 2001 terrorist attacks in the United States required an indefinite 'war' against terrorism abroad, accompanied by curtailment of legal rights at home. Despite criticisms by civil liberties groups, both the British and American governments introduced severe

*This chapter was written while the author was Visiting Professor, Osgoode Hall Law School, York University, Toronto.

anti-terrorism measures, including detention without trial and proscription of organisations.[1] Amnesty International condemned the Bush administration for breaching the ICCPR and other international protocols against arbitrary detention and inhuman treatment of prisoners.[2]

Significantly, the first two sets of Australian legislation pre-dated September 11, indicating that the anti-democratic trend is more fundamental than a response to the events in New York and Washington. Rather, these atrocities, and later the Bali bombing of 12 October 2002, were seized upon retrospectively to justify, as well as to introduce new, far-reaching alterations to the legal and constitutional framework.

These political and legal shifts, as this chapter will review, are profoundly anti-democratic. They were not the result of any popular demand for such measures; on the contrary, each legislative package aroused considerable public opposition. The purpose of their introduction is to strengthen the repressive capacities of the state against the free movement of people and other perceived threats to the political establishment. This chapter will suggest that these legislative responses highlight essential contradictions of the increasing globalisation of economic and political life.

THE MILITARY CALL-OUT LEGISLATION

Amid considerable public controversy, the Australian Labor Party combined with the Government of Prime Minister John Howard to pass military call-out legislation through both houses of the Commonwealth Parliament in September 2000. Both the Government and the Opposition declared that it was necessary to have the legislation in place before the Sydney Olympic Games. In the brief parliamentary debate, references were made to the need to counter possible terrorism at the Olympics, where some 4000 military personnel were deployed.[3] After expedited examinations by two Senate committees, whose recommendations for minor amendments were partially adopted,[4] the legislation was ultimately

[1] For a comparison of the US and British legislation, see N Hancock, *Terrorism and the Law in Australia: Supporting Materials* (Canberra, Parliament of Australia, Department of Parliamentary Library, Research Paper No. 13 2001–2002) 2–8.

[2] *Amnesty International's concerns regarding post September 11 detentions in the USA*, Amnesty International March 2002.

[3] M Head, 'Olympic Security: Police and military plans for the Sydney Olympics — a cause for concern' (2000) 25 *Alternative Law Journal* 131.

[4] Senate Foreign Affairs, Defence and Trade Legislation Committee, Defence Legislation Amendment (Aid to Civilian Authorities) Bill 2000 (2000) The Parliament of the Commonwealth of Australia, <http://www.aph.gov.au/senate/committee/submissions/fadt_civbill.htm> (16 August 2000); and Senate Standing Committee for the Scrutiny of Bills, *Alert Digest No 10 of 2000*.

passed on the last day of sitting before the opening of the Games. Despite this haste, the Act was not invoked during the Olympics.[5] This suggests that Olympics merely provided a pretext for the legislation, which in fact has more underlying purposes.

Under the amended *Defence Act 1903*, the Federal Government has the power to call out the armed forces on domestic soil against perceived threats to 'Commonwealth interests', with or without the agreement of a state government. Once deployed, military officers can order troops to open fire on civilians, as long as they determine that it is reasonably necessary to prevent death or serious injury. Soldiers will have greater powers than the police in some circumstances, including the right to shoot to kill someone escaping detention, search premises without warrants, detain people without formally arresting them, seal off areas and issue general orders to civilians.[6]

The legislation authorises the Prime Minister, the Defence Minister and the Attorney-General, or 'for reasons of urgency', one of these 'authorising ministers', to advise the Governor-General (the Commander-in-Chief of the armed forces under the Australian Constitution) to call out military personnel to deal with 'domestic violence'. The term 'domestic violence' does not correspond to the modern sense of the phrase, which refers to violence within homes or families. It is a vague expression, undefined legislatively or judicially, found in section 119 of the Australian Constitution, which provides that 'the Commonwealth shall protect every State against invasion and, on the application of the Executive Government of the State protect such State against domestic violence'. Unlike section 119, however, the new provisions do not require any invitation from a State government before troops are called out.

Both the Government and the Labor Party proposed limited amendments in an effort to meet certain objections from some State governments and to head off public concern about the impact on civil liberties, but the legislation's essential content remained the same: to authorise the use of the military to deal with civilian disturbances, including political and industrial unrest. The fact that such legislation was passed suggests a bipartisan expectation in official political circles that, in the coming period, troops will be required to deal with disturbances that the police forces cannot contain.

[5] It has since been revealed, however, that elite SAS personnel were deployed undercover in plain clothes, assisting the New South Wales police to monitor crowds during the Olympics, without approval by the Defence Minister or Federal Cabinet. Cabinet's National Security Committee subsequently approved the deployment, without any reference to the Act. See *The Sydney Morning Herald*, 9 February 2001, 6.
[6] Section 51.

Historical Context

For more than 100 years, the domestic deployment of troops has been politically contentious and clouded by legal uncertainties. In the words of one author, although Australia was established as a penal colony under military administration, 'with the passage of time, the evolution of the Australian political system ensured a clear distinction between military powers and civil powers'.[7] During the 19th century, martial law was declared several times to deal with riots and rebellions, but the last clear exception to the military-civil division of power occurred in 1891 when the Queensland Government used troops to help the police suppress a sheep shearers' strike.[8]

This division of power was enshrined in the Australian Constitution at Federation in 1901. The military power was handed to the Commonwealth under section 51(xxxi), the colonial defence forces were transferred to the Commonwealth by section 69, and under section 114 the States were forbidden to raise military or naval forces without the consent of the Commonwealth Parliament. Residual authority over domestic law and order remained in the hands of the States and their police forces.

The constitutional demarcation became embedded in public consciousness. Domestic use of the armed forces was widely regarded as conduct to be expected of a military or autocratic regime, not a democratic government. On the only occasion since Federation that a Commonwealth government called out the military in an urban situation — following a bomb blast outside a regional Commonwealth Heads of Government meeting at the Sydney Hilton Hotel in 1978 — the sight of armed soldiers patrolling highways and the streets of the New South Wales town of Bowral caused public consternation.[9]

The legislation challenges a political and legal tradition opposing the use of the military to suppress domestic unrest — a principle that dates back to the 17th-century struggles against the absolutist monarchy in Britain. In the lead up to the English revolution of the 1640s, the 1628 *Petition of Right* demanded that Charles I remove the 'great companies of soldiers and mariners [who] have been dispersed into diverse counties of the realm … against the laws and customs of this realm and to the great grievance and vexation of the people'. The *Petition* is regarded as making it unconstitutional for the Crown to impose martial law on civilians.[10] As a result of the 1688 settlement between the monarchy and the parliament,

[7] C Doogan, 'Defence Powers Under the Constitution: Use of Troops in Aid of State Police Forces — Suppression of Terrorist Activities' (1981) 31 *Defence Force Journal* 31.
[8] *Ibid*.
[9] T Molomby, *Spies, Bombs and the Path of Bliss* (Sydney, Potoroo Press, 1986), and J Hocking, *Beyond Terrorism: The Development of the Australian Security State* (Sydney, Allen & Unwin, 1993).
[10] W S Holdsworth, 'Martial Law Historically Considered' (1902) 18 *Law Quarterly Review* 117.

the Bill of Rights declared it illegal for the Crown to raise or keep an army without parliamentary consent.[11]

By the early 19th century, the emergence of mass protests fuelled by the conditions of the Industrial Revolution caused the British authorities to resort to military suppression at times. In the 1832 case of *R v Pinney*[12] three officers were tried before a Grand Jury after riots in Bristol. Two officers who had refused to order the troops to fire without a magistrate's sanction were found guilty of neglect of duty, causing one to commit suicide. The third officer, who had fatally shot someone during the incident, was acquitted of manslaughter.

Notwithstanding the *Petition of Right*, British law was also prepared to support the imposition of martial law if civil unrest threatened the existence of the state. According to Halsbury, martial law applies 'when a state of actual war, or of insurrection, riot, or rebellion amounting to war, exists'.[13] Martial law has been somewhat loosely described as 'the right to use force against force within the realm in order to suppress civil disorder'.[14]

Doubt exists as to the legal basis of martial law. It is said to be either an example of a common law right to employ force to repel force or, alternatively, a royal prerogative.[15] Despite this fundamental uncertainty, the Privy Council in the 1902 *Marais* case, an appeal from the Cape Colony, extended the doctrine of martial law to apply even where the ordinary civilian courts were still sitting.[16]

There has been no recorded case of martial law in Australia since Federation in 1901 but it was invoked several times during the 19th century to suppress convicts, Aborigines and workers.[17] The strike struggles of the 1890s saw troops mobilised against specific demonstrations and gatherings, with orders to shoot to kill strikers and their supporters. In one infamous incident, Colonel Tom Price issued the following instruction to a volunteer unit during the extended Australian maritime strike of 1890:

> [I]f the order is given to fire, don't let me see any rifle pointed in the air; fire low and lay them out so that the duty will not have to be performed again.[18]

[11] S Greer, 'Military Intervention in Civil Disturbances: The Legal Basis Reconsidered' [1983] *Public Law* 573.
[12] (1832) in St Tr (1891), N S Vol 3; 5 C & P 254.
[13] Lord Hailsham (ed), *Halsbury's Laws of England* (4th ed, 1973–), vol 8(2), para 821.
[14] R Heuston, *Essays in Constitutional Law* (2nd ed, 1964) 152.
[15] *Halsbury's Laws of England*, above n 13, para 821.
[16] *D F Marais v The General Officer Commanding the Lines of Communication and the Attorney-General of the Colony* [1902] AC 109.
[17] S D Lendrum, 'The "Corrong Massacre": Martial Law and the Aborigines at First Settlement' (1977) 6 *Adelaide Law Review* 26. See also Victor Windeyer, 'Certain Questions Concerning the Position of Members of the Defence Force When Called Out to Aid the Civil Power' in Robert Hope, *Protective Security Review Report* (Canberra, AGPS, 1979) Appendix 9.
[18] Quoted in B McKinlay, *A Documentary History of the Australian Labor Movement, 1850–1975* (Melbourne, Drummond Publishing, 1979) 377. Such instructions — to 'fire low and lay

The turmoil of the 1890s led to s 119 being inserted in the Constitution, to allow the military to be mobilised against an 'uncontrollable situation'.[19] The expression 'domestic violence' was borrowed from Article IV of the United States Constitution, s 4 of which specifies that the United States shall protect each State, on the application of its legislature, against 'domestic violence'. The statutory embodiment of this provision in 10 USC §331 (1964) uses the more specific term 'insurrection', suggesting that an extremely serious level of rebellion must be involved — one that threatens the very existence of a State government.[20]

In the early years of the 20th century, Australian State governments requested military intervention on at least six occasions, to deal with such anticipated incidents as 'general strike riot and bloodshed', 'disturbances', wharf strike 'violence', 'labour troubles' and the 1923 Victorian police strike. On each occasion, it seems, the Federal Government declined on the basis that the State police were capable of dealing with the threat (although troops were sent to guard Federal buildings, including post offices, during the Victorian police strike).[21] Only one of those requests — by Queensland in 1912 — was formally made under s 119. Thus, s 119 has never been applied.

The Legislation

Once deployed under the amended Defence Act, the military forces will have wide-ranging powers that they currently do not have in civilian situations. The most revealing measures are those contained in s 51T on the use of 'reasonable and necessary force'. Soldiers will be permitted to cause death or grievous bodily harm where they believe 'on reasonable grounds' that such action is necessary to protect the life of, or prevent serious injury to, another person — including the soldiers involved. A person 'attempting to escape being detained by fleeing' may be killed or caused grievous bodily harm if they have been called on to surrender and a soldier believes on reasonable grounds that the person cannot be apprehended in any other way.

them out' — are still mirrored in the Australian Military Regulations. Regulation 421(6) specifies that: 'Care shall be taken to fire only upon those who can be seen to be implicated in the disturbance'. H P Lee, *Emergency Powers* (Sydney, Law Book Co, 1984) 242. Regulation 410 requires the commander of the forces to warn those present that, if the troops are ordered to fire, the fire will be effective. *Call Out the Troops: an examination of the legal basis for Australian Defence Force involvement in 'non-defence' matters* (Canberra, Australian Parliamentary Research Paper 8, 1997–98) 5.

[19] A R Blackshield, 'The Siege of Bowral — The Legal Issues' (1978) 4 *Pacific Reporter* 6.
[20] See generally M Cherif Bassiouni, *The Law of Dissent and Riots* (Illinois, Charles C Thomas, 1971).
[21] Lee, above n 18, 201.

Confronted by public hostility to its earlier unconditional endorsement of the Act, the Labor Party moved an amendment forbidding troops to 'stop or restrict any protest, dissent, assembly or industrial action, except where there is a reasonable likelihood of the death of, or serious injury to, persons'. The Government added a final clause 'or serious damage to property', which Labor accepted. The resulting section 51G opens the way for wide use of the call-out power. Likelihood of property damage can be alleged easily. As Independent MP Peter Andren put it, 'a rock thrown through the front door of the Crown Casino [the venue of the 2000 World Economic Forum in Melbourne] could give rise to such a call-out'.[22] As for the likelihood of injury, that could be created by a police attack on demonstrators.

Doubts remain about the constitutional validity of the provisions, notwithstanding the fact that a number of authorities have taken a generous view of the Commonwealth's powers to call-out the military.[23]

It is clear that the implications of the legislation go far beyond the Sydney Olympics. The Government and the Opposition rejected amendments to insert a sunset clause that would revoke the legislation after the Games. In the words of shadow attorney-general Robert McClelland: 'These measures should not be seen as simply a short-term measure that can be sunsetted after the Olympics. They are in themselves important measures that are certainly required'.[24]

One can only conclude that the Act has given effect to a permanent shift in the military's role. Australia's constitutional and legal framework has been altered to allow for military intervention to deal with any potentially destabilising internal unrest or political dissent.

THE *TAMPA* CASE AND THE 1951 REFUGEE CONVENTION

The strains produced by globalisation can be seen clearly in the crisis that has developed in the existing international system for dealing with refugees. According to the available statistics, the flight of people from their countries of birth grew dramatically in the final two decades of the 20th Century and this mass movement is likely to grow in the 21st.[25] In many cases, they are resorting to unauthorised methods of entry, often at great risk to their lives.

[22] Commonwealth, *Parliamentary Debates*, House of Representatives, 7 September 2000, 18447.
[23] M Head, 'The Military Call-Out Legislation — Some Legal and Constitutional Questions' (2001) 29 *Federal Law Review* 1.
[24] Commonwealth, *Parliamentary Debates*, House of Representatives, 28 June 2000, 18420.
[25] S Castles and M J Miller, *The Age of Migration: International Population Movement in the Modern World* (London, Macmillan, 1993) 5–8.

Despite implementing increasingly draconian measures, governments are having considerable difficulties, logistically, diplomatically and politically, in removing those denied refugee status.[26] Governments are spending mounting sums on detecting and detaining unwanted arrivals, deciding their fate and administering the outcomes, while giving decreasing funds to the UNHCR, which is responsible for most of the world's displaced persons.[27]

More fundamentally, the increased demand for asylum has occurred amid an unprecedented globalisation of the world economy since the mid-1980s, creating massive flows of international capital, the rapid shift of production processes from country to country, and a worldwide labour market.[28] At the same time, the ever-widening gulf between the capital-rich, technologically advanced and militarily powerful countries and the rest of the world has fuelled the demand for the right to escape poverty.[29] According to the 1998 United Nations World Development Report, the three richest people in the world have assets exceeding the combined Gross Domestic Product of the 48 least developed countries, the 15 richest people have assets worth more than the total GDP of sub-Saharan Africa and the 32 richest more assets than the GDP of South Asia. The wealth of the richest 84 individuals exceeds the GDP of China with its 1.2 billion inhabitants. In 1997, the richest one fifth of the world's population received 86 percent of world income, with the poorest fifth receiving just 1.3 percent. More than 1.3 billion people are forced to subsist on less than $1 per day, a life-threatening situation.[30]

Ultimately, the efforts of national governments to restrain the global movement of people are akin to King Canute trying to hold back the tides. Whether governments like it or not, there is a growing trend for millions of people to live outside their countries of birth, with or without official status. As a senior Canadian immigration official has observed:

> Almost all parts of the world are witnessing major migratory movements. While in 1965, 65 million people were living long term outside their countries of normal residence, by 1990 there were 130 million and in 2000 an estimated 150 million. Some are persons with legal status in their adopted countries. Most are in an irregular situation and try by various means to regularise their status.[31]

[26] G Van Kessel, 'Global migration and asylum', (2001) 10 *Forced Migration Review* 10 at 11.
[27] J Telford, 'UNHCR and emergencies: a new role or back to basics?' (2001) 10 *Forced Migration Review* 42.
[28] International Committee of the Fourth International, *Globalization and the International Working Class: A Marxist Assessment* (Sydney, Mehring Books, 1999). See also Castles and Miller, above n 25.
[29] A Zolberg, 'International Migrants and Refugees in Historical Perspective', (1992–1993) *Refugees* 36–42.
[30] *United Nations World Development Report 1998* (Geneva, 1998).
[31] Van Kessel, above n 26 at 10. Van Kessel is the Director General, Refugees Branch, Department of Citizenship and Immigration Canada.

While embracing the global restructuring of economic life, opening their borders to the movement of investment funds, many Western governments have sought to erect new barriers to the movement of ordinary working people. British writer Harding has observed that 'for a growing list of governments the best interpretation of the Convention Relating to the Status of Refugees can only be to run it through the shredder'.[32]

In Australia, successive governments during the 1990s have taken the policy of seeking to block and deter unwanted arrivals to its logical end by compulsorily detaining asylum seekers, usually in remote, inhospitable semi-desert locations, and, since August 2001, by militarily barring entry to refugees. Severe police and security methods, including the use of mass arrests, water cannon, tear gas and solitary confinement, have failed to quell the unrest in the camps, expressed in hunger strikes, mass breakouts and determined protests, and this has fuelled concerns that damage is being done to Australia's international reputation.[33]

In late August 2001, the Australian government deployed SAS troops to prevent the asylum seekers rescued by the Norwegian container ship, the *MV Tampa*, from landing in a safe harbour at Australia's Christmas Island. The soldiers detained the rescuees on the ship's deck and ultimately transferred them to the *HMAS Manoora*, a naval troop carrier, for transportation to far-distant Nauru. The government was aware that it probably lacked any lawful power to do so. It tried to rush retrospective legislation — the Border Protection Bill 2001 — through parliament to authorise its actions, but the Bill was initially defeated in the Senate. The apparent purpose of the SAS operation was to evade the Migration Act 1958, which requires government officers to detain all 'unlawful' arrivals. Under the 1999 'border protection' amendments to the Act, military officers who board refugee vessels, even on the high seas, are obliged to bring the people on board ashore, to be placed in detention.[34]

On the Federal cabinet's instructions, steps were taken to ensure that the *Tampa* rescuees could not contact lawyers to challenge the legality of the government's conduct or seek their release from the ship. The government was determined to prevent them from applying for refugee status and protection visas.

According to the agreed facts in the case:

> The ship has been forbidden by Australian authorities from proceeding any closer to Christmas Island and from entering the port ... The effect of the continuing presence of the SAS officers is that the captain and crew are

[32] J Harding, *The Uninvited: Refugees at the Rich Man's Gate* (London, Profile Books, 2000).
[33] P Mares, *Borderline: Australia's treatment of refugees and asylum seekers* (Sydney, University of New South Wales Press, 2001).
[34] Migration Act 1958 (Cth) ss 189, 245.

> unlikely to attempt to move the ship into the port. This is a consequence desired by the Australian government…
>
> The evidence justifies an inference that many of the rescuees would, if entitled, wish to apply for protection visas, and would wish to leave the ship and enter Australia. The rescuees have no access to communications with persons off the ship and persons off the ship are unable to communicate with them.[35]

Federal Court Justice Tony North ruled that the refugees had been illegally detained. In his judgment, the government had determined 'at the highest level' to 'use an unlawful process to detain and expel the rescuees'. It had breached one of the most basic legal principles, dating back hundreds of years, that no person, whether a citizen or non-citizen, can be held in detention arbitrarily. In granting a writ of *habeas corpus* for the immediate release of the refugees, he declared: 'An ancient power of the Court is to protect people against detention without lawful authority.'[36]

Despite this ruling, the government continued on its course, having obtained an agreement from the lawyers challenging its actions that it would return the rescuees to Australia if it lost an appeal to the Full Federal Court. The refugees were shipped thousands of kilometres away to Nauru. En route, the government crammed 237 more refugees, seized off Ashmore Reef, onto the *Manoora*.

In the Full Federal Court, Chief Justice Michael Black upheld Justice North's ruling. However, two judges, Robert French and Bryan Beaumont, held that the government's actions were authorised by section 61 of the Constitution, which invests the government with executive power, including the so-called prerogative powers formerly exercised by the British monarchy.[37]

On 27 November 2001, the High Court brought the *Tampa* case to an abrupt halt.[38] A panel of three justices refused to consider an appeal from the Full Federal Court despite the undeniable existence of 'questions of law' of 'public importance'.[39] In a one-page judgment, they declared that the claim for a writ of *habeas corpus* had been 'overtaken by events,' namely the government's forced transfer of the *Tampa* refugees to Nauru. In fact, the government had undertaken to bring the refugees back to Australia should it lose the appeal. Nevertheless, it presented the High

[35] *Victorian Civil Liberties Council Incorporated v Minister for Immigration and Multicultural Affairs* [2001] FCA 1297, para 35.
[36] *Ibid* at para 19.
[37] *Ruddock v Vadarlis* [2001] FCA 1329.
[38] *Vadarlis v MIMA and Ors* M93/2001 at <http://www.austlii.edu.au/au/other/hca/transcripts/2001/M93/2.html> (30 November 2001).
[39] The Judiciary Act 1903 (Cth) s 35A provides that in considering whether to grant an application for special leave to appeal, the High Court shall have regard to whether the proceedings involve a question of law of public importance.

Court with a *fait accompli*, arguing that Australia was no longer detaining the refugees, because they had been removed to Nauru. In effect, the three High Court judges rewarded the government for thumbing its nose at the legal process.

By the time the case reached the High Court, the government, supported by the Labor Party, had pushed through parliament a package of legislation retrospectively authorising its conduct and giving military officers wide-ranging authority to board, search, detain and turn around refugee boats, using whatever means are considered 'necessary and reasonable,' including force.[40] The legislation does not define 'necessary and reasonable force' but even if it did, the definition would seem to be academic because all conduct under the legislation is protected from legal challenge. One section states: 'All action to which this Part applies is taken for all purposes to have been lawful when it occurred.' Another specifies that no legal proceedings can be commenced or continued against the Commonwealth in relation to such action.[41]

These provisions could allow refugees to be brutally treated or their boats to be sunk deliberately to prevent them landing on Australian soil. This is not far-fetched. Shots have been fired in the direction of at least one over-crowded and sinking boat, whose occupants government ministers then falsely accused of throwing children overboard.[42] Prime Minister Howard defended the use of capsicum gas and possibly electric prods by Australian military personnel to force asylum seekers to sail back to Indonesia in an unseaworthy boat that was later shipwrecked off West Timor.[43]

Other precedents established by the *Tampa* operation and the ensuing legislation include:

- — creation of excision zones where Australian migration law does not apply to parts of the country;
- — denial of basic legal rights, including the right to seek legal advice, to detainees held in the excision zones or in Nauru or PNG;
- — insertion of a sweeping privative clause in the Migration Act to effect a blanket exclusion of judicial review of nearly all refugee and immigration visa decisions.

[40] The legislation includes Migration Amendment (Excision From Migration Zone) Act 2001, Migration Amendment (Excision from Migration Zone) (Consequential Provisions) Act 2001, Border Protection (Validation and Enforcement Powers) Act 2001, and Migration Legislation Amendment Acts (Nos 1, 5, 6) 2001.

[41] Border Protection (Validation and Enforcement Powers) Act 2001, Part 2 ss 6, 7.

[42] See M Head, 'Australian election: The Howard government's big lie unravels', *World Socialist Web Site*, 10 November 2001, <http://www.wsws.org/articles/2001/nov2001/refu-n10.shtml> (10 November 2001).

[43] 'PM backs troops over electric prod claims,' *Sydney Morning Herald* 16 April 2002, <http://www.smh.com.au/articles/2002/04/16/1018333497326.html> (16 April 2002).

Even though the latter provision does not seek to override the constitutionally-entrenched jurisdiction of the High Court, some of these measures may be unconstitutional, including on the grounds that they block the exercise of Federal judicial power.[44] The High Court has since held that the privative clause is ineffective in blocking access to the High Court.[45]

The Refugee Convention

Human rights groups, refugee advocacy groups and the United Nations have criticised the Australian government's unprecedented response to the *Tampa* asylum seekers.[46] Amnesty International has condemned the Australian Government, saying the course of action taken 'is a flagrant violation of the 1951 UN Refugee Convention to which Australia is a state party.'[47]

The government rebuffed these criticisms, denying any breach of the Convention. The *Tampa* affair highlights four glaring deficiencies in the Convention.[48] First, its narrow focus on *individuals* who are *persecuted* does not allow for mass exoduses in the face of suffering, injustice or discrimination that is not considered serious enough to amount to persecution. Secondly, the Convention does not create a right to enter another state; only a limited obligation on a national state not to expel or return a refugee to a state where he or she faces persecution. Thirdly, even those accepted as refugees have no right to permanent residence and hence can be consigned to a tenuous and insecure status. Fourthly, the Convention only assists asylum seekers who manage, invariably by means designated as 'illegal,' to arrive physically in the country where they seek refuge. It does not impose any obligation on a country to take off-shore applicants, that is, the overwhelming majority of people languishing in refugee camps throughout the poorest parts of the world, whether in their own countries or neighbouring states.

A number of authors have suggested possible models for replacing the Refugee Convention with new international frameworks for protecting

[44] Even though the High Court has previously upheld the validity of non-judicial detention of asylum seekers. See *Chu Kheng Lim v Minister for Immigration, Local Government and Ethnic Affairs* (1992) 176 CLR 1.
[45] *Plaintiff s157/2002 v Commonwealth of Australia* [2003] HCA 2.
[46] UN High Commissioner for Refugees, 'Australia passes new laws to deter boat people' 14 October 2001, <http://www.unhcr.ch/cgi-bin/texis/vtx/home/+XwwBmZelc_dwwww RwwwwwwwmFqnN0bInFqnDni5oFqnN.../opendoc.html> (14 October 2001).
[47] Amnesty International Australia 'Amnesty international calls for Urgent Action against Australia' 30 August 2001 <http://www.amnesty.org.au/news/tampa30Aug2001-press.html> (3 October 2001).
[48] J Hathaway, *The Law of Refugee Status* (Toronto, Butterworths, 1991) at 6–11.

and assisting refugees, usually with a wider definition of refugee status.[49] None of these models, however, challenge the underlying assumption that nation-states and national borders will continue to exist throughout the 21st Century. Instead, they seek ways to dilute the refugee obligations of nation-states according to what the authors consider politically palatable. Hathaway has argued specifically for tailoring proposals for change to meet the needs of national governments. 'In an international legal system based on the self-interest of states, it is critical that principled reform proceed in a manner which anticipates and responds to the needs of governments,' he stated. Hathaway proposed a 'broader (if shallower) level of protection for most of the world's refugees'.[50]

Aside from leaving refugee policy in the hands of national governments, this approach is based on maintaining the strict distinction between refugees and migrants. In a global world, and one increasingly dominated by social inequality, this is a spurious, misleading and ultimately unreal perspective. If the oppressed are to be given the same right to travel and live as the wealthy and if the right to immigrate as well as to emigrate is to be recognised, a new form a citizenship is needed, global citizenship. As currently instituted, citizenship is confined to a given nation-state, and does not extend beyond its borders. However, this conception stands in opposition to the development of the global economy, which has transcended the limits of the nation-state.[51]

'COUNTER-TERRORISM' LAWS

Similar contradictions arise in the 'war on terror'. Basic democratic rights are being undermined, not just for asylum seekers but for others as well. Unprecedented measures are being introduced on the pretext of combating terrorism, but which have far-reaching implications. For example, in the United States, according to Amnesty International, more than 1200 people have been detained without trial under anti-terrorist provisions since the

[49] See A Ahilan, 'Restructured safe havens: A proposal for reform of the refugee protection system' (2000) 22 *Human Rights Quarterly* 1; P Schuck, 'Refugee burden-sharing: a modest proposal' (1997) 22 *Yale Journal of International Law* 243; P Freedman, 'International intervention to combat the explosion of refugees and internally displaced persons' (1995) 9 *Georgetown Immigration Law Journal* 565; J Hathaway, 'A reconsideration of the underlying premise of refugee law' (1990) 31 *Harvard International Law Journal* 129; E Burton, 'Leasing rights: a new international instrument for protecting refugees and compensating host countries' (1988) 19 *Columbia Human Rights Law Review* 307.

[50] J Hathaway, 'Can International Refugee Law be Made Relevant Again?' in Hathaway (ed), *Reconceiving International Refugee Law* (The Hague, Martinus Nijhoff Publishers, 1997) xxix.

[51] M Head, 'Whither the Refugee Convention – a new perspective for the 21st Century', (2002) 21 *Mots Pluriels*, <http://www.atrs.uwa.edu.au/MotsPluriels/MP2102mh.html> (30 August 2003).

events of September 11, 2001. Of these prisoners, 347 were still in custody in March 2002, deprived of basic protections against arbitrary detention under international law.[52]

In June 2002, the Australian government, again assisted by Labor, secured passage of a raft of 'counter-terrorism' Bills, handing unprecedented powers to the executive government and the intelligence and police agencies. The Bills introduce sweeping definitions of terrorism and treason, both now punishable by life imprisonment, which could outlaw many forms of political protest and industrial action. They contain powers to ban political parties, freeze their funds and jail their members for alleged support of 'terrorism'. In addition, they reverse the burden of proof for a range of serious offences, effectively requiring defendants to prove their innocence.

Because of public opposition and adverse parliamentary committee reports, the government temporarily withdrew one measure, the Australian Security Intelligence Organisation Legislation Amendment (Terrorism) Bill (ASIO Detention Bill), which sought to authorise ASIO, the domestic spy agency, to detain people without charge and interrogate them incommunicado. With Labor's support, the Bill was finally passed in June 2003 with limited amendments, along the lines proposed by parliamentary committees.

Many submissions to parliamentary committees, including those of the Law Council of Australia and the Civil Liberties Councils of NSW and Victoria, questioned the need for the entire legislative package.[53] Indeed, the laws appear to have little to do with protecting the Australian people against terrorism. As pointed out by a parliamentary library report, any conceivable terrorist activity, such as a bombing, kidnapping or assassination, was already a serious crime under existing law.[54]

Context and Pretext

It is ironic that fifty years after the *Australian Communist Party Case*[55] and the subsequent defeat of a referendum to ban the Communist Party, the main political parties passed legislation that goes beyond the measures of

[52] Amnesty International, <http://web.amnesty.org/aidoc/aidoc_pdf.nsf/index/AMR510442002ENGLISH/$File/AMR5104402.pdf> (30 August 2003).

[53] Submissions to the Senate Legal and Constitutional Committee for the Committee's Inquiry into the Security Legislation Amendment (Terrorism) Bill and Related Bills, Vol. 1, pp 157–65 and Commonwealth, *Parliamentary Debates*, Senate Legal and Constitutional Committee, Reference: Security Legislation Amendment (Terrorism) Bill and related bills, 17 April 2002, pp 82ff and 18 April 2002, pp 95ff.

[54] N Hancock, *Terrorism and the Law in Australia: Legislation, Commentary and Constraints* (Canberra, Parliament of Australia, Department of Parliamentary Library, Research Paper No. 12, 2001–2002).

[55] *Australian Communist Party v Commonwealth* (1951) 83 CLR 1.

1950–51 in its potential to outlaw dissenting political activity. The Cold War, which provided the setting for the Menzies government's proposals, has ended but instead of a new period of political freedom, we are witnessing far-reaching moves against traditional democratic norms.

The government rejected previous advice, adhered to by successive administrations since the Hilton Hotel bomb blast, that it was unnecessary, inadvisable and constitutionally questionable to introduce generic anti-terrorism laws. In the 1979 *Protective Security Review Report*, Justice Robert Hope, while recommending a major boost to the powers and resources of the police, intelligence and security forces, did not recommend the creation of new criminal offences, stating that: 'Terrorism by its nature involves breaches of the ordinary criminal law.'[56] In an opinion commissioned by the Fraser government as part of Justice Hope's review, former High Court Justice Victor Windeyer came to the same view.[57]

One must ask why the government has now overturned these precepts. The legislation punishes violent or other criminal activity far more severely if offenders are motivated by political, religious or ideological considerations than if they are acting for revenge, rage, greed, lust or other motives. This indicates that it is political motives, rather than the conduct itself, that the government is seeking to punish. This suggests that the 'war on terrorism', like the 'war on communism' a half century ago, is being used for political ends.

Certainly, the Howard government's rhetoric is reminiscent of the campaign waged a half century ago. After winning the 1949 election in the wake of the coal miners' strike, Prime Minister Robert Menzies claimed a 'political mandate' to place Australia on a 'semi-war footing' against communism.[58] Against a backdrop of global anti-communism, the Communist Party Dissolution Bill was the incoming government's first piece of legislation. The Bill's recitals claimed that its measures were required for the 'security and defence of Australia' in the face of a dire threat of violence, insurrection, treason, subversion, espionage and sabotage.[59]

The Australian High Court, however, rejected the use of these recitals to validate the government's claim to be exercising the defence, incidental and executive power of the Commonwealth. The judges warned of the corrosive dangers of unfettered executive power. Dixon J stated:

> History and not only ancient history, shows that in countries where democratic institutions have been unconstitutionally superseded, it has been done not seldom by those holding the executive power. Forms of government may

[56] R Hope, *Protective Security Review* above n 17 at 13.
[57] V Windeyer in *ibid* at 291.
[58] K Lindsay, *The Australian Constitution in Context* (Sydney, LBC, 1999, 72–76). For the political and social context of the Communist Party case, see G Winterton, 'The Significance of the Communist Party Case,' (1992) 18 *Melbourne University Law Review* 630–58.
[59] Communist Party Dissolution Act 1950 (Cth) Preamble.

> need protection from dangers likely to arise from within the institutions to be protected.[60]

The Court's stance was, in effect, vindicated by the defeat of the 1951 referendum. It remains to be seen whether today's High Court will restate these principles, if and when the current legislation is challenged.

Terrorism, Treason and Espionage

Central to the legislative package are far-reaching definitions of terrorism, treason and espionage. These offences will become some of the most serious on the statute books, with severe penalties. The first two are punishable by life imprisonment; the third by 25 years' imprisonment. Under the Security Legislation Amendment (Terrorism) Bill, terrorism extends to acts or threats that advance 'a political, religious or ideological cause' for the purpose of 'coercing or influencing by intimidation' any government or section of the public. 'Advocacy, protest, dissent or industrial action' is exempted but not if it involves harm to a person, 'serious damage' to property, 'serious risk' to public health or safety, or 'serious interference' with an information, telecommunications, financial, essential services or transport system.[61]

The legislation imposes jail terms ranging from life to 10 years for preparing, planning or training for 'terrorist acts' and for possessing documents or other objects used in the preparation of such acts. A person can be jailed for possessing such a 'thing' even if they did not know it was used for terrorist purposes, but were merely 'reckless' as to that fact.[62] This definition could cover any demonstration or strike action in which a person was injured or felt endangered. The 'coercion or intimidation' clause is practically meaningless, given that the purpose of many protests and strikes is to apply pressure to a government, employer or other authority. Nurses taking strike action that shuts down hospital wards in support of a political demand for greater health spending, for example, could be accused of endangering public health and thus be charged as terrorists.

The various, related, terrorist offences could apply to a wide range of political activity, such as planning or participating in a protest outside government buildings or facilities where damage is alleged to have occurred. Demonstrators who block roads or entrances to financial institutions, such as the stock exchange, could be charged as terrorists, as could computer hackers.

[60] (1951) 83 CLR 1, 187.
[61] Criminal Code 100.1.
[62] Criminal Code 101.2, 101.4, 101.5, 101.6.

During questioning in a Senate committee hearing on 8 April 2002, the Attorney-General's representatives admitted that someone who cut through a fence at the Easter 2002 protest at the Woomera refugee detention centre or who invaded the parliament building during a 1996 trade union rally could have been charged with terrorism.[63] The officials acknowledged that a picketing striker who caused property damage or a person who possessed a mobile phone used to discuss a violent act could be prosecuted under the new provisions.[64]

While citing the September 11 attacks in the United States as its justification, the government has adopted a definition of terrorism that goes beyond the Bush administration's USA Patriot Act, which covers activity that is dangerous to human life and violates existing criminal laws. The Howard government's version is based on the British Blair government's Terrorism Act 2000, but goes further in specifying disruption to various communications systems.[65]

Power to Outlaw Organisations

Under the original version of the Terrorism Bill, the Attorney-General could have proscribed any organisation on a number of vague grounds, including his view that a group had 'endangered, or is likely to endanger, the security or integrity' of Australia or another country.[66] In the light of the wide meanings that can be given to the term 'national security' and the difficulties of obtaining judicial review of its use by government and intelligence agencies,[67] these criteria opened up wide scope for political abuse.

In the face of public opposition, the government was compelled to back down on its original proposal. But the amended version allows the government to issue regulations to outlaw parties or groups if the UN Security Council has listed them as terrorist. A court can also declare an organisation to be 'terrorist'.[68]

Proscription orders may have far-reaching implications. Any person who directs or provides support to the activities of a terrorist organisation, knowing it to be terrorist, can be jailed for 25 years or, if they are 'reckless' as to whether the organisation is terrorist or not, for 15 years. A member of a group banned under a regulation faces up to 10 years imprisonment.

[63] Senate Legal and Constitutional Committee, above n 53, 8 April 2002 at 19.
[64] *Ibid* at 14–15.
[65] For a comparison of the US and British legislation, see N Hancock, *Terrorism and the Law in Australia: Supporting Materials* (Canberra, Parliament of Australia, Department of Parliamentary Library, Research Paper No. 13, 2001–2002) 2–8.
[66] Proposed Section 102.2 of the Criminal Code Act 1995 (Cth).
[67] See *Church of Scientology v Woodward* (1982) 154 CLR 25 and H Lee, P Hanks and V Morabito, *In the Name of National Security, The Legal Dimensions* (Sydney, LBC, 1995) chapters 1–2.
[68] Criminal Code 102.1.

Membership is defined to include 'informal membership' or taking 'steps to become a member'. It is a defence to have taken 'reasonable steps' to cease membership 'as soon as practicable' after knowing the organisation was terrorist, but the burden of proof lies on the defendant.[69]

The legislation also retains a backdoor method for banning organisations by freezing their funds, even if they have not been formally declared terrorist. The Attorney-General can freeze assets or proscribe groups if a UN Security Council freezing order has been issued. Either the Minister can 'list' an organisation by Gazette notice or the Governor-General may make proscription regulations. Anyone collecting or providing donations for the organisation can be jailed for five years. If the funds are used for terrorist purposes, the penalty is life.[70] Under regulations introduced in October 2002, the government has outlawed several lists of political groups.[71] They include the PKK, the Kurdish separatist organisation, and the Sikh Youth Federation.[72]

Detention Without Charge

Following the ultimate passage of the ASIO Detention Bill, ASIO now has the power to detain and question people without charge or trial. ASIO and Federal Police officers can raid anyone's home or office, at any hour of the day or night, and forcibly take them away, interrogate and strip-search them and hold them incommunicado, effectively indefinitely through the issuing of repeated warrants.[73]

Detainees do not need to be suspected of a terrorist offence, or any other criminal offence. The Attorney-General can certify that their interrogation would 'substantially assist the collection of intelligence that is important in relation to a terrorism offence,' even if no act of terrorism has occurred.[74] This power could be used to detain journalists and political activists, as well as the children, relatives or acquaintances of supposed terrorism suspects. Any detainee who refused to answer ASIO's questions would be liable to five years imprisonment.

Those detained have no right to know why they are being hauled off for interrogation. If they resist, violent force, including lethal force, can be used against them. If they refuse to answer any question or hand over any

[69] Criminal Code 102.2, 102.3, 102.4, 102.5, 102.6, 102.7.
[70] Suppression of the Financing of Terrorism Act 2002, Schedule 3, amending the Charter of United Nations Act 1945.
[71] Charter of the United Nations (Anti-Terrorism Measures) Regulations 2001 and A Downer and D Williams, Joint Media Release, 'Further Steps to Prevent the Financing of Terrorism,' 18 April 2002.
[72] Senator Bob Brown, *Senate*, 24 June 2002, 2248.
[73] Sections 34A to 34Y of the Australian Security Intelligence Organisation Act 1979 (Cth).
[74] Section 34C.

material that ASIO alleges they possess, they face five year's jail. Detainees, including teenagers as young as 16, will be unable to contact their families, friends, political associates or the media. If they know the name of a lawyer, they can contact them for legal advice, but only if ASIO does not object to the lawyer.

Even if ASIO accepts a detainee's choice of lawyer, questioning can commence without the lawyer being present. In any case, the lawyer cannot object or intervene during questioning—if they do, they can be ejected for 'disrupting' ASIO. If they inform a detainee's family or the media about the detention, they too face up to five years in jail. A lawyer who is provided information by a client may also be detained for interrogation. The Act does not protect legal professional privilege in communications between lawyer and client.

Initial detention can last for up to seven days, including three eight-hour blocks of questioning over three days, but the Attorney-General can easily approve further seven-day periods. To justify serial extensions, ASIO and the government simply have to claim that 'additional to or materially different' information has come to light.[75]

In a significant departure from established law, the Act effectively reverses the burden of proof, overturning a basic protection against police frame-up. If ASIO alleges a person has information or material, the onus is on the individual to prove otherwise.

Section 34JB, permits police officers to use 'such force as is necessary and reasonable' in breaking into premises and taking people into custody. This clause gives police the power to kill or cause 'grievous bodily harm,' as long as they believe it necessary to protect themselves. In addition, officers may use 'reasonable and necessary' force to conduct strip-searches.[76]

Interrogation must be video-taped[77] and conducted in the presence of a 'prescribed authority,' that is a judge, retired judge or presidential member of the Administrative Appeals Tribunal.[78] Video-taping of questioning, currently required for police questioning in most Australian jurisdictions, is no guarantee against the planting of evidence and extraction of false confessions.[79] And a government can readily appoint retired judges or tribunal members, with no judicial tenure, who may be amenable to its requirements.

The legislation has radically extended ASIO's powers. The agency currently has no powers of arrest or interrogation. The State and Federal police can detain people, but only on suspicion of committing a criminal

[75] Section 34C.
[76] Section 34L.
[77] Section 34K.
[78] Sections 34B and 34DA.
[79] See M Chaaya, 'The Right to Silence Reignited: Vulnerable Suspects, Police Questioning and Law and Order in NSW,' (1998) 22 *Criminal Law Journal* 82. On police 'verballing' and

offence and those suspects must be either charged or released within a short period, and generally cannot be detained for interrogation.[80] Prisoners have the right to legal counsel, who can be present during questioning, and to remain silent.[81] With the notable exception of the detention of asylum seekers, detention without trial is regarded as unconstitutional.[82] A citizen is entitled to decline a request to attend a police station 'to assist police'.

The new powers are unparalleled. Not even during two world wars did an Australian government seek to overturn freedom from arbitrary detention (with the controversial exception of rounding up people of German, Japanese and Italian origin as 'enemy aliens') or abolish the centuries-old common law right to remain silent.

ASIO hardly needs detention powers to detect terrorists. Its considerable powers include those to bug phones, install listening devices in offices and homes, intercept telecommunications, open people's mail, monitor on-line discussion, break into computer files and databases, seize computers and use personal tracking devices.[83] The ASIO Director-General or his delegated officers can issue search and entry warrants, effectively giving officers a legal *carte blanche* to conduct operations against political activists and organisations.[84] Moreover, ASIO is part of an extensive security and intelligence network, which incorporates Defence Intelligence Organisation (DIO), ASIO, Australian Secret Intelligence Service (ASIS), Defence Signals Directorate (DSD), Office of National Assessments (ONA) and special State police units (formerly called Special Branches).[85]

Despite the level of public disquiet, the Labor Party has supported the entire legislative package, a fact underscored on April 5, 2002 when the leaders of the Australian States and territories, all currently run by Labor governments, agreed at a Conference of Australian Governments summit to formally refer their powers over terrorism to the Federal government. Their decision has the potential to give the Commonwealth substantially unfettered law-making and police enforcement power over politically-related crime for the first time since Federation in 1901, possibly freeing the Howard government of the need to find precise constitutional heads of legislative or executive power for its measures.[86]

video-taping in general see Brown, Neal, Farrier & Weisbrot, *Criminal Laws* (Sydney, The Federation Press, 2nd ed, 1996) 203–34.

[80] *Williams v R* (1986) 66 ALR 385.
[81] S Bronitt and M Ayers, 'Criminal law and human rights,' in D Kinley (ed), *Human Rights in Australian Law* (Sydney, The Federation Press, 1998).
[82] *Chu Kheng Lim v Minister for Immigration* (1992) 176 CLR 1.
[83] See generally, Australian Security Intelligence Organisation Act 1979 (Cth).
[84] See J Hocking, above n 9, chapter 8.
[85] *Ibid* and Lee, Hanks and Morabito, above n 67, chapter 3.
[86] Most states have legislated accordingly: D Williams, Reference of Terrorism Powers, News Release, 27 March 2003.

Even so, the potential constitutional problems with the laws are manifold,[87] arising from the Commonwealth parliament's lack of general power to legislate with respect to criminal law[88] or 'terrorism'.[89] as well as the Constitution's implied right to political communication[90] and, perhaps, freedom of association.[91] In addition, detention without trial may infringe on judicial power and the separation of powers.[92] The freedom of religion protected by section 116 of the Constitution could also be infringed if the measures interfere with the free practice of a religion, although the High Court has interpreted section 116 as only invalidating laws that specifically target religious practice.[93]

In order to secure passage of the final piece of the legislative package — the ASIO Detention Bill — the government agreed to insert a three-year sunset clause.[94] However, the government has made plain its intention to seek the legislation's renewal and has, in fact, foreshadowed amendments to strengthen ASIO's detention powers.[95] In October 2003, the recently-appointed Attorney-General Philip Ruddock stated that the detention powers had already been used, while refusing to provide details.[96] Thus, the indefinite 'war on terror' has been utilised to make another significant alteration to the legal fabric.

CONCLUSION

Taken together, these laws represent a grave threat to basic democratic rights. Serious inroads have been made into long-standing principles such as no detention without trial, the presumption of innocence and freedom of speech and association. The pressures of globalisation and the 'war on terror' have set the stage for measures that substantially expand the powers of the military and security agencies. Both the context

[87] M Head, "Counter-terrorism" laws: a threat to political freedom, civil liberties and constitutional rights', (2002) 26 *Melbourne University Law Review* 266.
[88] Per Higgins J in *R v Kidman* (1915) 20 CLR 425, 448: 'There is not in our Constitution ... any power to make laws as to "the criminal law".'
[89] Royal Commission on Intelligence and Security (Commissioner Justice Robert Hope), *Fourth Report: Volume 1* (Canberra, Commonwealth Government Printer, 1978) 60–65, Royal Commission on Australia's Security and Intelligence Agencies (Commissioner Justice Robert Hope), *Report on the Australian Security Intelligence Organisation* (Canberra, AGPS, 1985) 88–89, and V Windeyer, above n 17 at 291.
[90] *Nationwide News Pry Ltd v Wills* (1992) 177 CLR 1 and *Australian Capital Television Pty Ltd v Commonwealth* (1992) 177 CLR 106.
[91] *Kruger v Commonwealth* (1997) 190 CLR 1.
[92] *Chu Kheng Lim v MILGEA* (1992) 176 CLR 1.
[93] See *Krygger v Williams* (1912) 12 CLR 366 and *Adelaide Company of Jehovah's Witnesses v Commonwealth* (1943) 67 CLR 116.
[94] Section 34Y of the ASIO Act.
[95] C Banham, 'ASIO law inferior, insists Ruddock', *Sydney Morning Herald*, 4 November 2003, 1.
[96] K Walsh, 'ASIO uses new laws on terror', *Sydney Morning Herald*, 12 October 2003, 2.

of the legislation and the extraordinary reaches of its measures invite constitutional challenge, as well as public opposition.

More broadly, all three developments reviewed in this chapter — the military callout legislation, the anti-refugee provisions and the counter-terrorism laws — reveal contradictions at the heart of the processes of globalisation. The development of world economy demands global governance and, this chapter suggests, international democracy. Yet, globalisation is also producing staggering worldwide inequality, to which many governments have increasingly responded by shutting their borders to the poor while introducing anti-democratic measures domestically. On the one hand, transnational corporations and the most economically powerful governments forcefully insist upon the dismantling of all limits on the movement of investment funds and production. On the other, they support ever more draconian measures that flout human rights, restrict freedom of movement and threaten legitimate political dissent. Existing refugee and human rights conventions have proved to be no barrier to these tendencies. These contradictions will loom large in coming decades.

3

Human Rights in Times of Economic Crisis: The Example of Argentina

SABINE MICHALOWSKI

INTRODUCTION

In his book *Globalisation and its Discontents,* Joseph Stiglitz writes that:

> [F]or millions of people globalisation has not worked. Many have actually been made worse off, as they have seen their jobs destroyed and their lives become more insecure. They have felt increasingly powerless against forces beyond their control. They have seen their democracies undermined.[1]

THIS GENERAL STATEMENT sounds like an accurate description of the current situation in Argentina, where during the latest serious economic crisis unemployment figures have rocketed,[2] savings and pensions have been devalued, poverty rates have reached an unprecedented level, and the social protection of large sectors of the Argentinian society has dropped to a worrying level.[3] While there can be no doubt that factors inherent in the political culture of Argentina have

[1] J Stiglitz, *Globalisation and its Discontents* (London, Allen Lane, 2002), at p 248. See also, eg, M Rapaport, *Tiempos de crisis, vientos de cambio* (Buenos Aires, Grupo Editorial Norma, 2002).
[2] See A M Morello, 'Suspensión del pago de la deuda pública. Fundamentos jurídicos', *El Derecho* 196 (2002), 839-46, at pp 839–40.
[3] The public health system, for example, has almost collapsed, see *Estado de los hospitales públicos del país* (Situation of the public hospitals in the country), an *Annex to the Report on Health in Argentina,* presented by the NGO Centre of Legal and Social Studies (CELS) to the Interamerican Commission on Human Rights, which gives an impressive overview of the disastrous situation of many hospitals in which even the most basic equipment, such as needles, anaesthetics etc., are missing, at <http://www.cels.org.ar> (24 August 2004). For statistics on health; social security; unemployment; poverty rates etc. see the web page of the National Instute of Statistics and Censuses: <http://www.indec.gov.ar> (24 August 2004).

significantly contributed to the desolate situation of the country,[4] it is equally clear that the current crisis in Argentina cannot be isolated from the phenomenon of globalisation.[5] Indeed, many of the acute problems that led to the breakdown of the Argentinian economy are the results of Argentina's neoliberal policies, backed and partly required by the IMF,[6] which eventually led to a comprehensive crisis, as the country faces external debts of unknown proportions,[7] while at the same time not being able to provide even for the basic needs of large parts of its population.

Many of the measures adopted by the Argentinian state in the context of this latest crisis have had an adverse impact on the protection of the rights of the country's population, particularly social rights and property rights. The justifications provided for this were mainly twofold: it was argued that these policies were a prerequisite for reaching much needed agreements with the IMF; and that the economic emergency made it factually impossible to protect the human rights of the citizens. Such arguments, if valid, could justify the disregard for human rights concerns on a very large scale. However, Argentina has adopted a constitution which guarantees individual rights and stipulates that the activities of all state authorities, including the Government and Parliament, have to respect the ambit of the Constitution. Human rights considerations can thus not be ignored when the Government enters into international agreements, when Parliament enacts legislation implementing the measures agreed therein, or when the Government formulates its economic and financial policy in the light of the country's economic crisis and international obligations. Furthermore, in Argentina the acts of all organs of the state are subject to constitutional review by the courts.[8] Consequently, the courts have the role and the power to control the compatibility of all decisions of the executive and the legislative branches with the human rights guarantees contained in the National Constitution and also in some international human rights documents that have been given constitutional status.[9] In the context of the latest crisis, Argentinian citizens, and also, for example, NGOs, have made use of the possibility of initiating judicial control of state acts to an hitherto unknown extent, challenging

[4] See, eg, A Ferrer, *La Argentina y el Orden Mundial* (Buenos Aires, Fondo de Cultura Económica, 2003), at pp 141–47; and M Mussa, *Argentina y el FMI: del triunfo a la tragedia* (Buenos Aires, Grupo Editorial Planeta, 2002), at pp 13–26.

[5] See, eg, Stiglitz, n 1 above, at p 69; and Rapaport, n 1 above.

[6] See, eg, R Sidicaro, *La crisis del Estado* (Buenos Aires, Libros del Roja, 2002); and J V Paddock, 'IMF policy and the Argentine Crisis,' (2002) *University of Miami Inter-American Law Review*, 155–187.

[7] For figures see, for example, C Juliá, *La memoria de la deuda* (Buenos Aires, Editorial Biblos, 2002), at p 21.

[8] H J Zarini, *Derecho Constitucional* (Buenos Aires, Editorial Astrea, 2nd ed. 1999), at pp 87–93.

[9] R House, and M Mutua, 'Protecting Human Rights in the Global Economy: Challenges for the WTO' (2000) *Rights and Democracy* Website, www.ichrdd.ca (24 August 2004).

the constitutionality of emergency measures such as the freezing and pesification[9a] of bank accounts,[10] the cut in public salaries and pensions,[11] and also alleging the unlawfulness of other policies, such as attempts to increase the charges for public services,[12] the lack of provision of basic medication,[13] and even the repayment of Argentina's external debts.[14] This has triggered an important discussion of the role of the courts in the context of litigation questioning political and economic policies. The main problems addressed in this context are the more general question of the distribution of powers between the judiciary and the other branches of government, and the more specific questions of whether constitutional standards should change, and citizens be required to tolerate a greater restriction of their rights, in times of crisis.

Argentina's constitutional system is based on that of the US and has also many similarities with that of European countries. An analysis of the current crisis in Argentina thus provides an excellent opportunity to examine not just the way in which one particular country is dealing with a critical situation, but also the more general question of whether a constitution based on the ideals of a liberal Western tradition, providing the protection of such principles as the separation of powers, the independence of the judiciary, the protection of individual rights, and the justiciability of state actions, provides an appropriate framework for the resolution of problems that lie in the political and economic sphere. This paper will use the example of Argentina to analyse the prospects and potential problems of enforcing human rights protection through the courts in the context of economic crises. It will be argued that particularly in times of crisis, it is essential for the protection of human rights that an independent judiciary with a clearly defined role and which is acting according to clearly defined standards, has the power to ensure that the acts of the executive and the legislature respect the tenets of the Constitution.

EMERGENCY MEASURES

As a reaction to the current crisis, both Parliament and the executive have issued such a large amount of emergency legislation that it is impossible to

[9a] Pesification means the conversion of the balance of bank accounts that were held in US dollars into Argentinian pesos.
[10] *Banco de Galicia y Buenos Aires SA s/solicita intervención urgente en Smith, Carlos A c PEN s/Sumarísimo*, Fallos 325: 28 (2002); *Provincia de San Luis c Estado Nacional*, La Ley, 2003–B, 537.
[11] *Tobar, Leonidas c Estado Nacional. M°Defensa — Contaduría General del Ejército — Ley 25.453 s/amparo;* La Ley, 2002–E, 428.
[12] D Azpiazu, M Schorr, *Crónica de una Sumisión Anunciada* (Buenos Aires, Siglo XXI de Argentina Editores, 2003), at pp 86–89, and 242–49.
[13] J Rossi, C Varsky, 'La salud bajo la ley del mercado', in CELS, *Derechos Humanos en Argentina, Informe 2002* (Buenos Aires, Catálogos Editora, Siglo XXI de Argentina Editores, 2002), at pp 343–51.
[14] Juliá, n 7 above, at pp 163–204.

give a comprehensive overview, and it must therefore suffice to introduce some key measures that are of particular concern in the context of the protection of individual rights. In July 2001, Parliament enacted the so-called Zero Deficit Act (ley 25.453), the aim of which was to achieve a balanced budget. The Act empowered the executive to reduce, inter alia, pensions and the salaries of public employees if public spending exceeded the State's revenue. The executive made use of this empowerment in August 2001 and reduced, retrospectively as of 1 July 2001, both salaries and pensions by 13 per cent.[15] In August 2001, the Inviolability of Bank Deposits Act (ley 25.466) was enacted in order to increase trust in the financial system. However, on 1 December 2001, Government enacted Decree 1570/2001, which introduced the so-called *corralito*,[16] limiting cash withdrawals by individuals to 250 pesos or 250 dollars[17] per person per week. On 6 January 2002, the Public Emergency and Reform of the Monetary System Act (ley 25.561) was enacted. This Act declared the public emergency in social, economic, administrative, financial and monetary matters and delegated far-reaching powers to the executive to proceed with the reorganisation of the financial and banking system. The Act suspended the applicability of the provisions of the Inviolability of Bank Deposits Act, but emphasised that the federal executive would take measures aiming at the preservation of the capital of the savings accounts that were in existence when Regulation 1570/01 came into force, including deposits that were made in foreign currency, by restructuring the original obligations in a manner compatible with the evolution of the solvency of the financial system. Finally, on 3 February, based on the empowering provision contained in the Public Emergency and Reform of the Monetary System Act and on its generic constitutional powers to enact emergency legislation under limited conditions,[18] the Argentinian government enacted Decree 214/2002 which, inter alia, declared the pesification of all bank accounts held in US dollars, the conversion rate being 1.40 pesos for 1 US dollar.[19] All debts with banks taken out in dollars were converted into debts in pesos, the conversion rate being one peso for one dollar. Creditors of bank deposits of up to $30,000 were given the opportunity to opt for a Treasury bond to compensate for the devaluation of their accounts.

Decree 214/2002 was the immediate response of the executive to the decision of the Argentinian Supreme Court in the case of *Smith*[20] in which

[15] Decreto 1.060/01.
[16] The literal translation of *corralito* is playpen!
[17] At that time the Convertibility Act that had pegged the peso to the dollar at an exchange rate of one peso to one dollar was still in place.
[18] See Art 99 (3) of the Constitution.
[19] At that time, dollars could be bought for about two pesos for one dollar, but the exchange rate went up very quickly, and within 2 months more than three pesos needed to be paid for one dollar.
[20] See n 10 above.

the provisions of Decree 1570/01 establishing the *corralito* were declared unconstitutional because they violated the property rights of the depositors. The new decree suspended the processing of all judicial proceedings related to the emergency measures contained in Decree 1570/01 and Ley 25.561 for 180 days. As the courts continued to declare the *corralito*,[21] the pesification of bank accounts in dollars[22] and also the suspension of judicial proceedings[23] unconstitutional, in July 2002 Government issued Decree 1316/2002, suspending for 120 days the execution of judicial decisions that invalidated the emergency measures.

What becomes clear when looking at these measures is that the Argentinian authorities decided to react to the emergency by restricting the rights of the citizens, particularly property rights. The frequent changes to the legal framework governing the use and also the value of one's assets moreover took away any legal certainty. At the same time, the protection of social rights was drastically reduced.[24] The suspension first of the processing of litigation against the emergency measures and later of the execution of court decisions affected the right of access to the courts[25] and arguably also the principle of the separation of powers, as the Government restricted the judiciary in the exercise of its functions.[26] The latter was also put at risk by the Government's excessive and often questioned use of the powers delegated by Parliament.

JUSTIFICATION OF THE EMERGENCY MEASURES

The Government, predictably, presented its emergency measures as inevitable in order to overcome the crisis, and argued that they were based on a careful balancing of the rights of all individuals and of society as a whole. The *corralito*, that is the freezing of the bank accounts, for example, was justified by the necessity to fight the dramatic decrease of the total of deposits in the financial system. When the courts intervened and declared these measures to be unconstitutional, the Government suspended court proceedings and the execution of judicial decisions for the same reasons for which the emergency measure had been introduced, that is that in a situation in which the banks did not have enough money to pay back all the deposits, the risk of a financial crisis which could harm

[21] *Ibid.*
[22] *Provincia de San Luis c Estado Nacional*, La Ley, 2003-B, 537.
[23] *A, A S B c PEN y otros s/amparo, Federal Court of La Plata*, El Derecho, 196 (2002), 252; *Santos, Claudio Roberto c PEN s/amparo, Federal Court of Bahía Blanca*, El Derecho, 196 (2002), 257.
[24] See, eg, Rossi, Varsky, n 13 above, at pp 331–54.
[25] As guaranteed by Article 18 of the Constitution.
[26] S Cayuso, 'Acción de amparo e inconstitucionalidad de los decretos 214 y 320/2002', *La Ley*, 2002–A, 807–810, at p 809.

the deposit holders as well as the economy as a whole could only be limited by temporarily restricting the free withdrawal of bank deposits, thus impinging upon the property rights of individuals. The Government argued that the litigation both against the *corralito* and against the pesification of bank accounts threatened the common good, as a positive decision would only benefit those individuals who managed to obtain favourable court decisions, to the detriment of all other individuals whose rights would be put at risk by the execution of such decisions. If, for example, some individuals were to secure court decisions allowing the withdrawal of large sums of money that were caught in the *corralito,* there would then not be enough money left in the banking system to satisfy the rights of those deposit holders who either did not initiate court proceedings at all, or who obtained favourable decisions at a later point in time, thus creating a first-come-first-served approach to the satisfaction of rights, instead of the balanced solution the Government had worked out when introducing the *corralito*. Indeed, according to the Government, litigation threatened the preservation of social peace, and it went as far as accusing the Supreme Court judges of deepening the economic crisis and delaying any agreement with the IMF, as

> those who observe the situation from the outside and need to provide the necessary funds will abstain from making available funds to a country whose judges do not seem to understand that to resolve partially the problem of this or that deposit holder means to delay indefinitely the overall solution and to jeopardise even more a system in crisis.[27]

A further justification provided for the suspension of the execution of judicial decisions was, consequently, that the judiciary stood in the way of achieving the stability that was needed to improve the country's position in the negotiations of the external debt with private creditors and international organisations. Based on its role as the prime negotiator with international organisations such as the IMF, the Government moreover put pressure on Parliament to delegate extensive powers to the executive and to reduce its role to rubberstamping legislation proposed by the Government. On 14 February 2003, for example, the newspaper *Clarín* reported that Lavagna, the Secretary of State for the Economy, urged Parliament with regard to the enactment of a bill on tax reforms, that:

> if we change as much as one comma of what has been agreed with the IMF, the whole agreement falls through.

[27] *Clarín*, 31 October 2002. In a similar vein, see, for example, J C Rivera, 'Como debe ejercerse el control de razonabilidad de leyes que incursionan en materia socio-económica', *La Ley*, 2002–D, 1116–37, at p 1135.

Thus, the necessity to reach agreement with the IMF was relied on by way of a double justification: first, in relation to the content of some of the emergency legislation, and secondly, to turn the Government into the main actor in times of crisis, not only determining all policies but also being exempt from all judicial control — the government alleging that it is not only best placed, but in fact the only state organ that is able to balance the rights of all citizens and the interests of society as such within the constraints imposed by the reality of the economic crisis and of the country's international obligations.

THE ROLE OF THE JUDICIARY

The extent to which the citizens challenged the various emergency actions in court suggests that many Argentinians do not accept that they should tolerate restrictions of their rights based on the Government's, and to some extent Parliament's, assessment of what is best for them and for the country, and that they rely on the judiciary as a corrective power. Given that liberal and democratic constitutions such as that of Argentina provide for the separation of powers, for constitutional guarantees of human rights, and for constitutional review of executive and legislative activities precisely because they do not accept that one branch of the state should be allowed to take all decisions it deems necessary without any control by the other state organs, in normal times the Government's arguments in favour of limiting the judicial control of its activities would not be valid under such a constitution. However, what needs to be examined is whether it can be argued with the Argentinian government that emergency situations are sufficiently distinguishable from normal situations to justify the applicability of different, laxer, constitutional standards, and the concentration of power mainly in one organ, government. In particular, how should the courts react to the Government's argument that only the short-term restriction of constitutional guarantees can in the long run ensure that these rights can be upheld, or to the argument that there is only one possible solution to the crisis, and this solution requires the restriction of individual rights?

The Argentinian Supreme Court itself defined its role in relation to the control of the other state organs as follows: It is not the task of a court to pronounce itself upon the policies that should be adopted by the other state powers, and the Court will therefore not control economic policies as such, but in the context of litigation it is the task of the Court to assess their necessity and reasonableness.[28] The Government and also some legal commentators suggested that while judicial control of reasonableness

[28] *Peralta y otro c Nación Argentina (Ministerio de Economía* — BCRA), Fallos, 313: 1513 (1990), at para 48; *Prodelco c Poder Ejecutivo Nacional*, Fallos, 321: 1253 (1998), at para 7.

might be the right approach in normal times, it was not appropriate in times of crisis, because in a situation of economic emergency, coupled with the economic impossibility of satisfying the rights of all individuals, it can never be reasonable that courts declare an emergency measure to be unconstitutional, even if it restricts individual rights. Rather, as the only way out of the crisis, and the only possibility to prevent the break-down of the state as such, and to guarantee an optimisation of the rights of all citizens, such measures are automatically reasonable. The very concept of the control of reasonableness, it was argued, obliges the courts to take into account the social consequences of their decisions,[29] so that a concept of property rights that favours the interests of those few who initiated court proceedings very quickly, but leads to the bankruptcy of the financial system and endangers the rights of the great majority of depositors, cannot be acceptable.[30] Therefore, if the courts when assessing the constitutionality of the emergency measures had asked themselves what would have happened had the state not enacted the challenged emergency measures, they would have had to decide differently.[31] In failing to show judicial realism, the courts were accused of standing in the way of governmental acts that aim to resolve the country's financial problems[32] and of paralysing governmental activities.[33] Even some of the commentators who thought that the decisions of the Supreme Court in *Smith*[34] and *San Luis*,[35] declaring the *corralito* and the pesification of dollar accounts unconstitutional, respectively, were legally impeccable, suggested that the Court should nevertheless have decided differently, as it cannot dissociate itself from the dramatic consequences of its decisions for the financial system and the survival of the state as such.[36] It was furthermore suggested that it was not reasonable for the courts to make decisions the enforceability of which is economically impossible.[37] Thus, given that those critics accepted that the Government had chosen the one possible and potentially successful path forward,[38] they regarded the courts' challenges of these policies on constitutional grounds as unreasonable and even destructive.[39]

[29] Rivera, n 27 above, at p 1128.
[30] *Ibid*, at p 1129.
[31] E Conesa, 'La crisis económica y el regimen legal de la moneda', *La Ley*, 2003–F, 24 September 2003, 1–6, at p 2.
[32] R Boqué, 'Esperando a la Corte: el derecho de necesidad en el campo contractual a partir de la emergencia', *La Ley*, 2003–A, 1239–52, at p 1249.
[33] Rivera, n 27 above, at p 1137.
[34] See n 10 above.
[35] See n 10 above.
[36] W F Carnota, 'La Corte Suprema y el fallo del "corralito"', *La Ley*, 2002–B, 1231–32, at p 1231; Boqué, n 32 above, at p 1247.
[37] *Ibid*. See also Rivera, n 27 above, at p 1135.
[38] Conesa, n 31 above, at p 2; C G Gerscovich, 'Sobre la inconstitucionalidad del "corralito" declarado por la Corte', *Jurisprudence Argentina* 2002–I, 26–34, at pp 32–34.
[39] E Conesa, 'La sentencia de la Corte en el caso "San Luis"', *La Ley*, 2003–C, 1397–1404, at p 1399.

The main criticism against the court decisions that declared the unconstitutionality of the emergency measures seems to be that they questioned the Government's assessment of the necessity of the particular emergency measures. Indeed, the courts were accused of overstepping their competencies and of usurping the prerogative of the executive and the legislature in determining economic and financial policies.[40] But is this really the case? Consider, in this context, the analysis of the constitutional roles of the different state powers presented by McLaghlin J, as she then was, in the Canadian case of *RJR MacDonald v Canada*,[41] where she stated that:

> Parliament has its role: to choose the appropriate response to social problems within the limiting framework of the Constitution. But the courts also have a role: to determine, objectively and impartially, whether Parliament's choice falls within the limiting framework of the Constitution. The courts are no more permitted to abdicate their responsibility than is Parliament. To carry judicial deference to the point of accepting Parliament's view simply on the basis that the problem is serious and the solution difficult, would be to diminish the role of the courts in the constitutional process and to weaken the structure of rights upon which our constitution and our nation is founded.[42]

Thus, all state organs have different constitutionally allocated roles to fulfil, and, while the executive and the legislature have the prerogative of formulating and implementing policies, this power finds its limits in the Constitution, and it is the prerogative of the judiciary to oversee and determine whether or not these limits have been respected.

It then needs to be asked whether economic emergencies justify an attitude of complete judicial deference, as the Argentinian government demanded. It is conceded that courts cannot dissociate their decisions from the economic, social and political context in which they are being made,[43] that is in the cases under discussion that Argentina was suffering a grave economic emergency. There can also be no doubt that the survival of the state as such, or the rescuing of institutions that are vital for its functioning, is an important, if not the most important goal, and that constitutional guarantees should not be applied in a way that in a moment of crisis might result in the break-down of the state and/or its fundamental institutions.[44] However, it is submitted that it does not follow that emergency measures that are intended to overcome a crisis

[40] See, eg, Boqué n 32 above, at p 1249.
[41] [1995] 3 SCR 199.
[42] *Ibid*, at para 136.
[43] *Provincia de San Luis c Estado Nacional*, La Ley, 2003–B, 537, at para 53.
[44] *Peralta y otro c Nación Argentina (Ministerio de Economía – BCRA)*, Fallos, 313: 1513 (1990), at para 59.

and/or to address a situation of economic impossibility are therefore automatically constitutional. If the very existence of a crisis and an allegation of economic impossibility automatically led to the constitutionality of all emergency measures that might be adopted, or at least to the exclusion of judicial control of these matters, this would have far-reaching consequences for the protection of constitutional guarantees in times of emergency.

First of all, the Government, when negotiating agreements with the IMF or other international bodies in the context of an economic crisis, would then be free to formulate its policies without regard to its constitutional and human rights obligations, and it would not be possible to challenge policies that favour the economic interests of certain individuals, companies or organisations over the constitutionally protected rights of the Argentinian people, in court. This is worrying, given that it is the logic of negotiations of economic and financial policies that economic and financial interests dominate the debate. Indeed, it is clear that the IMF, the most influential organisation in this context, does not have human rights considerations at the forefront of its agenda for Argentina. The IMF, for example, supports the emergency measures that restrict property and other constitutional rights of the Argentinian people, while at the same time requiring that the IMF and other international organisations be regarded as preferential creditors whose loans need to be repaid in full, including interest, as a matter of priority;[45] demanding that the Government accelerate the negotiations of the external debt with private creditors;[46] and putting pressure on the Argentinian government to allow for an increase in the rates that the owners of privatised public service providers, mainly influential foreign companies, can charge.[47] Without any possibility to challenge the domestic implementation of such policies in court, the IMF might put more pressure on the Government to disregard its constitutional obligations. The Government, on the other hand, could be tempted to carry out policies that might not be compatible with their human rights obligations towards their own people, by hiding behind their impotence when negotiating with powerful international institutions. Given the IMF's emphasis on legal certainty and the importance of a political consensus within the country,[48] it is submitted that the courts can play an important role in this context. If they give out clear

[45] *Clarín*, 21 September 2003.
[46] See, eg, *Clarín*, 16 and 17 December 2003.
[47] See, eg, *Clarín*, 21 September 2003. For an account of Government's repeated attempts to increase the rates for public service providers in the light of this pressure, and the consistent frustration of these attempts by the courts which held that Government had not respected the provisions of the enabling statute that gave Government the power to renegotiate these only within strict limits, see Azpiazu, Schorr, n 12 above.
[48] See, eg, *yahoo news*, 11 October 2002.

signals that they intend to exercise their task of controlling the constitutionality of all state measures, including those implementing internationally agreed policies, this will necessarily influence the content of these negotiations. The importance attached to the role of the Supreme Court in the context of the negotiations of the latest agreement between Argentina and the IMF proves this point.[49]

If the judiciary were excluded from the control of emergency measures, governments could moreover easily justify the restriction of individual rights in the domestic context. They would only have to assert a situation of economic emergency and to present their palliative measures as the only possible way out, in which case the courts could not reasonably question these policies, even if they restricted individual rights or violated other constitutional principles. In this context, it needs to be borne in mind that situations of economic emergency do not befall a nation without the responsibility of those who have determined past economic and financial policies. This means that if a government that has driven a country into an economic crisis can then use the very same economic emergency as a reason to act outside of the constraints of the Constitution, and if in such a situation no effective judicial control of its policies is possible, the Government is in fact given the opportunity intentionally to create a situation in which it can justify the exercise of almost unlimited powers. In a country such as Argentina, where many argue that the abnormality has been institutionalised by the way of permanent emergencies, and it is therefore normal that the state needs to be rescued by a restriction of individual rights, it is difficult to accept that emergencies can in themselves justify restrictions of constitutional guarantees, particularly when bearing in mind that human rights violations do not seem to have had a rescuing effect.[50]

The dangers of an attitude that uncritically allows for the conferring of special powers in times of emergency have been forcefully delineated by the former Attorney General of Argentina, Don Sebastián Soler. He warned that when a state organ, in order to cure an extraordinary problem, resorts to faculties with which it is not vested, it creates a more serious danger than that which it originally tried to avert, namely that of blurring the line between a legitimate exercise of power and power excesses. According to him, the authority will get accustomed to overstepping constitutional boundaries, and what in the beginning was justified with reference to exceptional situations or by invoking necessities of primary magnitude, will sooner or later be perceived as the normal conditions of the exercise

[49] See, eg, *Clarín*, 26 October 2002.

[50] C D Gómez, 'Las reducciones salariales y las emergencias económicas', *La Ley*, 2002–F, 450–54, at p 453. See also G J Bidart Campos, 'Las reducciones salariales por emergencia económica', *La Ley*, 1998–A, 62–64, at pp 62–63.

of state power.[51] Thus, governments that know that in times of crisis they can exercise extraordinary powers and act outside of the strict limitations imposed by the country's Constitution, might get used to this and be tempted to rely on this as a means of economic policy.[52] Indeed, many commentators hold the deferential attitude of the Argentinian Supreme Court in the decade of the Menem Government responsible for the 'emergency culture' of government.[53] In *Peralta*, the Court had emphasised that the limitations on state actions contained in the Constitution cannot stand in the way of the efficient exercise of state power, and that in times of major economic and social upheavals, the biggest threat is not the temporary suspension of legal principles, but rather the consequences following from their strict application.[54] In *San Luis*, the decision on the redollarisation of bank accounts, the Court reversed this attitude and declared that the violation of the fundamental order would merely aggravate the crisis, as in addition to the rights that are already affected by the crisis itself, the remaining constitutional guarantees would also be endangered.[55] While it can by no means be excluded that the shift in the Supreme Court's case law has more to do with political power considerations than with legal concerns,[56] as a matter of legal principle it is nevertheless submitted that this is the right approach, because:

> the Court cannot stay mute when in the name of an emergency the constitutional order has been infringed upon, as it would otherwise violate its constitutional mandate.[57]

It then remains to be discussed how this control should be performed in the context of economic crises. It is submitted that when exercising its task of controlling the constitutionality of emergency measures, the courts are not prevented from exercising judicial realism and from allowing for a restriction of the normal enjoyment of constitutional rights, if otherwise the common good or the rights of others would suffer irreparable harm.[58]

[51] Fallos, 247: 121 (1960).
[52] B Campos, n 50 above, at pp 62–63; B L Jacobs, 'Pesification and economic crisis in Argentina; the moral hazard posed by a politicized Supreme Court', (2003) *University of Miami Inter-American Law Review*, 391–434, at pp 394–95; see also A B Bianchi, 'La Corte Suprema ha establecido su tésis oficial sobre la emergencia económica', *La Ley*, 1991–C, 141–71, at p 154.
[53] Gómez, n 50 above, at p 453; A M Hernández, *Las emergencias y el orden constitucional* (Buenos Aires, Rubinzal-Culzoni Editores, 2002), at p 74; Jacobs, n 52 above, at p 429.
[54] *Peralta y otro v Nación Argentina (Ministerio de Economía — BCRA)*, Fallos, 313: 1513 (1990), at para 44.
[55] *Provincia de San Luis c Estado Nacional*, La Ley, 2003–B, 537, at para 43.
[56] See, eg, Jacobs, n 52 above, at p 412.
[57] *Provincia de San Luis c Estado Nacional*, La Ley, 2003–B, 537, at para 55. See also *RJR MacDonald v Canada* [1995] 3 SCR 199, at para 136 per McLaghlin J.
[58] *Peralta y otro c Nación Argentina (Ministerio de Economía – BCRA)*, Fallos, 313, 1513 (1990), at para 37.

However, I would argue that this does not require special rules for constitutional review in emergency situations, but rather constitutes no more than an application of the generally accepted principles that constitutionally guaranteed rights are not absolute, but rather find their limits in the rights of others and in other competing constitutional interests. The particularities caused by the situation of economic emergency could be considered in the context of the courts' assessment of whether or not the restrictions imposed are proportionate to the aims pursued, as extreme crises might make necessary extreme measures and might justify requiring that all citizens contribute to the effort of overcoming the crisis by sacrificing parts of their rights.[59] According to the Argentinian Supreme Court — this being a jurisprudence that is at least verbally accepted by the other state powers — in times of grave emergencies, emergency measures can temporarily *suspend* the full enjoyment of constitutionally guaranteed rights. What they cannot do, on the other hand, is take away altogether such constitutional rights, or alter them in their core.[60] Thus, in the context of the proportionality analysis, the situation of emergency can be used to justify a more intense restriction of constitutional rights, but not their elimination. This obviously requires a stringent judicial control of these measures in order to ascertain whether there was in fact a situation of emergency, whether the restrictive measures were, in fact, proportionate, and whether or not they crossed the line between the temporary suspension of the full enjoyment of a constitutional right or its permanent alteration or deprivation. This is in line with the approach suggested by McLaghlin J in the context of the Canadian Charter, when she emphasised that:

> While remaining sensitive to the social and political context of the impugned law and allowing for difficulties of proof inherent in that context, the courts must nevertheless insist that before the state can override constitutional rights, there be a reasoned demonstration of the good which the law may achieve in relation to the seriousness of the infringement. It is the task of the courts to maintain this bottom line if the rights conferred by our constitution are to have force and meaning ... No matter how important Parliament's goal may seem, if the state has not demonstrated that the means by which it seeks to achieve its goal are reasonable and proportionate to the infringement of rights, then the law must perforce fail.[61]

It is submitted that these arguments apply a *forteriori* to acts of the executive. Thus, instead of being free to restrict individual rights in times of crisis

[59] *Provincia de San Luis c Estado Nacional*, La Ley, 2003–B, 537, at para 44.
[60] See, for example, *Peralta y otro c Nación Argentina (Ministerio de Economía — BCRA)*, Fallos, 313, 1513 (1990), at para 38; *Provincia de San Luis c Estado Nacional*, La Ley, 2003–B, 537, at para 23.
[61] *Provincia de San Luis c Estado Nacional*, La Ley, 2003–B, 537, at para 129.

based on their own evaluation of the necessity and inevitability of certain measures, governments and parliaments must be prepared to justify the existence of an emergency and the content of the measures taken and to convince the courts of the reasonableness of the chosen measures within the constitutional framework.[62] While the Government always stressed the necessity, inevitability and even vitality of the emergency measures taken, it is submitted that these are political questions that usually depend on a value judgment of what is considered necessary in a given situation.[63] Thus, from the fact that an emergency measure is presented as an essential, the most effective, or even the only means to react to a crisis, it does not follow that this assessment contains an objective truth that the courts need to accept without further investigation, and without subjecting the measures justified this way to a constitutional analysis. If the judiciary takes its task of controlling the constitutionality of emergency measures seriously instead of adopting an unduly deferential approach to governmental policies, even in times of crisis constitutional rights and guarantees cannot easily be undermined.

PROBLEMS THAT NEED TO BE RESOLVED IN THE CONTEXT OF THE JUSTICIABILITY OF EMERGENCY MEASURES

Given that constitutional review of emergency legislation, if taken seriously, has an enormous political impact on the exercise of governmental powers as well as on the protection of individual rights and constitutional guarantees, it is essential that it is being performed in a consistent and predictable manner. In this respect, the Argentinian example shows some ground for concern. First of all, from the point of view of Argentinian constitutional law, the validity of legislation and other state measures stands and falls with its reasonableness. It is then essential that clear criteria exist according to which reasonableness can be assessed. The application of this principle by Argentinian courts, as well as its discussion in legal texts, demonstrates that the principle is extremely vague, which is worrying, as court decisions are then neither predictable for the Government nor for individuals who initiate court proceedings. It is, for example, not clear whether the control of reasonableness should start from an assumption in favour of the constitutionality of governmental activities,[64] or whether it is the Government that has the burden of

[62] See also the discussion of closely related issues by R E Edwards, 'Judicial Deference under the Human Rights Act', (2002) 65 *MLR* 859–82.
[63] R A Guibourg, 'Norma, coyuntura y emergencia', *La Ley*, 2003–E, 1060–1065, at pp 1064–1065.
[64] See N P Sagües, 'Derecho constitucional y derecho de emergencia', *La Ley*, 1990–D, 1036–1058, at p 1057; J Cianciardo, 'Una aplicación cuestionable del principio de razonabilidad', *La Ley*, 2002–B, 953–61, at p 960.

showing the reasonableness of its emergency measures that restrict individual rights.[65] Nor is it entirely obvious how a control of reasonableness can be separated from controlling the policy choices as such. These problems, which are by no means exclusively Argentinian,[66] need to receive more academic attention in order to achieve more legal certainty and predictability.

As a matter of procedural law, Argentina has adopted a system whereby every court, federal or provincial, of first or last instance, can declare legislation or other state acts to be unconstitutional.[67] However, court decisions, even those of the Supreme Court of the Argentinian Nation, only have *inter partes* effect.[68] This raises two serious problems, that of contradictory decisions by different courts regarding the constitutionality of the same piece of legislation or other state measures; and that of the invalidity of the provision or measure only with regard to the parties to the litigation. Leaving aside the general question of the disadvantages of such a system, it is submitted that in the context of emergency legislation that affects large parts of society, such a system becomes untenable. The fact that the emergency legislation continued to be valid and applicable, even though the Supreme Court had declared its incompatibility with constitutional guarantees in the case of *Smith*,[69] for example, made possible the subsequent decision in *Banco Francés*.[70] In this latter case, a federal judge decided that, based on the expert evidence that was made available to him and which, as he pointed out, had not been considered by the Supreme Court in *Smith*, the *corralito* was reasonable. This, of course, further added to the already immense judicial uncertainty created by the regularly changing emergency legislation. Thus, some individuals with bank accounts in dollars could obtain a decision allowing them to withdraw an unlimited amount of money in US dollars according to the real exchange rate, not the one that was artificially determined in Decree 214/2002. Meanwhile, to those who were waiting for their cases to be processed, the outcome of the litigation was not predictable, while those who, for example because they did not have the means to do so, did not challenge the emergency measures, had to tolerate the application of provisions that the Supreme Court of the country had declared to be unconstitutional! All of this could call into question the adequacy of an individualised approach to the protection of rights in a situation in which

[65] R L Lorenzetti, 'Nunca más: emergencia económica y derechos humanos', *La Ley*, 2003–A, 1207–1221, at p 1215; B Campos, n 50 above, at pp 62–63.
[66] For a discussion of this problem, drawing on the example of different jurisdictions, see Edwards, n 62 above, at pp 864–65.
[67] Zarini, n 8 above, at pp 87–88.
[68] *Ibid*, at p 93.
[69] See n 10 above.
[70] *BBVA Banco Francés SA c Estado Nacional-Ministerio de Economía s/proceso de conocimiento*, La Ley, 2002–A, 904.

the rights of the vast majority of citizens are affected by emergency measures, but where the claims of all citizens cannot be fully satisfied. For, it might violate the principle of equality if the claims of those who first secure favourable judgments, which will mostly be individuals who can afford the costs of court proceedings, will be fully met, while the majority of citizens will be left with nothing.[71] However, it is submitted that these arguments cannot justify the use of emergency legislation that restricts constitutional guarantees, and even less the suspension of judicial proceedings or of the execution of judicial decisions. Instead, it is submitted that what is needed is a concentration of decisions on the constitutionality of legislative measures in one court. Even more importantly, such decisions need to have *erga omnes* effect, so that once it is decided that a piece of emergency legislation is, in fact, unconstitutional, it can no longer be applied to anybody. It then needs to be decided what mechanisms to introduce in order to decide the effect of a declaration of unconstitutionality. It would, for example, be possible for the courts to refer the legislation back to the state authority from which it emanated[72] with a deadline within which it needs to be amended based on the Supreme Court's guidance on the constitutional problems the original provisions had raised.[73]

A problem that has so far been left aside is that of the protection of social rights. Given the limited justiciability of such rights, one argument against the justiciability of emergency legislation could be that the latter favours justiciable negative rights over social rights, in forcing the Government to adopt economic policies that respect property rights and therefore redistributing the little available funds that might otherwise have gone into the social protection of the population. However, it is submitted that this argument cannot stand in the way of the justiciability of negative rights, such as the right to property. Instead, what is essential is that social rights equally become justiciable,[74] and that principles are being developed whereby the Government can justify the restriction of negative rights to some extent when it can show that these restrictions are essential for the upholding of social rights.

Finally, in the context of Argentina, it cannot be left unmentioned that the Argentinian Supreme Court has the reputation of being corrupt and

[71] See Rivera, n 27 above, at p 1128; H M Lynch, 'Emergencia, derecho, justicia y seguridad juridical (reflexiones sobre la crisis y las libertades económicas)', *La Ley* 2002–C, 1287–1312, at p 1291; J C Crivelli, 'El fallo San Luis: un grave error que debe subsanarse', *La Ley*, 2003–C, 1474–79, at p 1474.

[72] See R Gargarella, *La justicia frente al gobierno* (Barcelona, Editorial Ariel, 1996), at pp 174–77.

[73] For an overview of the German approach to this issue see S Michalowski, L Woods, *German Constitutional Law — The Protection of Civil Liberties* (Aldershot, Ashgate, 1999), at pp 43–44.

[74] For an excellent discussion of this subject see V Abramovich, C Courtis, *Los derechos sociales como derechos exigibles* (Madrid, Editorial Trotta, 2002).

highly politicised.[75] Indeed, at the peak of the crisis, in early 2002, many Argentinians demanded in regular political demonstrations in front of the court house the replacement of the Supreme Court judges. At the same time, whenever the Supreme Court, or also lower courts, issued decisions that the Government regarded as a menace to its policies, they were threatened with impeachment proceedings, and in the case of the Supreme Court, impeachment proceedings against all judges were, in fact, initiated after the Court's decision in *Smith* that declared the unconstitutionality of the *corralito*.[76] While this paper tried to show that the mechanisms of constitutional review as foreseen in liberal democratic Constitutions can be a powerful means to uphold individual rights and constitutional principles in times of crisis, this presupposes a strong and independent judiciary which might not always be in place in countries in which such situations most frequently arise. However, it is submitted that this is not an argument against constitutional review of governmental activity, but rather an argument in favour of strengthening judicial independence and the legal excellence of the judiciary.

CONCLUSION

The example of Argentina has shown that in a globalised world, in times of economic crisis threats to the protection of human rights can come from the outside, in that powerful international organisations try to induce, or indeed impose, policies that adversely affect the rights of the population of a country in crisis, and from the inside, in that the government of such a country might resort to emergency legislation that restricts the rights of its citizens. Ways to reduce these threats accordingly need to be found at the national and the international level. While more and more arguments are being developed in favour of holding international organisations such as the IMF accountable for the human rights implications of their policies,[77] this is an objective that needs to be pursued at an international and global level, and individual states, particularly underdeveloped states in an acute economic crisis, are not necessarily in the best position to push for such a far-reaching policy change when negotiating with the IMF a much

[75] See, eg, Jacobs, n 52 above, at p 412.
[76] These proceedings were later dropped, partly because of the pressure of the IMF; see, eg, *Clarín*, 12 October 2002. But the current Government of President Kirchner has again taken up the impeachment issue, and so far one Supreme Court Justice has been suspended from his office as a result of impeachment proceedings, proceedings against one Justice are pending, and two Justices have resigned as a consequence of planned impeachment proceedings against them.
[77] For a detailed discussion of these questions see S Skogly, *The Human Rights Obligations of the World Bank and the International Monetary Fund* (London, Cavendish, 2001).

needed agreement that will help the country to avoid a default on debt repayment and isolation from the international financial market. Before the purpose of making governance subject to considerations of justice and the protection of human rights has been achieved at the global level, it is thus important to find ways in which individual countries can achieve a more just and human rights friendly globalisation.

This is where the importance of judicial control of governmental activities comes in. Particularly in times of acute economic crises, there is a serious imbalance of power between international financial organisations, on the one hand, and the government of an underdeveloped country in crisis, on the other,[78] so that international interests can to a large extent influence the policies the country has to implement. If, however, the government is subject to constitutional review of its policies, this means that the content of agreements reached at the international level must be compatible with the country's human rights obligations, which, in a country that not only provides for the protection and enforceability of traditional negative rights such as the right to property, but that also grants international documents that protect social rights constitutional status, provides great potential for the protection of human rights.

At the domestic level, the example of Argentina demonstrates the tendency of governments to perceive constitutional guarantees of individual rights, and constitutional mechanisms aiming to ensure that none of the state organs exceed their constitutionally designated powers, as obstacles preventing it from doing its job of rescuing the country in crisis. Especially in times of crisis, however, when citizens are particularly vulnerable because of the overall uncertainty of the social, economic, and political situation of their country, and when it is particularly easy for the other state powers to find arguments justifying an erosion of a political culture based on constitutional principles, it is essential that the judiciary does not shy away from fulfilling its constitutionally designated task of ensuring that the other state powers have not, in fact, overstepped their powers and chosen means that run counter to the demands of the Constitution.[79] While it is for the political powers to find solutions to overcome the crisis, solutions which violate the basic and inalienable rights of the citizens are excluded because they are unconstitutional.[80] Thus, in exercising constitutional review of emergency measures, the courts encourage government to find solutions that are compatible with

[78] See Stiglitz, n 1 above, at pp 42–43; Paddock, n 6 above, at p 166. The most recent and still ongoing struggle between the Argentinian Government and the IMF which has already led to the postponement of World Bank loans for Argentina, provides yet another demonstration of this, see *Clarín*, 9 January 2004.

[79] See also A A Gordillo, 'El estado de derecho en estado de emergencia', *La Ley*, 2001–F, 1050–1057, at p 1056.

[80] *Provincia de San Luis c Estado Nacional*, La Ley, 2003–B, 537, at para 44.

the Constitution instead of restricting individual rights whenever it deems this to be necessary. Furthermore, being able to question emergency measures in court and to trust in an independent judiciary that will uphold constitutional standards in times of crisis empowers the citizens of a country in crisis to bring human rights considerations into the equation.

4

Collateralism

SHELDON LEADER

THE SETTING

AS POWER MOVES away from the nation state — either below it to bodies such as commercial corporations, or above it to bodies such as those regulating international trade — certain basic rights are slipping from their central place. They do not disappear, but are relegated to being collateral constraints on institutional power. What does this shift involve, and why is it a problem? Whereas many states aim to hold the whole range of basic rights in an equitable balance with one another, limiting the exercise of one so as to make room for another, in the work of these organisations located in international and national civil society the balance is transformed. Some basic rights are recognised, but at the cost of systematically limiting their exercise for the benefit of other rights, and the latter do not always merit such priority. The balance of basic entitlements is thereby skewed in civil society, and the resulting social cost is high.

Consider some illustrations:

International Trade

Several of the treaties supervised by the WTO provide space for members to refuse the entry of goods or services on grounds that the refusal is necessary for the protection of public morals, as well as a list of other possible priorities.[1] Among the reasons that a country could potentially give for this exclusion is that it would be placed in violation of its own human rights obligations towards its subjects were it to do otherwise.[2] These

[1] See Article XX of the General Agreement on Tariffs and Trade, and Article XIV of the General Agreement on Trade in Services.

[2] See S Leader, 'Human Rights and International Trade: Mapping the Terrain' in P Macrory, *et al* (eds), *The World Trade Organization: Legal Economic and Political Analysis* (Berlin, Springer,

rights are grounded on the need to protect the health and safety of the users of products; the protection of children; protection of access to adequate education and medical facilities; and other concerns.[3] If it is to succeed in carving out a right to refuse to trade — to resist market pressures against the presumption that, as a member of the WTO, the member state is meant to open its borders — the exclusion must usually be shown to be necessary in order to achieve the objective sought.[4] 'Necessity' here has a special meaning: it does not indicate that this measure is essential for a policy to succeed but rather that, as compared with reasonably available alternatives, the policy has least impact on what is seen as the central objective of a trading treaty: the integration of markets.

It is important to notice two features of the balance being sought in this example. We need to distinguish between *ultimate* priority accorded to a basic right, and priorities in the *adjustment* of that right against the demands of competitors. In the trading regime, a state is entitled to give ultimate priority to, say, its citizens' right to protection from dangerous products such as certain cigarettes or cars. This is allowed to take priority over the competing basic right to free disposal of property that is said to underpin the right to trade.[5] However, before a non-trading right can acquire that priority, the excluding state must satisfy the 'least impact' principle. The result is that a member state may have a preferred *level* at which it would like to provide protection of a basic right (such as a right to a safe environment), but may be forced to choose a lower degree of protection if that would prove less of an obstacle to producers in selling their products on the market.[6] The right to a safe environment in our example

2004) pp 2235–68. Several leading commentators feel that the state could refuse to open its markets for human rights reasons via the freedom of action given by Art XX of the GATT, which permits members to refuse entry of a product if doing so is 'necessary to protect public morals'. On this point, see S Charnovitz, 'The Moral Exception in Trade Policy' (1998) 38 *Virginia Journal of International Law*, 689.

[3] These rights, and their vulnerability to the pressures of trade, are considered in J Oloka-Onyango and D Udagama, 'Human Rights as the Primary Objective of International Trade, Investment and Finance Policy and Practice', a paper submitted in accordance with UN Sub-Commission Resolution 1998/12 E/CN 4/Sub 2/1999/11; UN Sub-Commission on the Promotion and Protection of Human Rights, 'Liberalization of Trade in Services and Human Rights,' Sub-Commission on the Promotion and Protection of Human Rignts, E/CN4/Sub 2/2002/9, June 25, 2002, 25 June 2002 para ¶ 7; *cf* UN Commission On Human Rights, Fifty-Ninth Session, The Fundamental Principle of Non-discrimination in the Context of Globalization, E/CN 4/2003/50, December 2002.

[4] On the dimensions of this 'necessity' requirement, see S Leader, above n 2, at p 2257ff.

[5] The status of this latter right is debated, but for our purposes we shall accept it as among the fundamental rights that a democracy should protect.

[6] For an example see the *Thai Cigarettes* case, *Thailand — Restrictions on Importation of and Internal Taxes on Cigarettes*, BISD 37S/200, adopted on 7 November 1990, discussed in S Leader, above n 2, 2259f. For a case that gives greater latitude for to a member state's setting of its own level of commitment to a non-trading interest, see the *Asbestos* case,

is given ultimate priority, but the right to trade is given priority in adjustment: it sets the benchmark against which candidates for rights protecting a non-trading interest are evaluated. The latter has become a collateral concern of the trading system.

Corporate Governance

Private companies are gradually being drawn to recognise obligations to respect certain human rights. However, here again certain of these rights have a lower priority in adjustment as compared with others, and the former have this quality because they are collateral to the objectives of the corporation in question. As in the international trade example, the rights are taken seriously in that they are given ultimate priority, but they are shaped in a particular way that reflects the fact that they fall to one side of the direct concerns of the organisation. A recent example has emerged in a large infrastructure project, the Baku-Ceyhan petroleum pipeline between the Caspian and Mediterranean. The consortium of multinationals building and operating this pipeline has made it clear that it intends to respect all relevant human rights during the lifetime of the project. However, in working out its legal liabilities, it drew a sharp line between its obligation to compensate someone once damage occurs and an obligation to allow the state to intervene proactively, stopping the project if necessary in order to prevent risk from such damage arising in the first place. The consortium was willing to assume the former liability, but only a shrunken version of the latter — one that falls short of the evolving requirements of international human rights law.[7] It refused any significant interference by the state with the running of the project — even for valid human rights reasons — on the ground that limiting itself to the compensation strategy will have less of an impact on revenue. The company has thereby given ultimate priority to a right to a safe environment, but it has given priority in adjustment to the property rights of its investors. It has sought this adjustment not because it simply has a preference for building and operating the pipeline at a profit, but because it feels that this is its primary mandate. Health, safety, and environmental protection thereby take their place as collateral concerns — not because

European Communities — Measures Affecting Asbestos and Asbestos-Containing Products Appellate Body WT/DS135/11, also discussed in Leader, above n 2.

[7] For a fuller account, see *Human Rights on the Line: the Baky-Tibilisi-Ceyhan Pipeline* (Amnesty International, UK, 2003) para 4.1.1. These restrictive conditions have been modified by a legally binding *Human Rights Undertaking* <http://www.caspiandevelopmentandexport.com/Downloads/Human%20Rights%20Undertaking.pdf> (Accessed 12 September 2004).

they are thought to be less worthy of protection per se, but because this is what the corporation believes fidelity to its legitimate role requires.

Perhaps certain basic rights can only ever succeed in playing this secondary role in institutions such as trading bodies or commercial corporations. But we should not be too quick to accept this relegation. Some rights should be brought back to a more central place on the agenda of bodies such as the WTO and commercial corporations. The obstacle to achieving this is that such institutions are not states, and cannot for fundamental reasons we shall consider be treated as if they were. This is not an insurmountable problem: it is possible both to hold on to the basic fact that we are dealing with non-state actors and to require these organisations to give a central place to certain basic rights that seem at first glance to lie beyond their remit.

In developing this argument, and a set of principles that flow from it, we will concentrate on the example of world trade, leaving for a later occasion its application to the commercial corporation.

THE ROOTS OF COLLATERALISM: FUNCTIONALIST PRINCIPLES

The prospects for moving beyond collateralism depend on an investigation of its roots. These are to be found in a functional outlook, which is defined via an approach taken to three related issues: the character of institutional objectives; the scope of that institution's responsibility; and a particular approach taken towards competing basic rights.

Two Types of Institutional Objective

To appreciate the thrust of a functional approach, we need to distinguish between what can be called general objectives of an institution on the one hand, and special objectives on the other. General objectives set the basic direction which an organisation is taking. Often these goals are shared across a range of bodies, each with quite distinct qualities. The WTO, for example, is assigned by the preamble to its articles several such aims, including the raising of standards of living; expanding the production of, and trade in, goods and services; ensuring full employment; and promoting sustainable development.[8] It shares several of these objectives with other international organisations such as the World Bank and IMF. General objectives can be either found in the explicit text of the organisation's constitution — often in its preamble — or they may be considered to be in the constitution implicitly, as several authors

[8] Preamble, para 1.

argue when they claim that the constitution is tacitly bound by certain elements of international human rights law.[9] Alongside this set of goals is the second category of special objectives: those that pick out a particular role for an organisation that sets it apart from the other institutions with which it shares general objectives. The WTO's special objective says that the organisation is to aim, across the world, at '... reciprocal and mutually advantageous arrangements directed to substantial reduction of tariffs.' It is to do this by developing '... an integrated, more viable and durable multilateral trading system.' [10] The special purposes of the IMF are, inter alia, 'to promote international monetary cooperation through a permanent institution...; to promote exchange stability; to shorten the duration and lessen the degree of disequilibrium in the international balances of payments of members,' and so on.[11]

Now, the functionalist focuses on these special objectives rather than on the shared, general ones. The WTO's legitimate powers, on this view, flow from its mandate to integrate markets by mutual and non-discriminatory reduction of obstacles to trade. It is only via the pursuit of this special objective that the organisation may legitimately aim to attain the general ones. It may not rely on general objectives as a reason for compromising those goals that give specific and special content to its mission. Take as an example the WTO's general objective of promoting sustainable development. From a functionalist perspective, any development strategy that might encourage a member state to prevent the penetration of trade into its domestic market is a strategy that either falls outside of the remit of the WTO altogether, or insofar as there is a place made for it, this must always be a secondary — collateral — one. An extreme version of functionalism sees no place at all for other goals while a more moderate species of the position provides some opening for objectives that cut across the primary one. We shall see more of this point below. Functionalism has the following results:

The Scope of Responsibility

Appeal to special objectives, in the hands of the functionalist, shapes the boundaries of institutional responsibility. It fixes, that is, the range of those to whom that responsibility is owed. For example the WTO is, on this functionalist view, primarily responsible to the *producers* of goods and services who will benefit from its exercise of its particular mandate. Its

[9] R Howse and M Mutua, 'Protecting Human Rights in the Global Economy: Challenges for the WTO,' (2000) *Rights and Democracy* 31ff <http://www.ichrdd.ca> (Accessed 12 September 2004).
[10] Preamble, para 4.
[11] Articles of Agreement, Arts 1 (1, 3, and 6).

dominant concern should be that these producers in an exporting state not suffer discrimination at the hands of an importing state. That exhausts what 'fair trade' means. The interests of others affected by trade, such as the users of goods and services, may be taken into account but will of necessity be secondary in order of importance as compared with producer interests.[12] From this perspective, the WTO is not accountable for the fact that in opening markets up to foreign competition certain local businesses might be forced into bankruptcy with the social consequences that this carries. Insofar as the organisation does pay attention to this damage, says the functionalist, it must do so in a way that is subordinate to its primary mission of market integration.

Directions of Adjustment Among Basic Rights

The functionalist way of fixing priorities among institutional objectives, and its way of identifying those to whom primary responsibility is owed, lead inexorably to the relegation of certain basic rights to a collateral role. This is not, once again, because these rights are thought to have less intrinsic value, but simply because of the structure of the situation. If you begin with a functional outlook, the rest follows. It does no good to berate the functionalist for failing to take rights seriously. She will reply, hand on heart, that she does. She is not willing to sacrifice all basic rights to the pursuit of institutional goals per se. She is willing, as has been seen, to give ultimate priority to those rights that call for a limitation on the institution's ability to pursue what we called its particular, defining goals. She is, for example, willing to see the right of a local population to a safe environment take ultimate precedence over the right to trade. At the same time, however, she systematically looks for a mode of exercising that right that will do the least to prejudice other basic rights which run with the grain of institutional goals.

Varying Strengths of a Functional Position

The most austere of functional outlooks often bars human rights concerns altogether.[13] Unless a commitment to support such rights is clearly within the special objectives of an organisation, and is not simply located in what is often seen as the thinner atmosphere of its general goals, then for some functionalists the rights have no substantial regulative force. An example

[12] For an account of the producer bias, see E Petersmann, 'Human Rights, Cosmopolitan Democracy, and the Law of the WTO' in I Fletcher *et al*, (eds) *Foundations and Perspectives of International Trade Law* (London, Sweet & Maxwell, 2001) para 8–023.

[13] I owe the distinctions between different strengths of collateral position to a suggestion from Prof Roger Brownsword.

is the position taken by the General Counsel to the IMF, François Gianviti. He considers the IMF's Articles of Agreement to fix exhaustively the competence and powers of the organisation. It follows for him that the '... the social rights to health or education ... [as found in the International Covenant on Economic, Social and Cultural Rights]... lie outside the mandate [of the Fund].'[14] He points to what he believes is a wall between the IMF's obligations and the terms of the Covenant. This is in Article 24 of the Covenant itself, which says that

> nothing in the Covenant shall be interpreted as impairing the constitutions of the specialized agencies which define the respective responsibilities of the various organs of the specialized agencies in regard to the matters dealt with in the Covenant.

For Gianviti, this means that, 'the Covenant does not affect the Articles of Agreement of the Fund, including its mission and governance structure.'[15] The guiding principle, on this view, picks out what the Covenant calls the *respective* responsibility of each international organisation: the responsibility that it has which is distinct from those of other bodies with overlapping general objectives. This in turn fixes the boundary to its mission.

The more moderate species of functional approach moves one step closer to basic rights. We can see this version in the WTO administered trade treaties already mentioned. They allow member states ultimately to refuse to trade for certain overriding non-trade concerns, but then they also require that the way in which the latter is carried out does least damage to the institution's special purpose. Basic rights appear to receive their due respect, but practice can fall well short of what we normally think of as required.

MOVING BEYOND COLLATERALISM: CIVIC PRINCIPLES

The functionalist approach stands in sharp contrast to a conception of institutional authority and responsibility grounded on what can be called civic principles.[16] The contrast can be drawn along each of the three dimensions: institutional objectives; the scope of responsibility; and directions of adjustment among basic rights.

[14] F Gianviti, 'Economic, Social and Cultural Rights and the International Monetary Fund' ECOSOC document 07/05/2001; E/C 12/2001/WP 5 para 23. For a contrary view, see S I Skogly, *The Human Rights Obligations of the World Bank and the International Monetary Fund* (London, Cavendish, 2001) Ch 7.

[15] Gianviti, above n 14, para 15.

[16] For an exploration of the distinction between functional and civic principles, see S Leader, 'Three Faces of Justice and the Management of Change' (2000) 63 *Modern Law Review* 55. Compare the treatment of civic justification in L Boltanski and L Thevenot, *De La Justification* (Paris, Gallimard, 1991) at 137 ff, and Parts III–V.

Institutional Objectives

Civic principles invert the functionalist's order among goals. Where the functionalists claim that shared, general objectives can guide the organisation via its pursuit of its special goals, civic principles turn that priority around. The special objectives fall into place as a particular way of fulfilling a larger mandate, and the latter may sometimes call for compromises in the pursuit of the former. These are compromises that may be far stronger than moderate functionalism allows.

To go back to our central example, were the WTO's constitution to be interpreted from a civic perspective then the special objective of promoting market integration would have to be pursued in a way that least compromised the institution's need to achieve a balanced pursuit of the *full range* of shared, general objectives we have seen in its preamble: from promoting sustainable development to expanding the production of, and trade in, goods and services. It would no longer temper its commitment to such a balance by having to find and pursue a version of these general objectives that did least damage to the special imperative to integrate markets. As before, there are some concrete implications of this outlook.

The Scope of Responsibility

Civic principles widen considerably the balance and range of institutional responsibility. It is a range that enlarges the accountability of the organisation for the effects of its policies, and it is a balance that places all of those affected on a par. The result brings the responsibilities of the non-state actor in some ways closer to those of the state itself, though vital differences remain. Thus, where *states* open their markets each is responsible for the effects of that decision on users, producers, and third parties. There is no legitimate basis for giving any one of these interests automatic priority over the other. Similarly, the state's decision to operate an oil pipeline, or to close a factory, renders it responsible to all affected parties equally: to those whose working lives, land ownership, or environments are affected; as well as to those shareholders who may have invested in the project if it mixes private and public finance. From a civic perspective, the powerful non-state actor should hold in equal balance the interests of the same range of individuals: they are all affected by what it does, and none should find in advance that they take second place.

Directions of adjustment among rights

As with institutional objectives, so with rights: when basic rights compete with one another, civic principles require that the exercise of one such right is not always to be compromised in favour of another.[17] The compromise can run in both directions: the right to adequate health care is sometimes to be adjusted in favour of the right to trade, and at other times the opposite is true. There is, on civic principles, a quality of reversibility about these adjustments between competing basic rights. To illustrate this feature from another domain, consider the right to life as it competes with the right to freedom of movement. Preservation of life is ultimately more important than is the interest in freedom of movement along the highway. But it is not true that each and every level of risk of death is more important to prevent than is any given level of freedom of movement.[18] Assume that evidence shows that the death rate on highways is reduced by a significant but decreasing number for every mile per hour of reduction in permitted speed. Assume that the reduction is 10,000 deaths in a given population for every mile of reduction between 100 and 90 mph; 1000 from 50 to 40 mph; 100 from 40 to 20 mph, and 10 between 20 and 10 mph. Even though the preservation of life is ultimately more important than is freedom of movement along the highway, it does not follow that the right to freedom of movement must always be adjusted downwards so as to have the least impact on the death rate. At a certain point a polity may, and sometimes must, reverse the direction of compromise. In this example, it must at a certain point limit the attention paid to the risk of death in favor of the right to freedom of movement, however clearly a certain number of deaths is linked to a further reduction in speed.

This point should help us to pin down further what is involved in moving a basic right away from a collateral position towards being a central concern of an institution. A right plays such a central role if it forms part of a set, each one of which sometimes serves as the benchmark against which the exercise of another is adjusted. If there is to be any prospect of combining civic principles with the imperatives of specialized organisations in civil society, then it is this capacity for mutual and reversible adjustment among rights that is crucial: it is the domain in which that marriage must succeed in practical terms.

COMBINING CIVIC PRINCIPLES AND FUNCTIONAL IMPERATIVES

At first sight, the prospects for this marriage look meagre. It is tempting to think that civic balances underpin the work of the state, but not that of the species of specialised organisation we are concerned with here. The

[17] See S Leader, 'Integration, Federation, and the Ethics of Rights' in M Costillo (ed), *Morale et politique des Droits de l'homme* (Zurich and New York, Georg Olms Verlag, 2003) p 63 ff.
[18] *Cf* Jeremy Waldron, 'Rights in Conflict' (1989) 99 *Ethics* 503, esp 509–12, 516–18.

issue turns around institutional identity. Many think that it undermines the very nature of the WTO to think of holding it, like the state, responsible for damage to the full range of human rights. We seem to be faced with an insurmountable difference in kind between the two institutions.

Such an objection can be grounded as an article of faith among some political theorists. According to this, there is a fundamental difference between what Michael Oakeshott called enterprise and civil associations. The former corresponds to what in today's parlance would be a non-state actor, and the prime example of the latter is the state itself. The enterprise association exists to further its members' common purposes, says Oakeshott, and distinct common purposes define the character of distinct associations. These range from the Vegetarian Society to the commercial company and the WTO.[19] The state, as a civil association, is said not to be the product of such common purposes. Instead, it provides the background against which such purposes are pursued by the enterprise association. The state properly exists to provide a framework of public order, and this framework could extend to include human rights. [20] But it would be a mistake to transfer a civic responsibility for these basic rights from one domain to the other: from the state to the non-state actor. The reason is that on this analysis the latter are inherently unsuited to a civic role. The rules and rights enterprise associations adopt must, Oakeshott thinks, inevitably have an instrumental quality to them: they are tailored to the pursuit of common purposes, and if they don't serve these purposes they must be discarded.[21] It would be fundamentally wrong to force this sort of organisation to respect any basic right that takes it away from its dedication to what we have called its special purposes, defining the field of concrete agreement among its members. From this perspective, the WTO or the commercial corporation cannot *coherently* see themselves as having a primary responsibility to further the full set of human rights with the range and balance that we have seen civic principles require. That scope of commitment manifests a fundamental confusion between the logic of enterprise and civic association.[22]

How convincing is this approach? If it is successful, collateralism is built into the fabric of globalisation — of that portion, that is, which has witnessed the transfer of power from states to international and domestic non-state actors. The question is, is it possible to bring collateral responsibilities for certain basic rights, such as access to health care in the case of the WTO, into the set of primary responsibilities of that body, and yet still

[19] M Oakeshott, *On Human Conduct* (Oxford, OUP, 1975) p 114 ff.
[20] *Ibid* p 118, fn 1, though Oakeshott does not make this extension to a consideration of human rights.
[21] *Ibid* p 117.
[22] For a sustained statement of this functionalist view in relation to the International Monetary Fund, see F Gianviti, above n 14, at para 23.

not abandon the particular character of the institution? Is it, in short, fatal to an attempted transformation of priorities that the WTO could complain that it is being asked to duplicate the functions of the state in addition to its own?

The answer is that it is possible to hold on to and to do justice to both of these elements that are pulling against one another. It is possible, that is, that the WTO can carry on as an organisation with the particular role assigned to it of integrating markets, while at the same time having a responsibility to promote rights such as the right to health care. In fact, with no loss to its fundamental mission, it might at some points properly give that right priority in adjustment over the right of its members to fair access to one another's markets. It might, in other words, reverse the direction of compromise between basic rights. The reason for working with basic rights in this way is that it is also possible to reverse the order between general and special institutional objectives without sacrificing the identity of an organisation. If the WTO has the shared, general goal of promoting the right to health as part of its stated commitment to sustainable development, at some points it must be prepared to adjust its mission of promoting access to markets so as to have least negative impact on that development objective. If it does so, it does not cease to be the particular type of body it is: it is not submerged into other types of institution.[23]

This argument could be thought to founder on one further objection that is often advanced against this larger set of responsibilities. This is the objection based on institutional lack of competence. The WTO is not a development or health agency. Its rule making authorities, like its dispute settlement mechanism, do not have the experience or knowledge which will enable them to make assessments about what is or is not an essential measure for the protection of health or a policy that will make development truly sustainable. The urge to give primacy to what we have called special over general objectives simply mirrors the expertise of the institution: it cannot be expected to have responsibility for satisfying the full range of human rights, simply because it would be no good at doing so.

There are two faults in this line of argument. One is that the trading system already makes assessments of the nature of measures designed to protect health or the environment whenever it decides whether one will have less of an impact on trade as compared with another. It must not only look at this impact, but must be in a position to compare alternative measures protecting non-trading interests that might reasonably be selected. True, two different exercises are involved in deciding about the impact

[23] For this point in relation to the potential range of human rights obligations for the IMF and World Bank, see the argument advanced in S Leader, 'Review of Skogly, "The Human Rights Obligations of the World Bank and the International Monetary Fund,"'(2002) 2 *Kings College Law Journal* 147.

of a health measure on trade, and deciding about the impact of a trade measure on health, which this proposed approach to balances among rights involves. The second sort of balance does require a higher degree of knowledge about the health strategy in question. But it is quite possible — and it happens already — for other specialised bodies, such as the WHO, to provide expert evidence to WTO dispute settlement bodies on these issues.[24]

This heightened responsibility for non-trading rights on the part of the WTO also does not require that a basic right to *trade* be written out of the script, as is sometimes advocated.[25] It is possible for the WTO to give occasional priority in adjustment to other rights than the right to trade, but it does not follow that the latter does not exist as part of the cluster of basic rights that the body must respect. Instead, the transformation towards fidelity to civic principles would mean that the institution is brought to place the right to trade alongside others that compete with it.

REVISITING THE DISTINCTION BETWEEN STATE AND NON-STATE ACTOR

If this line of reasoning is sound, then — to go back to Oakeshott's vocabulary — the line between the roles of civic and enterprise associations can be drawn differently. One cannot collapse enterprise associations, with their particular defining purposes, into states. But it is nevertheless possible to inject civic principles into the internal priorities of enterprise associations. In doing so, it is possible to move basic rights from their status as collateral concerns into the core of the organisation's responsibilities.

The result is a widened range of responsibility by these institutions that often dominate national and international civil society. It is a responsibility to the following:

People

It should be possible to give priority at various points in institutional work to users of goods and services; to potential victims of damage from these goods and services who are not users; and, of course, to producers of those goods and services. The first two types of person to whom the WTO is

[24] For an example, see the evidence provided by the WHO to a WTO panel in the famous *Thai Cigarettes* case. Report of the GATT Panel, *Thailand — Restrictions on Importation of and Internal Taxes on Cigarettes*, GATT No. DS10/R, BISD 37S/200, adopted on November 7, 1990.

[25] P Alston, 'Resisting the Merger and Acquisition of Human Rights by Trade Law: A Reply to Petersmann' (2002) 13 *European Journal of International Law* 815. *Cf* S Leader above n 2.

responsible have interests that lie beyond the special purposes of the organisation, but their protection does fall within its general purposes.

The Range of Basic Rights

Similarly, there are basic rights whose protection lies beyond the WTO's special objective of market integration but well within its general goals, such as the rights associated with the promotion of sustainable development. If so, then these rights should enter into the set that are mutually adjusted against one another, along the lines demanded by civic principles.

An Illustration

To end with an illustration, consider the example of a country that wants to ban imports of a certain product on grounds of risk to health. Consider two such products: the higher per capita consumption of one carries a marginally higher risk of life-threatening illness, and another that carries a substantially higher risk of a life-threatening illness. An example of the former could be a food that, beyond a certain level of consumption, tends to cause obesity which in turn can marginally increase the incidence of certain diseases such as cancer; and an example of the latter could be another product, such as cigarettes, which radically increase the incidence of that cancer. Assume finally that it is not practical or desirable for a country to totally ban the domestic consumption of these cigarettes, the local variety of which is much less attractive to the population than a foreign product would be.[26]

In the first situation, if the local production and sale of food causing obesity is allowed then it seems appropriate for the WTO to demand that foreign producers of similar products have equal access to the market. Pointing in the other direction, it is also legitimate that a member state aim to limit consumption of such food as part of its public health concerns, some of these falling within the basic right to adequate access to health protection. Bringing the two considerations together, it seems right that the public health objective be accomplished in the least trade restrictive way: such as by non-discriminatory labeling requirements that carry appropriate warnings rather than by outright bans on importation. This solution would be likely to yield a greater number of cases of obesity than would a complete ban of the import. Nevertheless, it would be an equitable way of balancing the two competing concerns of sustaining

[26] Compare the facts of the *Thai Cigarettes* case, above n 24.

non-discriminatory access to markets and protecting this domain of public health.

In the second situation, the tables are turned. If the state allows increased consumption of a product which poses a substantial threat to life, it might be in violation of relevant international conventions for a failure to act.[27] How should the trading system approach these situations? As with the first case, the options for controlling cigarette consumption range from labelling requirements through to total bans on imports. Here, it is submitted, the state should be allowed to choose the import-reducing measure that will do most to reduce the risk to life. The direction of adjustment is reversed: rather than finding a method of protecting human life that has the least negative impact on trade, the state would be allowed here to adjust the flow of trade in a way that has the least impact on human life.

It is, of course, not easy to draw lines between degrees of risk of harm arising from the import of different sorts of goods and services, and hence to know when it would be appropriate to alter the direction of adjustment between trading and non-trading interests in the light of human rights requirements. However, as suggested earlier, the bodies charged with the primary duty of interpreting the meaning of these basic rights do provide us with guidelines — either from organisations that specialise in a particular domain, such as the ILO or WHO; or from bodies with a more general mandate, such as the Committee on Economic Social and Cultural Rights' General Comments and Statements on the meaning of provisions in the ICESCR. These can be drawn upon in order to see when a state should be given scope by the trading treaties to adjust the requirements of trade so as to do least damage to a non-trading interest, and when it should be required to adjust the non-trading interest to the requirements of trade.

CONCLUSION

Globalisation poses a threat to basic rights. I have argued that it is not a threat stemming from a failure to take such rights seriously: from a failure, that is, to appreciate the special weight that any given right must have over against the optimal pursuit of values such as economic efficiency. It is instead a threat that comes from a particular way of giving priority to some basic rights as compared with others. This we have called priority in adjustment as opposed to the ultimate priorities that competing rights

[27] For a recent example in which the failure by the state to secure individuals against a reasonably apprehended danger to health and safety that was so grave as to amount to a violation of the right to life under Article 2 of the European Convention on Human Rights, see *Oneryildiz v Turkey* No 48939/99 2002 FCHR 491.

receive. Civic principles insist that this adjustment potentially run in two directions: at some points adjusting one right in order to minimise the impact on another, and then by reversing the direction of compromise. The vice of globalisation is that it upsets this mutuality among basic entitlements. The *spread* of commitments that human rights impose is overtaken by a *hierarchy* of commitments that specialised bodies in civil society see themselves as bound to further. The state is, in turn, often pushed into mirroring the same hierarchy of commitments, whatever the international and constitutional law applying to it might say. The social cost of this transformation is considerable.

We cannot blur lines: it is neither possible nor desirable to assimilate the capacities of a body such as the WTO to those of the nation state. The former is primarily concerned to further the integration of world markets. But it is possible and desirable to ask it to pursue this objective in a way that aims to do least damage to the full range of rights that it can potentially affect.

Looking at the issue in more general terms, the adequate protection of human rights is a matter of equilibrium. That is part of what is meant by the claim that the full set of such rights is indivisible.[28] Indivisibility does not mean that the satisfaction of one right requires the satisfaction of all others, but that the compromise of one right be accomplished on the same terms as all other rights must face. The enjoyment of no single right is to be automatically preferred, and none is to be systematically allocated a collateral role. Globalisation is a threat to human rights when it upsets this particular facet of indivisibility among basic rights. The challenge is to find that balance again, in settings very different from those which the nation state has long provided in jurisprudence and politics.

[28] For the most recent assertion of this point in a UN analysis of the relation between world trade and human rights, see the 'Report by the UN Special Rapporteur on Health,' *Commission on Human Rights* E/CN 4/2003 Nov 2003 para 11.

5

The (Im)possibility of the European Union as a Global Human Rights Regime

ANDREW WILLIAMS

INTRODUCTION

SOME YEARS AGO Armin von Bogandy asked provocatively whether the EU was a 'Human Rights Organisation', one with human rights at the core of its institutional framework.[1] Although he may have answered the question in the negative, he nevertheless raised numerous concerns about the constitutional, legal and even moral direction of the EU's approach to human rights. These concerns were not limited to the internal policies of the EU. They straddled the internal/external divide, identifying national, regional and global dilemmas that the Union faces with increasing frequency. In following such a theme, von Bogandy established an implicit enquiry: how should human rights inform the future trajectory of the EU?

Now that the EU is engaged upon a fundamental reappraisal of its existence and development, von Bogandy's key theme has attained added pertinence. With the drafting of a Constitutional Treaty in 2003 that seeks to place human rights at the heart of the Union's values *and* objectives and with the prospect of an enlargement that will significantly alter the dimensions of the European Project and the human rights issues it needs to address, the EU is consciously or unconsciously embracing the question. It is locating human rights within its sphere of operations and it is doing so at all levels of governance. There is even a suspicion that the EU now seeks to promote a vision of itself as a global human rights regime, for which its 'one boundary is democracy and human rights'.[2]

[1] A von Bogandy, 'The European Union as a Human Rights Organization? Human Rights and the Core of the European Union' (2000) 37 *Common Market Law Review* 1307-1338.
[2] See Declaration of the Laeken Council at <http://european-convention.eu.int/pdf/LKNEN.pdf> (Accessed on 31 July 2003).

The purpose of this chapter is to consider the potential role of human rights in the EU in this context. In particular, it is to contemplate the possibility or impossibility of the EU developing into a human rights organisation at the global level, transcending borders and traditionally expected institutional constraints. It does so in three parts.

First, the chapter contemplates a possible definition of a global human rights regime and whether there is any evidence that the EU has attained such a status. In four specific fields, the political, the constitutional, the practical, and the institutional, the EU's current human rights profile is reviewed to determine if there is any evidence of a transformation.

Second, the question whether it is desirable for the EU to take the institutional path towards its foundation as a global human rights regime is considered. The advantages and disadvantages are assessed in the context of the present functioning of the EU and its enlargement.

Finally, the practicability of a transformation of the ethos required to install the EU as a functioning global human rights organisation is analysed. Does the EU possess the capacity, from legal, political, and practical perspectives to undergo such a conversion whether or not its ambitions lie in that direction?

THE RECORD OF THE EU AS A GLOBAL HUMAN RIGHTS REGIME

It is unlikely that consensus could be reached on a definition of a global human rights regime. But perhaps that is not the point. We are dealing here with characteristics that might shape the projection and self-perception of an institutional polity/organisation like the EU. Essentially then a working definition might be any collective, state agreed institutional structure or international organisation that purports to intervene in human rights matters regardless of jurisdiction, and which administers itself with human rights as a (if not the) key principle of governance. Potentially, such a definition could incorporate the UN, the Council of Europe and other regional entities, and potentially organisations like the World Bank.

By contrast, for some time the EU has been criticised because it lacks the second limb of such a definition. Palpably, it has failed to possess a clear constitutional statement that records the central role of human rights in its creation, operation and evolution. Critics have regularly and rightly pointed to the absence of ethical guidance within the EU's shaping documents.[3] Similarly, although the EU may intervene in human rights matters across a wide range of subjects both within and outside its borders, it is difficult to present a case that respect for human rights has been the administering principle behind all its actions and interventions since the EU's inception.

[3] See for instance, I Ward, *The Margins of European Law* (Basingstoke, Macmillan, 1996).

Rather the history of human rights and the EU is one of ambiguity and confusion, where for all the advancements that are proclaimed there still remains an underlying uncertainty as to the exact influence human rights should wield.

On this basis alone, any conclusion that suggested the EU had become a human rights regime, global or otherwise, would be in direct contravention to the evidence. Nonetheless, there is still significant indication on various levels that the EU has begun to develop along these lines since at least the end of the Cold War. In four areas, the political, the constitutional, the practical, and the institutional, numerous initiatives imply that a coordinated attempt to reinvent the EU as a human rights organisation operating regionally and globally has been instituted.

Political Transformations

The prospect of enlargement has enthralled the EU since the Iron Curtain was torn down. Before then expansion was a tentative affair, involving tepid and protracted negotiations with states in Western Europe and firmly rebuffing those from further afield, most notably Turkey. Come the end of the Soviet Union enlargement was re-presented as a passion for the reunification of Europe, the healing of an unnaturally divided continent. All those values and histories that bound the peoples of Europe, from the Atlantic to beyond the Carpathians, were rediscovered to give hope to that old dream of unity and 'perpetual peace' for Europe. The newly democratised states of Central and Eastern Europe embraced this rhetoric, perhaps even inflamed it, with great enthusiasm. The EU itself used the promise (and continues to do so) to apply pressure to those states that were largely unstable (most noticeably with regard to the Balkan countries). Enlargement became the EU's immediate project for the end of the 20th century and the beginning of the new millennium.

Throughout the evolution of this enlarging rhetoric human rights were deployed as vital moral components to define what was and what was not acceptable for the new Europe. By 1996 and Agenda 2000,[4] which set in train the practical admission procedure for all applicant states, respect for human rights was placed firmly as a standard of development against which applicants would have to measure themselves. The whole admission procedure emphasised the significance of abiding by the 'Political Criteria' that included respect for human rights and the protection of minorities. Through various evaluative reports and recommendations applicant states were shepherded towards an improvement in their human rights structures.

[4] Agenda 2000 'For a Stronger and Wider Union' *EC Bull Supp* 5–1997.

The process culminated in the Accession Treaty at Athens in April 2003.[5] The Athens Declaration that accompanied the Accession Treaty reaffirmed the need to commit the Union to 'furthering respect for human dignity, liberty and human rights' and maintained that '[w]e will continue to uphold and defend fundamental human rights, both inside and outside the European Union'.[6] Such a statement of intent indicated the seriousness with which the EU held its perceived responsibilities in human rights promotion and protection. Drawing together the two dimensions, the internal and external, emphasised the willingness to address the resulting issues beyond the enlargement procedure and to develop the Union's future introspective role in human rights affairs.

The process of enlargement was not the only area in which the EU's activities have suggested an ambition for recognition as a global player in human rights. Development policy underwent some considerable rearrangement with the re-negotiation of the Lomé Conventions in 1990 and 1995 and the ratification of the replacement Cotonou Convention of 2000.[7] These have seen the steady increase in frameworks for intervention on human rights grounds into the affairs of developing states. The institution of regular political dialogue, the possibility of a gradation of action to 'encourage' respect for human rights', and the mainstreaming of human rights considerations into the development projects supported by the EU have all contributed to construct a human rights based development model.[8]

The central rationale for such a progression of policy has been both moral and economic. Moral because the EU maintains that it owes a duty to ensure that it supports states in a process of development that accords with the European model, at least in so far as its fundamental values of human rights, democracy and the rule of law are concerned. Economic, because the EU insists that it should seek value(s) for money from those states with which it deals as a response to European political and public demands.

Similar passions have influenced the evolution of the EU's Common Foreign and Security Policy. Human rights have consistently played a role in uniting Member States to act in concert in matters of foreign policy. The imposition of sanctions where extreme examples arise have been a convenient method for indicating unity and consensus.[9] The debâcle that was

[5] See Accession Treaty 2003 at <http://europa.eu.int/comm/enlargement/negotiations/treaty_of_accession_2003/> (Accessed on 31 July 2003).

[6] Athens Declaration made at the Athens Informal European Council April 16th 2003 at <http://www.eu2003.gr/en/articles/2003/4/16/2531/index.asp?> (Accessed on 31 July 2003).

[7] Partnership Agreement between ACP States and the EC and Member States, Cotonou [2000] OJL 317/3.

[8] For a recent review of the Cotonou Agreement see K Arts, 'ACP — EU Relations in a New Era: the Cotonou Agreement' (2003) 40 *Common Market Law Review* 95–116.

[9] The EU's Annual Reports on Human Rights take pride in identifying those occasions where action has been taken.

the EU's attempts to act as one in relation to the conflict in Yugoslavia may have demonstrated the difficulties of building a common foreign policy but speedily imposed sanctions and condemnations for human rights matters on other occasions have suggested the benefits of coordination and co-operation. Human rights actions as a 'problem-free' territory for those seeking 'ever closer union' have therefore appeared as an essential impetus for further integration in this traditionally Member State preserve. Thus, the EU has sought to present itself as speaking with one voice on human rights matters at global institutions such as the UN. Indeed, it sometimes adopts a rather oleaginous manner in its self-representation as a unique entity that illustrates the value of harmonious relationships between states.

Many of the developments above have been reflected in the constitutional changes that have characterised the EU's progression at the end of the 20th and beginning of the 21st centuries.

Constitutional Transformations

Few could have imagined in the 1970s that Member States would be able to renegotiate the basis upon which the EU was constructed and operated with such increasing frequency as occurred after the Single European Act of 1986. Since that time, the Treaties of Maastricht, Amsterdam and Nice have all contributed to change the EU in fundamental ways. On each occasion human rights have achieved an increasingly important constitutional presence.

So it has been seen from those aspirational preambular statements in the SEA that respect for human rights has been enshrined as a fundamental principle of EU law and a specific consideration in development policy, foreign and security policy, refugee and asylum matters, and accession policy. Individual constitutional 'moments' have also been applauded for their advancement of human rights. Articles 7 TEU and 13 EC Treaty have often been touted as evidence of the EU's increasing commitment to establish itself as a polity bound by human rights principles.

Similarly, the creation of the EU Charter of Fundamental Rights did much to indicate the willingness of the EU to promote an evolving constitution that looked to human rights as a means of acquiring legitimacy for the whole edifice.

Now, at the time of writing, the narrative has advanced even further. The draft Constitutional Treaty that emanated from the Convention on the Future of Europe in May/June of 2003 indicated a willingness to draw human rights into the very core of the new Europe.[10] The Union's values

[10] See draft Constitutional Treaty 26/2752003 available at <http://european-convention.eu.int/bienvenue.asp?lang=EN&Content=> (Accessed on 31 July 2003).

included 'respect for human rights' under draft Article I–2 and Article I–3 proclaimed that the Union's aim included the promotion of its values. Further explicit reference was made to human rights in the draft's identification of the objectives of the Union. The protection of children's rights was given specific prominence in both the external and internal spheres. Fundamental rights continued to operate as 'general principles of the Union's law'. Respect for human rights remained a conditioning factor in development and foreign policies. Most publicity, however, has been reserved for the newly enshrined commitment by the Union to 'recognise' the EU Charter of Fundamental Rights and to 'seek accession' to the ECHR.[11]

The effect of these constitutional amendments may be difficult to predict but undoubtedly the environment for human rights in the EU will be subject to much debate and institutional activity. Whether this will lead to the Union managing its continuing development with human rights promotion and protection as key directive elements is impossible to tell. There may be flaws in the whole re-constitutional process that has revolved around the Future of Europe Convention and draft Constitutional Treaty but at least there is now greater evidence for the proposition that human rights are attaining a position of fundamental influence. The case is strengthened when the practical initiatives introduced by the institutions of the EU over the last decade are taken into account.

Practical Transformations

Although the political and constitutional developments outlined above have encouraged an optimistic view of the EU's human rights potential to flourish, it has been in the realm of the day-to-day practice of rights speak and rights promotion that a transformation is particularly evident. The inherent caution that seemed to characterise the EU's actions prior to the end of the Cold War has not exactly evaporated but has certainly been substantially liberated. Even the Council is now apt to embrace rhetoric that prioritises human rights. In its 2002 Annual Report on Human Rights it contends that the protection and promotion of human rights constitute 'defining principles of the EU' and that the TEU represented a 'significant strengthening of human rights as a priority issue for the EU in its internal as well as external policies'.[12]

[11] Article I–7 draft Constitutional Treaty.

[12] EU Annual Report on Human Rights 2002 at 12 <http://europa.eu.int/comm/external_relations/human_rights/doc/report02_en.pdf> (Accessed on 1 September 2003).

Equally, it claimed that the importance attached to the principle of respect for human rights

> is reflected in its increased commitment to mainstreaming human rights and democratisation objectives into all aspects of EU external and internal policies.[13]

Similar language is frequently produced by all the institutions. However, of greater significance are the practical activities that give force to the professed claims. In this respect, we can see that both in terms of scrutiny and promotion the EU has introduced a number of important initiatives that have transformed the level of intervention and concern in human rights matters. These can be separated between internal and external measures and are worth reviewing briefly to consider the scope of action.

On the internal front much emphasis has been placed on the fight against racism and discrimination. The EU Annual Report prioritises the subject. Article 13 EC Treaty has spawned two directives and an action programme. The EU has funded a Monitoring Centre on Racism and Xenophobia. And specifically in the employment sector it has supported an initiative to test 'new ways of tackling discrimination and inequality'.[14]

On a broader front there has been an expressed intention to mainstream human rights across the policy spectrum. Although most activity in this respect has surfaced in external affairs some precedent has been set by the approach towards issues of gender, praised for its success in embedding an issue across the legislative spectrum.

Equally, the institution of the European Ombudsman and the promotion of a policy of transparency have helped to instil a sense of human rights concern into the fabric of internal affairs. The recent concern to turn institutional attention towards the human rights impact of corporate behaviour might also presage a shift to practical enforcement measures where they can have a significant influence for communities currently victim to non-state rights violations.

Externally, the scope of practical activity has been even more adventurous. For some time, most prominently since 1989, human rights have occupied an increasingly prominent position in the various aspects of the EU's foreign affairs. In development policy, trade relations, accession policy and in the day-to-day management of the Common Foreign and Security Policy, they have established themselves as key issues of and for political action. In development policy, for instance, procedures for a graded scale of potential action, from 'political dialogue' and diplomatic pressure to sanctions of varying descriptions (trade, economic, political or diplomatic),

[13] *Ibid* at 11.
[14] *Ibid* at 23.

now represent a recognised tool for addressing human rights concerns. The EU has not been slow to employ the full armoury provided.[15]

The powers invested in the EU institutions in relation to the accession process and foreign affairs have also spawned an array of supportive measures as well as scrutiny and enforcement devices that have been deployed on applicant and other states. From the reporting process that has become the hallmark of the accession procedure, encompassing a regular assessment and identification of objectives for improvement, to the provision of financial support for projects in human rights matters through the European Initiative in Democracy and Human Rights, an array of practical measures now lie in the hands of the Commission and the Council. The Parliament adds its voice through commentary, political resolutions and *rapportage*. Whether all this has led to a meaningful change in respect and realisation of human rights in these countries is difficult to determine with any certainty.[16] Nonetheless, the evidence suggests that many states have at least been encouraged to transform their institutional structures in order to establish a culture of human rights within their systems. The measures certainly represent as wide a range of possible interventionist actions available to any international organisation whatever the reality of their application.

Institutional Transformations

Whilst commentators and institutional actors alike readily identify the most apparent manifestations of change (as sketched above) we should not ignore other aspects of transformation that are based on institutional culture or behaviour rather than pronouncement.

Specifically, the adoption of systems of decision making that purport to involve a wider constituency is suggestive of a transformation capable of enhancing the role of human rights regionally and globally. The processes by which the EU Charter was drafted and now the draft Constitutional Treaty has been prepared, indicate an institutional willingness to hear (if not listen to) the voices of people beyond the narrow cadre of politicians and bureaucrats. The development of a network society operating within the EU, in which human rights actors have the ability to draw on both the rhetoric and the resources of the Union to lobby for human rights action, may also suggest a progression towards an inclusive approach in the development of human rights.

[15] The EU Annual Report on Human Rights regularly recounts action taken. See for instance the Annual Report 2002 38–49 at <http://europa.eu.int/comm/external_relations/human_rights/doc/report02_en.pdf> (Accessed on 1 September 2003).

[16] Voices have begun to emerge criticising the impact of the EU's activities on the ground. See for instance H Arikan, 'A Lost Opportunity? A Critique of the EU's Human Rights Policy Towards Turkey' (2002) 7 *Mediterranean Politics* 19–50.

More theoretically, we can also point to the arguments that accompany the debate about European citizenship, some of which make the case for the evolution of the EU as a post-national polity able to transcend national interests that so frequently seem to prevent moral progress in the promotion and protection of human rights.[17]

The four aspects of transformation sketched above strongly support the notion that the EU has begun to evolve a skeletal-like human rights framework that inhabits the whole Union structure. Even if one can point to the many instances of double-standards, hypocrisy or straight absence of concern for human rights in whatever field, the fact remains that substantial progress has been made over the past decade with the promise of more to come. This is without taking into account the oft-reviewed legal developments in the Court of Justice.

There is more than just a suspicion, therefore, that the EU is undergoing a transformation, one that could turn it into a human rights regime as defined at the beginning of this essay. But how desirable is this metamorphosis?

THE DESIRABILITY OF TRANSFORMATION

Should the EU allow itself to become a human rights organisation or regime, assuming the political will existed for such a move? The question provokes both positive and negative responses.

Arguments for Transformation

As I have outlined, there is much to suggest that the EU has already embarked on a transformation of its ethos so as to re-incorporate itself as some form of human rights entity. Institutional acceptance and acknowledgment of this trend to the extent that the EU is consciously so transformed would therefore be a logical extension to an existing pattern of development. It would represent recognition of the political reality of the EU in the world that is better embraced than ignored.

Nevertheless, more persuasive and specific arguments for the transformation cannot be eschewed in favour of a simplistic adoption of change merely because it already appears to have taken place. Some readily suggest themselves.

First, the structure of the EU offers greater dialogic possibilities for the progression of human rights regionally than any other European organisation, such as the Council of Europe and the Organisation for Security

[17] See in particular J Habermas 'Citizenship and National Identity: Some Reflections on the Future of Europe' (1992) 12 *Praxis International* 1–19.

and Co-operation in Europe. Due to the institutional obsession with bringing the EU closer to its people, constantly monitoring public views through the *Eurobarometer* and agonising over the results, there is perhaps a greater tendency towards reacting to public concern over human rights issues than is the case with those other more isolated organisations. Also, the EU's increasing concern for public debate, consultation, and transparency as regards its own dealings, suggest that it is a polity already possessed of qualities that a human rights organisation ideally requires.[18] Whether that capability can be moulded to work *for* human rights is of course another matter. But the argument still remains.

Second, and related to the above, the EU is also a highly developed *democratic* polity. Certainly, it is deficient when matched against ideal standards of democratic accountability. The problems of a significantly unaccountable Council and Commission, and a vaguely representative but underpowered Parliament, cannot be dismissed. These, and other issues, remain serious defects of democratic legitimacy but only if measured against an institution constructed on ideal grounds. If compared to other international organisations, either in Europe or wider afield, the EU demonstrates a commitment to both possessing as well as improving its democratic structures that few if any can match. Does this enable the EU to be more effective as a regional and global human rights actor? Clearly not in itself. But the presence of a democratic strand in its framework is not insignificant. The Parliament's increasing influence on human rights matters, which has consistently evolved over the past twenty years or more, has done much to promote the issues on a widening stage. For this reason, the EU might well represent a nascent form of democratic human rights organisation that has greater claim to public legitimacy than any other international institutional regime.

Third, the EU occupies a unique position in international affairs that suggests a role as a human rights promoter would be both effective and efficient. It has access to financial, diplomatic and bureaucratic resources that are reasonably secure and it concerns itself naturally with all aspects of economic and political life. Its economic character also brings into its field of vision possible avenues to apply pressure on states guilty of human rights abuses. The fact that the EU is the largest donor of aid to the South and has a massive market capacity ensures that countries from outside the EU must at least appear to listen to approaches related to human rights. The rewards or sanctions that the EU can deploy should not, therefore, be underestimated. Influence relies on such matters of power.

Fourth, through its Member States histories as well as the very nature of its aspiration to represent the peoples of Europe as a whole, the EU has

[18] The importance attached to transparency by the EU can be seen from the insertion of Article I–49 devoted to the issue in the draft Constitutional Treaty.

traditionally maintained a political perspective that is as much externally focused as it is internally. The possibility of an isolationist policy towards the rest of the world seems highly unlikely despite many of the xenophobic tendencies that Europe as a continent seems to own. This lends the EU with a balanced view on the world that could encourage a human rights regime to be developed that is equally appropriate for the interior condition as it is the exterior.

Fifth, the EU has a legal core to its constitution and operation that could provide any human rights regime with necessary jurisprudential safeguards that other organisations lack. The established nature of the Court of Justice's concern for human rights matters coupled with an increased jurisdiction to scrutinise the EU's external human rights activities would provide an exceptional basis for an organisation operating in the global human rights field. This may be a real possibility that no other human rights based international organisation could match. Whatever the disadvantages of self-scrutiny may be, the combination of Parliament, Commission, Court and Council involvement in progressing a human rights regime could be highly effective.

The arguments raised above for a transformation of the EU into a global human rights regime are not without counterpoint. They beg questions that infer opposing arguments.

Arguments against Transformation

Any move by the EU to embody itself as a human rights regime is bound to attract significant concerns, several of which are briefly outlined below.

First, the perennial fear for the EU is that it is controlled by the political interests of the powerful Member States and the elite group of politicians, bureaucrats and corporate executives that operates at the international level. Much critique aimed at the EU is based on this truism. And of course there is plenty of evidence to suggest that decisions are made by a few for largely economic reasons. Such is the implicit nature of rational choice theory, which appears to possess some ability to explain decisions made at EU level. Consequently, any further encroachment by the EU and these self-interested parties into the realm of human rights promotion and protection might (a) lead to partial decisions made without real concern for improving the quality of peoples lives, or (b) a conflict of interest undermining the very notion of human rights. As regards the latter, the argument would be that the current political structure of the EU enables decisions to be made on the grounds of self-interest rather than with the observance or improvement of human rights in mind. Economic values might therefore take precedence over moral or social concerns.

Second, and related to the last point, the EU has also been troubled by concerns over the lack of independence that the various institutions display. In other words, although the Commission and the Parliament may appear as autonomous bodies they remain beholden to Member State governments and the corporate world. They could not possibly be in a position to operate a human rights practice that was impartial and centred on the very principles implicit in the human rights discourse. Part of this concern would be the vulnerability of the EU bureaucracies to forms of corruption that would interfere with the proper promotion of human rights.

Third, the histories of the Member States' interventions in global affairs suggest that an organisation controlled by them would continue to demonstrate the unjust characteristics of colonial thinking and practice that potentially taints all European interventions in the developing world. Any attempts to promote human rights would only further the opportunities for neo-colonialist interference in the affairs of other states. Such a critique has been well rehearsed for the EU's human rights external policies in any event and therefore any supposed transformation into a regime more thoroughly involved in human rights could attract increased criticism on this basis. But the dangers of a human rights regime emanating from any location, and particularly Europe, are greater than this. The possibility of European values and European models of society being promoted through a European definition of human rights is significant. The consequences for human rights generally are profound unless one adheres to the notion that human rights are both static in their form and universal in their nature. Of course, the latter is a constant precept for the EU in all its external human rights dealings. Human rights are defined, mantra-like, as universal and indivisible. From this perspective there would be little of concern should rights be patrolled and promoted from one geographical location. But such thinking is by no means universal. Those who advocate for different conceptions depending on context are numerous and there is a constant debate over the nature of human rights interpretation in various cultural settings. It is possible that such questions will be resolved but even so the notion that the EU would be accepted as best placed to represent a united understanding of human rights is difficult to imagine.

Fourth, the development of the EU into a global human rights regime may threaten the vital progress made in the field by those more obviously independent organisations such as the UN and the ECHR systems. Although these international organisations are not without their critics it is indisputable that they have made significant contributions to the advancement of human rights since the Second World War. At the European regional level, the ECHR system has acquired an iconic status, setting standards against which European States are judged, providing important methods of scrutiny and enforcement, and acting as a precedent for other regional systems around the world. At global level, the

UN's sponsored human rights system has instituted an historically unique structure for developing, monitoring, promoting and protecting people's human rights. Whether a determined increase in the EU's interference into both fields, the regional and global, would adversely affect the work of these (and other) organisations is a legitimate concern.

No doubt other arguments against the EU's role altering can be made but those above are significant enough to question any conscious or unconscious development towards a global type regime. This begs the last question I wish to pose. Does the EU possess the capacity for a transformation and for overcoming the inevitable anxieties rehearsed above?

THE CAPACITY FOR CHANGE?

What would the EU require in order to establish itself as a legitimate human rights actor both for its Member States and the rest of the world? Clarity in four dimensions of human rights work, which I have termed the four 'C's, might be preconditional: conceptualisation, competence, coherence, and consistency.[19] These require considerable analysis on their own but a brief review of the issues might help determine how far the EU is from attaining any global regime status.

Conceptualisation

I have already alluded to the difficulties that would be sustained by any global regime that was incapable of promoting a human rights vision that could not gain acceptance across cultural and philosophical divides. This does not imply that universally acknowledged definitions and standards have to be set in place before any organisation can take action. However, it does mean that a capacity needs to be displayed for achieving consensus, coping with alternative interpretations and recognising that human rights are fluid and in a constant state of negotiation. The UN system, for instance, *has* acquired important credibility in these areas, not only adhering to the Universal Declaration of Human Rights but also overseeing a steady clarification of definition, principles and their application. So we have new conceptions of rights entering the human rights lexicon through a process of debate and documentary refinement.

Does the EU possess a similar capacity? At present, the answer must again be negative. The EU appears to participate fully in the international

[19] I have alluded elsewhere to these requirements in respect of the EU developing a legitimate human rights policy within its current guise. See A Williams, 'EU Human Rights Policy and the Convention on the Future of Europe: A Failure of Design?' (2003) *European Law Review* 794–813.

arenas that are offered by the UN system but it does so not as a recognisably independent global actor. Rather it presents itself as a representative body, looking after the interests of its Member States and the self-consciously parochial values that the EU has adopted.

A case in point was the EU's approach to the UN World Conference Against Racism. The EU was keen to promote its anti-racism initiatives as an inspiration to 'combat racism at a regional level throughout the world'.[20] It highlighted Article 13 EC Treaty and the accompanying racial equality directive as indicative of the commitment and method for tackling the issue. But such self-promotion, if not satisfaction, failed to recognise the ambiguous position the EU occupies. There are deep concerns about the racism that is inherent within the EU's constituency.[21] From Member States governments accused of following policies that fuel racism,[22] to 'popular' movements predicated in part on racist principles; from increasing xenophobia whipped up by narratives of asylum seekers and refugees 'swamping' States, to anti-Muslim hysteria fuelled by terrorist outrages,[23] the EU presides over a whole range of troubling conditions. The situation involving the case of Austria and the coming to power of Jörg Haider and the Freedom Party in 2000 merely accentuated the possibilities taking root in the EU. The position can hardly have been improved by the failure of many Member States to abide by the Racial Equality Directive deadline for its implementation.[24]

This is not simply a matter of questionable commitment to tackle racism. It becomes an issue of conceptualisation when one considers the means by which the scope of human rights is defined by the EU in this area. The EU Charter of Fundamental Rights may well provide for the right not to be discriminated against (supported to some extent by Article 13 EC Treaty) but it fails to take into account the wider context that makes such a right socially meaningful. So, the EU Charter's failure to incorporate any group rights focused upon minorities suggests that the

[20] Commission, 'European Union action to combat racism' Contribution to the World Conference Against Racism, COM(2001) 291 final at 12.

[21] One need only examine the results of a 1998 *Eurobarometer* survey that found that '33% of the persons interviewed stated openly that they were "quite racist" or "very racist"'. For the EUMC's report see <http://eumc.eu.int/eumc/index.php?fuseaction=content.dsp_cat_content&catid=3e1d59a357218&contentid=3e5a588134c4c> (Accessed on 1 September 2003).

[22] See the reports produced by the European Commission against Racism and Intolerance. The 2003 report on Spain, for example, concludes, 'Problems of racism and xenophobia, however, persist and concern particularly Roma/Gypsies and non-EU citizens. This situation appears to be partly linked to an inadequate implementation of the existing legislation to fight against these phenomena but also to the widespread use in public debate of arguments and imagery that create a negative climate around immigration and immigrants.' Second Report on Spain 13 December 2002 ECRI (2003) 40 at 1.

[23] Specific problems identified in the Amnesty International Report 2003 at <http://www.amnesty.org/ailib/aireport/index.html> (Accessed on 9 September 2003).

[24] Commission Press Release IP/03/1047 'Commission concerned at Member States' failure to implement new racial equality rules' Brussels, 18 July 2003.

EU concept of rights related to racism and discrimination (invariably a minority related issue) are steadfastly individualistic rather than collective. In the area of language rights in particular the EU has failed to establish any kind of internal understanding beyond a highly limited conception. This flies in the face of not only the international attempts to give support to group rights of minorities but also the EU's own position when dealing with external matters. For instance, in the accession process the EU has self-consciously promoted the rights of minorities, making them a pre-conditional concern.[25] Equally, in its development policy it has also recognised the need to promote group rights and specifically the right to use one's own language.[26]

Such mixed messages suggest strongly that the concept of rights remains highly uncertain in the EU's hands. This can only make pretensions to global regime status problematic to say the least. In the area of racism an argument can be made that the failure to tackle the issue effectively is the result of a refusal to incorporate an understanding of rights that would empower governments and other agencies to adopt successful strategies.

Whether the EU's response to such a critique will be to push a limited individualistic notion of rights both internally and externally (as seems possible given the increasing willingness to use the EU Charter as the basic expression of the EU's conception of rights) or whether it will amend its interior regime so as to cater for a collective notion, the matter has still to be resolved. In the meantime, the ambiguous status of group rights generally leaves the EU's conceptualisation open to question.

Could such a position be rectified to such an extent that the EU acquired international recognition and acceptance as a forum for human rights development? It would seem unlikely given the partisan nature of the EU's role vis-à-vis its Member States in particular. This would not preclude it from replacing the Council of Europe as the regional organisation best suited to promote respect for human rights but global pretensions would seem to be unrealisable. However, this is not say that the EU could not acquire global acceptance as a human rights player through its practice. In other words, the possibility remains that in many areas the EU's role could be both respected and welcomed *provided* that it demonstrated the ability to transcend its overwhelmingly representative role on behalf of its Member States. Could it sever that link sufficiently to make it appear independent? Perhaps. If the Commission, the Parliament

[25] See the requirements for accession set by the Agenda 2000 'For a Stronger and Wider Union' *EC Bull Supp* 5–1997.

[26] See, in particular, Article 2(1)(j) Council Regulation 975/1999 [1999] OJL 120/1. For a brief account of the treatment of minority language rights by the EU and the ECJ see N N Shuibhne, 'The European Union and Minority Language Rights' (2001) 3 *MOST Journal on Multicultural Societies* No 2 at <http://www.unesco.org/most/v13n2shui.htm.> (Accessed on 31 July 2003).

and those other institutions other than the Council were assigned greater control over human rights policy and practice some headway might be made towards providing the EU with that sense of moral control otherwise perceptibly exercised by Member States. This would not obviate the euro-centric critique but at least it would address some of the direct political concerns.

Competence

Any purported human rights regime must possess clear lines of authority to act. It requires a mandate, defined areas of competence that establish the limits of its activities.

At present the EU is incapable of determining the nature of competence it should possess to direct human rights policy. In the draft Constitutional Treaty the issue of human rights is left outside any policy definition. Although the EU institutions all exercise human rights practices they do so without any general mandate. Rather, human rights are treated as providing 'guiding principles' to govern policy not a policy field in itself. The result has been the institution of a confused and ambiguous condition. Who has the authority to govern human rights development in the EU's internal and external affairs? It remains far from clear. In many areas, development policy for instance, the field is consciously shared between the EU and its Member States. The same applies to foreign affairs in general.

Internally, the position is more complex with the EU constrained in what it can do and with the Court of Justice restricted to judging human rights matters only in so far as they are affected through the operation of European law. There are discrete areas where the EU has assumed a greater role, for instance in gender, equality, and anti-discrimination issues. Individual institutions, such as the Parliament, have also developed methods of scrutiny with respect to the Member States' human rights records. But internally the picture is one of confusion.

Again it cannot be said that the EU is incapable of acquiring clear lines of competence in the field of human rights. The re-constitutionalisation opportunity offered by the process of enlargement could have resolved many of the ambiguities currently affecting the EU. The fact that this opportunity was not grasped is perhaps a good indication of intent. Nonetheless sufficient proposals have been made to advance the human rights role of the EU that one could be forgiven for believing the EU has still to resolve a central conflict. The failure to define competences clearly means that the EU can still pursue practices that suggest global regime possibilities, with particular regional and internal ambitions, albeit with the possibility always of Member State intervention to rein in that tendency.

Coherence

No global regime can maintain a semblance of authority and acceptance if it discriminates between certain classes of state. Unfortunately, there remains for the EU a patent distinction between its internal and external approaches to human rights. In its definition of human rights, in its surveillance practices and in its enforcement measures, the EU manifestly displays different policies depending on location. The result is a system that has been severely criticised for developing insidious double-standards.[27]

The pattern is best illustrated in the application of accession policy. Applicant states have been subjected to a systematic review of their human rights records that possesses no equal within the EU. In particular they have been required to address numerous concerns related to the rights of minorities at a time when there is little recognition of minority rights operated internally by the EU. The charge of hypocrisy lies near at hand whilst such a condition persists.

The possibility for eradicating the incoherence, however, could be resolved. It requires institutional recognition of the condition and a political willingness to transform it. This is not outside the bounds of reason. With an enlarged Europe, with a number of new Member States lacking in decades of liberal democratic stability, the pressure may build to ensure similar powers are retained by the EU institutions with regard to surveying the internal human rights conditions as those applied externally. Already, Article 7 TEU offers some hope that a system of scrutiny and enforcement might be imposed. But so far little institutional flesh has been put on the bones of this provision to ensure that the EU has in place the capacity as well as the authority to act internally.

Consistency

A related issue to the incoherence critique is that of inconsistency, by which I mean the different approaches taken in respect of different states in the EU's external affairs when attempting to enforce human rights.

Can any global human rights regime, however, escape such a charge that it fails to replicate measures taken against weak states when dealing with violations perpetrated by economically powerful states? It seems unlikely. But the EU is perhaps more exposed to this criticism than those organisations that are not so self-consciously concerned with the

[27] See A Williams, *EU Human Rights Policies: A Study in Irony* (Oxford, Oxford University Press, 2004).

economic weight of those states with which it deals. The EU considers the implications of taking a stand on human rights matters because it still represents the interests of its Member States. Those interests are predominantly economic in nature. Thus moral considerations are malleable to the extent that they might be put to one side when the consequences of ethical action might be perceived to be financially significant.

There are of course many arguments deployed by the EU to justify inconsistency. It can claim persuasively that it would be ridiculous to assume the approach adopted with regard to say Malawi should or could mirror that applied to China. Each case has to be examined in isolation. Different measures will invariably be needed to achieve the same ends. However, unless the level of inconsistencies can be reduced to a minimum, and left untainted by suggestions that they are the result of self-interest, any human rights practice will be considered suspect. This might therefore be a matter of pure presentation, the ability of the EU to be persuasive in its justification for any responses applied in relation to human rights concerns.

CONCLUDING THOUGHTS

The *possibility* of the EU developing into some form of globally active human rights regime is no longer a fantasy. The progression of human rights within the full spectrum of institutional activity and construction has been too substantial to be mocked and discounted, a characteristic response by critics in the past. Rather, the EU demands to be taken seriously in its concern for all aspects of human rights.

The importance of recognising the potential and engaging with it has been rendered more appropriate with the increasing concern over the effectiveness of the traditional human rights organisations. In particular, the UN system seems caught in a financial and bureaucratic bind that threatens to undermine its authority as well as its practical activities related to the cause of human rights. Similarly, a constant complaint against human rights organisations has been the lack of bite they can deliver against both states and multinational corporations in relation to human rights violations. It may be high time, therefore, to evaluate the possibility of new regimes emerging in the 21st century, regimes that acknowledge the development of economic associations that are capable of incorporating a human rights element into their core activities. Economic-political organisations may well be seen to possess the resources and the institutional capacity to operate more effectively as global human rights actors than traditional structures.

Such a transformation for the EU is not beyond the bounds of reason. Indeed, it may already be interpreted as having arisen de facto regardless of the absence of political and critical recognition to that effect. Although there are considerable, perhaps insurmountable, barriers to such a development these should not preclude serious analysis of the possibility. In particular, there is a vital need to consider the safeguards against all the political and ideological arguments that accompany possible change. A failure to engage with the possibility would be tantamount to a neglect of human rights futures for the region of Europe and the whole world.

6

The EU and Human Rights: Never the Twain Shall Meet?

ELSPETH BERRY*

INTRODUCTION

THERE ARE A surprising number of parallels between the development of rights protection in the European Union (EU) and that in the United Kingdom. First, until recent times, human rights were protected under English law not by a written constitution but by the common law, and because they were largely residual, in that they existed in so far as the State had not been authorised to interfere with them,[1] they lacked transparency. Similarly, although certain economic rights, such as the right to move freely in search of employment, were set out in the Treaty Establishing the EEC 1957 ('the EC Treaty'), more fundamental human rights, such as the right to life, were not. Given that the roots of the European Communities and thus of the EU lay primarily in the horrors of the two world wars, this omission might seem curious, but the strategy chosen for the avoidance of further conflict was economic integration, and, as Lord Hope of Craighead has stated, 'It was not anticipated that the Communities would be operating in areas or by methods that were likely to violate human rights'.[2] In this legislative vacuum, human rights jurisdiction was assumed by the Court of Justice on the basis that 'Community law... is also intended to confer upon [individuals] rights

*Address for correspondence: Nottingham Law School, Nottingham Trent University, Burton Street, Nottingham NG1 4BU. Email: <elspeth.berry@ntu.ac.uk.> I wish to thank Simon Boyes, Senior Lecturer at Nottingham Law School, for his comments on an earlier draft. Any errors or omissions remain, of course, my own.

[1] See further A Dicey, *An Introduction to the Study of the Law and the Constitution* (London, Macmillan, 1959).

[2] Lord Hope of Craighead, 'Human Rights — where are we now?' (2000) 5 *European Human Rights Law Review* 439 at 440. See also the *H L Select Committee on the European Union Report 8th Report 1999–2000*, 144–46 and S Michalowski, 'Human Rights in Times of Economic Crisis: The Example of Argentina', ch 3 of this volume.

which become part of their legal heritage'.[3] However, the result of this is that it has been difficult for EU citizens to identify the existence and scope of rights not expressly set out in the Treaties.

The second parallel is that while the accession of the United Kingdom to the European Convention for the Protection of Human Rights and Fundamental Freedoms 1950 (ECHR) gave British citizens a set of easily identifiable and accessible rights, they could not invoke them directly in national courts, since those courts only relied on the ECHR as an aid to interpretation[4] or a source for the development of the common law,[5] and were not bound by rulings of the Court of Human Rights. Similarly, although the Charter of Fundamental Rights of the EU ('the Charter') has now provided EU citizens with an identifiable list of rights, the legal status of the Charter and whether it will become legally binding has yet to be decided.

Third, actions before the Court of Human Rights or the Community Courts involve compliance with strict admissibility criteria and considerable delay and expense, and accessing the latter through the preliminary reference procedure is neither simple nor guaranteed.

Where the parallels break down is that with the enactment of the Human Rights Act 1998 ('HRA'), which enshrined in British law most of the rights laid down in the ECHR, British citizens became able to enforce their rights directly in their national courts, whereas the Charter remains unenforceable by EU citizens.

This begs the question: is the human rights protection currently afforded by the EU, which appears to be less than that available at domestic level, proportionate to its powers. The purpose of this article is therefore to examine, first, the need for human rights protection at EU level; second, the current extent of such protection; and third, how protection might be improved.

THE NEED TO PROTECT HUMAN RIGHTS AGAINST THE EU

The case for human rights protection against the EU, and Member States when acting within the scope of EU law, is not a difficult one to make. The EU has competence in areas as diverse as employment, foreign policy, police co-operation and monetary policy,[6] in respect of hundreds of

[3] Case 26/62 *Van Gend en Loos* [1963] ECR 1 at 12. See also Case 4/73 *Nold v Commission* [1974] ECR 491 and Opinion 2/94 [1996] ECR I–1759, para 33.
[4] See, for example, *R v Secretary of State for the Home Department ex parte Brind* [1991] 1 AC 696.
[5] See, for example, *Derbyshire County Council v Times Newspapers Ltd* [1992] 1 QB 770.
[6] See further P Vila Maior, 'Is the ECB a Case for Institutional Adaptation to the Challenges of Globalisation? Implications for the EU's Democratic Legitimacy' in S Macleod and J Parkinson (eds), *Global Governance and the Quest for Justice, Vol 2: Corporate Governance* (Oxford, Hart Publishing, forthcoming 2005). See also C Villiers, 'European Integration and Globalisation: The Experience of Financial Reporting Regulation'.

millions of people and across an immense geographical area. It is therefore inevitable that its activities have a substantial impact on its citizens,[7] albeit less than that of the Member States, and in democratic societies functioning under the rule of law the recognition and enforcement of human rights are essential.

It is impossible to consider in full within this chapter all possible abuses resulting from EU measures, but a number of examples can be provided. Under Title IV EC the Community is empowered to adopt measures on the treatment of asylum seekers and immigrants, visa requirements for third country nationals, and the improvement of cross border enforcement of judgments. These measures could have an adverse impact, for example, on the rights not to be tortured or inhumanely treated (in a third country), to free movement, to a fair trial, or to property. Similarly, pursuant to Title VI EU, the police, customs authorities and courts may co-operate in a number of ways which have the potential for human rights abuses, including data collection and analysis, coordination of the investigation of offences, extradition, the introduction of a European Arrest Warrant,[8] and the adoption of minimum rules on the constituent elements of certain offences and the applicable penalties. Economic sanctions imposed pursuant to Title V EU on the common foreign and security policy have also given rise to allegations of breaches of the rights to property and to pursue a trade or profession.[9]

The European Parliament has identified a number of possible threats to human rights under EU law,[10] and while these are largely from Member States, a number of shortcomings at EU level are identified and it is submitted that many of its criticisms of the Member States should also be addressed to the EU. For example, it argues that the prohibition of torture and inhuman and degrading treatment is threatened by persistent misconduct in police stations and prisons throughout the Member States, but does not mention the possibility that the EU provisions under Titles IV EC and VI EU referred to above might lead to such abuses. It also argues that the widespread trafficking in persons and the failure to curb illegal immigration resulting in a pool of workers without employment rights indicates that Member States are failing to enforce the prohibition on slavery and forced labour. It is submitted that it is not just Member

[7] See I Bédoyan, P Van Alst and S Walgrave, 'The anti-globalisation protests and the success of transnational mobilisation: The protest against the EU summit, Brussels 2001', in D Lewis (ed), *Global Governance and the Quest for Justice, Vol 1: International and Regional Organisations* (Oxford, Hart Publishing, forthcoming 2005).

[8] Council Framework Decision 2002/584/JHA [2002] OJ L190.

[9] C–317/00 P(R) *'Invest' Import und Export GmbH and another v Commission* [2000] ECR I–9541.

[10] European Parliament Committee on Citizens' Freedom and Rights, Justice and Home Affairs, 'Report on the Human Rights Situation the European Union' (2001) (2001/2014(INI) in 12 December 2002 final A5–0451/2002.

State asylum and immigration policies which have failed, but also EU policies on free movement and employment and under Title VI EU.[11]

In relation to the right of privacy, the Parliament notes the risks of inadequate protection as a result of the storage of such data permitted by Directive 2002/58, and the absence of protection in respect of information held under the common foreign and security policy and police and judicial co-operation. In relation to access to documents, it urges more effective implementation of Regulation 1049/2001 concerning public access to the institutions' documents, but the Ombudsman has gone further and alleged that data protection rules, in particular Regulation 45/2001, are being used to undermine the principle of openness in public life rather than to protect personal privacy.[12] In relation to freedom of expression, the Parliament urges the Member States to act to protect the right to express opinions publicly, but it is submitted that EU action is also required, as witness the case of Paul Van Buitenen, a Commission employee who was disciplined and allegedly harassed as a result of his public allegations of fraud within the Commission.[13]

The Parliament calls on both the EU and the Member States to adopt adequate policies to outlaw racism. It is submitted that EU action in this area is essential since discrepancies in protection could deter free movement. The Parliament also calls on Member States to prohibit effectively discrimination on grounds of age or sexual orientation, on the Member States and the EU to provide for the recognition of unmarried partnerships as equivalent to marriage, and on the EU to consider the recognition of same sex marriage, to adopt anti-discrimination legislation which extends beyond the employment sphere, and to provide protection against sexual harassment and discrimination on grounds of disability. Failure to do so has obvious implications for the rights of those concerned and could, for example, impact on their right of free movement.

Finally, in the light of the large number of serious violations of the right to a fair trial and associated rights found by the Court of Human Rights against the Member States, the Parliament urges them to introduce reforms to guarantee these rights. However, it is submitted that if the EU adopts minimum standards for criminal proceedings, pre-trial orders and evidence, and harmonised rules on compensation,[14] this would bring it into potential conflict with the rights of suspects to review of detention and a fair trial. EU action to guarantee the right to a fair trial is therefore also necessary.

[11] See, for example, the Framework decision on combating trafficking in human beings 2002/629/JHA [2002] OJ L203/1.

[12] J Söderman, 'The Misuse of Data Protection rules in the EU' 25 September 2002. http://www.euro-ombudsman.eu.int/letters/en/20020925-1.htm (Accessed 24 August 2004).

[13] P Van Buitenen, *Blowing the Whistle* (London, Politico's Publishing, 2002).

[14] See the Presidency Conclusions of the Tampere European Council 15 & 16 October 1999 http://ue.eu.int/ueDocs/cms_Data/docs/pressdata/en/ec/00200-r1.en9.htm (Accessed 24 August 2004).

Limited protection of human rights at EU level therefore cannot be justified by the argument that the EU's competences are such that there is no real risk of human rights abuses. Furthermore, a number of other factors require that the human rights of EU citizens be protected. First, this is a precondition for the renunciation by the national courts of some Member States of their own jurisdiction over fundamental rights where Community law is at issue.[15] Second, a failure to protect human rights within the EU would reduce the legitimacy of Article 49 EU, which provides that any state wishing to join the EU must respect, inter alia, the principles set out in Article 6(1) EU, including human rights and fundamental freedoms. Candidate countries can hardly be required to demonstrate respect for human rights as a condition of entry if the EU itself is not obliged to offer a high level of human rights protection. Third, and similarly, while the EU lacks adequate human rights protection itself, its exhortations to third countries to improve their human rights record[16] must lack credibility. Finally, enlargement may make citizens feel even more remote from and unable to participate in EU policies, and the ability to enforce fundamental rights against the EU is an essential element in guarding against this.

Having identified the need for rights protection at EU level, it is now necessary to examine the current extent of the protection.

CURRENT HUMAN RIGHTS PROTECTION AGAINST THE EU

The Rights Recognised

In terms of rights recognised, the EU gives a good account of itself. For example, the EC Treaty grants the rights to free movement[17] and access to documents of the Community institutions,[18] and prohibits discrimination on grounds of nationality.[19] Secondary legislation provides further rights, such as protection of personal data[20] and certain workers

[15] See *Re Wünsche v Handelsgesellschaft (Solange II)* [1987] 3 CMLR 225, *Brunner and others v The European Union Treaty* [1994] 1 CMLR 57 and *Carlsen and others v Prime Minister Rasmussen* [1999] 3 CMLR 854.

[16] See, for example, Commission Communication 'The European Union's Role in Promoting Human Rights and Democratisation in Third Countries' COM (2001) 252 final. <http://www.europa.eu.int/comm/external_relations/human_rights/doc/com01_252_en.pdf> (Accessed 24 August 2004), Commission Staff Working Document 'Report on the Implementation of the European Initiative for Democracy and Human Rights' SEC (2001) 801. <http://www.europa.eu.int/comm/external_relations/human_rights/doc/sec01_801.pdf> (Accessed 24 August 2004), and Regulations 975/1999 and 976/1999 on the Development and Consolidation of Democracy and the Rule of Law and Respect for Human Rights and Fundamental Freedoms [1999] OJ L120/1 and /8. See further A Williams, 'The (Im)possibility of the EU as a Global Human Rights Regime' chp 5 in this volume.

[17] Articles 39 and 18 EC.

[18] Article 255 EC.

[19] Article 12 EC.

[20] Directive 95/46 [1995] OJ L281/31.

rights,[21] and the prohibition of discrimination in employment on grounds of religious belief, disability, age or sexual orientation.[22]

The jurisprudence of the Court of Justice has also recognised a number of human rights, drawing on the constitutional traditions common to the Member States and international treaties of which they are signatories,[23] particularly the ECHR[24] of which all Member States are Contracting Parties.[25] These include the rights to a fair hearing,[26] property,[27] privacy,[28] marry,[29] and freedom of expression.[30] However, the scope of rights drawn from the ECHR has on occasion been interpreted differently by the Court of Justice and the Court of Human Rights. For example, in *Hoechst v Commission*[31] the Court of Justice ruled that the right to respect for private life and home derived from Article 8 ECHR only protected individuals' private dwellings, while the Court of Human Rights ruled in *Niemietz v Germany*[32] that it included business premises. The Court of First Instance subsequently concluded in *Limburgse Vinyl Maatschaappij and others v Commission*[33] that protection against interference with personal privacy by public authorities was a general principle of EU law distinct from the right in Article 8 ECHR, and therefore *Hoechst* rather than *Niemietz* should be followed. The potential problems of such divergences will be examined further below.

The third source of rights in the EU is the Charter. Many of the Charter rights have already been recognised in legislation or by the Court, or would undoubtedly be recognised by the Court were an appropriate case to come before it. In some cases the scope of the rights is wider; for example, the right to marry in Article 9 of the Charter is not restricted to men and women. In addition, there are a small number of new rights, including the rights to dignity, asylum and protection against expulsion, and a number of social and civil rights such as education, access to health care, and the protection of the family.

[21] For example, Directive 94/45 on Works Councils [1994] OJ L254/64 as amended by Directive 97/74 [1997] OJ L10/20, Directive 89/391 on Health and Safety [1989] OJ L183/1 and Directive 92/85 on Pregnant Workers [1992] OJ L348/1.
[22] Directive 2000/78 [2000] OJ L303/116.
[23] However, it has held that the latter cannot extend the scope of the Treaties beyond the competences of the EU (C–249/96 *Grant v South West Trains* [1998] ECR I–621).
[24] The Court has also referred to Convention 111 of the International Labour Organisation (Case 149/77 *Defrenne v Sabena* [1978] ECR 1365) and the International Covenant on Civil and Political Rights of 19 December 1966 (*Grant v South West Trains*, see above n 23).
[25] Not all Member States have ratified all Protocols to the ECHR.
[26] See, for example, Cases 100–103/80 *Musique Diffusion Française v Commission* [1983] ECR 1825.
[27] See, for example, *Nold*, above n 3.
[28] C–404/92 P *X v Commission* [1994] ECR I–4737.
[29] *Grant v South West Trains Ltd*, above n 23.
[30] C–100/88 *Oyowe and Traroe v Commission* [1989] ECR 4285.
[31] C–46/87 & 227/88 [1989] ECR 2859.
[32] (1992) 16 EHRR 97.
[33] T–305–7, 313, 316, 318, 325, 328–9 & 335/94 [1999] ECR II–931.

Overall, therefore, the range of rights protected under EU law looks impressive. However, their real value can be assessed only by reference to their enforceability, and a number of factors which affect this will now be examined.

Nature of the Rights

It is submitted that, when the nature of the rights is examined, a less positive picture emerges. First, many lack real transparency because they are to be found only in the jurisprudence of the Court of Justice, a source not readily accessible or comprehensible to the average EU citizen.

Second, many of the 'rights' are in fact not really rights. For example, Article 13 EC merely empowers the Council to take action to protect the fundamental right of non-discrimination, and so the creation of any such rights is dependent on the existence and extent of such action. Other Treaty Articles also fall short of granting enforceable rights; for example, fundamental social rights *underpin* measures improving living and working conditions,[34] and EC policy on development co-operation is to *contribute* to the objective of respecting human rights (author's emphasis).[35] Similarly, in the Charter, the rights of children, the elderly and the disabled are only to be respected, and the rights to social security and health care are subject to 'national legislation and practices'.

Third, even if a right can be identified, it may not be freestanding. The right to free movement in Article 39 EC and certain of the rights to non-discrimination referred to above are notable examples of freestanding rights, but there are few others. In fact, the Court of Justice has described fundamental rights only as general principles used to interpret Community law[36] and Article 6(2) EU similarly provides only that the EU must respect fundamental rights as general principles of EU law. As a result, the enforceability of such rights will depend on whether another Community law right is infringed. For example, the right not to be deprived of liberty is not freestanding but dependent on the prior exercise of the right of free movement.[37] Thus no claim for unlawful imprisonment could be brought by an English national against the English authorities although a French national unlawfully imprisoned by the English authorities might bring such a claim. Similarly, in *Society for the Protection of Unborn Children (Ireland) Ltd v Grogan*[38] the Court of Justice considered only whether a

[34] Article 136 EC.
[35] Article 177 EC.
[36] Case 11/70 *Internationale Handelsgesellschaft v Einfuhr — und Vorratstelle für Getreide und Futtermittel (Solange I)* [1970] ECR 1125.
[37] C–299/95 *Kremzow v Austria* [1997] ECR I–2629.
[38] C–159/90 [1991] ECR I–4685.

national law prohibiting the distribution of information about abortion clinics in another Member State constituted a restriction on the freedom to provide services, concluding that it did not because the information was not distributed by or on behalf of the service provider. Since the right of free expression was not freestanding, no claim could lie in the absence of a breach of the freedom to provide services. This may be contrasted with *Open Door Counselling and Dublin Well Woman v Ireland*[39] in which the Court of Human Rights declared the same prohibition to be in breach of the right (freestanding under the ECHR) to free expression. Furthermore, freestanding rights such as free movement could be used to curtail fundamental rights such as the right to be protected against forced labour, on the grounds that measures intended to protect the latter interfere with the former.

Fourth, although the Charter was adopted in order to strengthen human rights and the Commission has described it as an 'indispensable instrument of political and moral legitimacy',[40] it cannot significantly advance the rights of EU citizens because it is not legally binding. The rights contained in it therefore currently have no direct legal effect[41] (although some of them merely duplicate existing EU rights which themselves have legal effect[42]), and while the Commission does examine proposals for legislation and other measures for compliance with the Charter,[43] it has so far been taken into by the Community Courts only as a reaffirmation of existing rights.[44]

It is therefore unclear whether Charter rights will be used to widen the interpretation of existing rights, either where legislation makes express reference to the Charter[45] or otherwise, although Advocate General Ruiz-Jarabo has strongly argued that the Charter extends the scope of the right to a fair trial.[46] In *BECTU v Secretary of State for Trade and Industry* Advocate General Tizzano described it as 'a substantive point of reference' and cited its inclusion of the right to paid leave in

[39] (1993) 15 EHRR 244.

[40] Commission Communication on the Charter of Fundamental Rights of the European Union COM (2000) 559 final.

[41] C–322/88 *Grimaldi v Fonds des Maladies Professionelles* [1989] ECR 4407.

[42] This duplication has a precedent in the introduction of EU citizenship and associated rights by the Treaty on European Union 1992. The majority of the rights (now contained in Articles 17–21 EC) existed prior to the introduction of citizenship.

[43] Commission, 'The Charter in the European Context; the Commission acts on its principles' <http://www.europa.eu.int/comm/justice_home/unit/charte/en/european-context-principles.html.> (Accessed 24 August 2004).

[44] See, for example, T–377/00 *Philip Morris International v Commission* [2003] 1 CMLR 21 and C–232/02 P R *Technische Glaswerke Ilmenaus GmbH*, judgment of 19 October 2002, not yet available in English. The Charter has only been referred to by the Court of Justice when summarising the parties' arguments (C–491/01 *R v Secretary of State for Health ex parte British American Tobacco (Investments) Ltd and others* [2003] 1 CMLR 14).

[45] See, for example, Regulation 1049/2001 on Access to Documents [2001] OJ L145/43.

[46] C–204/00 P *Aalborg Portland A/S v Commission* and C–205/00 P *Irish Cement v Commission*, Opinions of 11 February 2003, not yet reported.

support of the proposition that this right in the Working Time Directive constituted a fundamental right and that limitations on the right which effectively negated its substance were therefore contrary to EU law.[47] However, the Court of Justice reached the same conclusion without referring to the Charter.

Application to Member States

A further difficulty is establishing the extent to which EU rights may be enforced against Member States. First, fundamental rights can be used by the Court of Justice to review national implementing (including derogating[48]) legislation only where it is within the scope of the EU legislation which gave rise to it,[49] and it is not always clear what the scope of EU law is.

Second, discrepancies between national and EU human rights legislation could present a difficulty for British courts, since while s2(1)(a) of the HRA requires them to take account of the jurisprudence of the Court of Human Rights, they remain bound by the doctrine of supremacy to uphold EU law in the event of inconsistency.[50] Thus, for example, when dealing with Article 8 ECHR discussed above, the British courts would be obliged to follow *Hoechst*[51] rather than *Niemietz*,[52] and would therefore be in an unenviable position were the Court of Human Rights ever to rule national legislation implementing Community law to be contrary to the ECHR.

Third, when reviewing legislation the Court of Justice leaves some discretion to the Member States, stating that 'Community law does not impose upon the Member States a uniform scale of values as regards the assessment of [their] conduct'.[53] For example, while it has required that restrictions intended to protect public morality must be non-discriminatory,[54]

[47] C–173/99 [2001] ECR I–4881 at paras 26–8.
[48] C–260/89 *ERT* [1991] ECR I–292 at para 41.
[49] This competence has no Treaty basis and is derived solely from the Court's own jurisprudence; see, for example, Case 222/84 *Johnston v Chief Constable of the Royal Ulster Constabulary* [1986] ECR 1651.
[50] See Case 6/64 *Costa v ENEL* [1964] ECR 585 and Case 106/77 *Administrazione delle Finanze dello Stato v Simmenthal SpA* [1978] ECR 629. See also *Solange I*, above n 36 in which the referring court, the Bundesverfassungsgericht (German Constitutional Court) held that Community protection of fundamental rights was insufficiently developed for it to renounce its own jurisdiction over fundamental rights, even where this resulted in a conflict with Community law. However, it subsequently accepted the supremacy of Community law in this area in *Solange II*, above n 15. See also *Brunner* and *Carlsen*, above n 15.
[51] Above n 31.
[52] Above n 32.
[53] Case 115 & 116/81 *Adoui and Cornuaille v Belgium* [1982] ECR 1665 para 8. See also Case 249/86 *Commission v Germany* [1989] ECR 1263 para 19.
[54] *R v Henn and Darby* Case 34/79 [1979] ECR 3795.

it has otherwise allowed Member States a wide margin of appreciation in this area,[55] thus increasing the scope for the Member States to interfere with human rights, and permitting them to hinder the Single Market.[56] Therefore, even if the information in *Grogan*,[57] discussed above, had been distributed by the service provider, there is no guarantee that the Court of Justice would have agreed with the Court of Human Rights in *Open Door Counselling*[58] that there was a breach of the right of free expression (and thus a breach of the right to provide services). It might conclude instead that the restriction was within the margin of discretion afforded to Member States. It is submitted that the importance of fundamental human rights and the uniformity of Community law[59] necessitate a narrow margin of discretion. Indeed, the former requires that the discretion permitted to the Community and the EU[60] also be interpreted narrowly.

Access to the Courts

The enforceability of rights is also determined by access to the Courts. While the Court of Justice has argued that Articles 230, 234 and 241 EC constitute a complete system of legal remedies ensuring effective judicial review,[61] it is submitted that this is not the case, since applicants seeking to enforce their human rights under EU law face a number of hurdles.

First, an action against the national authorities under EU law must be brought initially in the national courts, with the possibility of a reference to the Court of Justice. In some cases the only way of bringing the issue before a national court might be for an applicant to breach the implementing measures in order to challenge the resulting sanctions or, in the absence of implementing measures, to breach the Community measure and then assert its illegality in proceedings against it. However, individuals should not be required to breach the law in order to gain access to justice. In addition, an applicant has no right to decide whether a reference to the Court of Justice is made, which measures are referred and on what grounds. It thus has no right of access to the Court of

[55] *Conegate Ltd v Commissioners of Customs and Excise* (Case 121/85) [1986] ECR 1007.

[56] See, for example, Case 120/78 *Rewe-Zentrale AG v Bundesmonompolverwaltung für Branntwein (Cassis de Dijon)* [1979] ECR 649.

[57] Above n 38.

[58] Above n 39.

[59] Cf, the development of a similar doctrine by the Court of Human Rights; see, for example, *Handyside v United Kingdom* (1976) 1 EHRR 737.

[60] C–280/93 *Germany v Council* [1994] ECR I–4973 at para 21. See also the jurisprudence concerning Article 288 EC (for example, Case 5/71 *Aktien-Zuckerfabrik Schöppenstedt v Council* [1971] ECR 975) and competition policy (for example, Cases 43 & 63/82 *VBVB and VBBB v Commission* [1984] ECR 19.

[61] C–50/00 P *Unión de Pequeños Agricultores (UPA) v Council* [2002] 3 CMLR 1.

Justice, yet a national court has no jurisdiction to annul a Community measure. Furthermore, the interests of legal certainty suggest that a general measure should be reviewable as soon as possible and not only when implementing measures have been adopted. Finally, a reference under Article 234 EC has a number of procedural disadvantages, such as substantial delays and costs.[62]

Second, an action against the EU institutions for breach of fundamental rights, either for annulment under Article 230 EC or for damages under Article 288 EC, must be brought in the Community courts. Although Article 288 EC has no *locus standi* restrictions, the requirement that the breach must be sufficiently serious effectively rules out many claims and, in any event, Article 288 EC cannot result in the annulment of the Community measure held to be unlawful.

Under Article 230 EC, organisations which lack legal personality have no standing, and a natural or legal person may apply only for the annulment of a Decision, or a Decision in the form of a Regulation, which is of direct and individual concern to it. The position is particularly problematic with Regulations because they are normally general measures, while the Court of Justice has held that an applicant will only have *locus standi* to challenge a Regulation where it is of specific rather than general application and thus in substance a Decision, or of individual concern to the applicant[63] and thus a Decision in his regard.[64]

Third, where the alleged breach of human rights arises not from secondary legislation but from a Treaty, the Court of Justice has no jurisdiction, although the effect of this may be mitigated by the Court of Human Rights' ruling that Member States may be liable for breaches of the ECHR caused by the Treaties. In *Matthews v United Kingdom*[65] it held a Member State liable for breaching its obligations under Protocol 1 to the ECHR to hold free elections by excluding Gibraltar from direct elections to the European Parliament, pursuant to an Act annexed to Decision 76/787. The Court argued that the transfer of powers to an international organisation was compatible with the ECHR only if fundamental rights were protected,[66]

[62] Opinion of Advocate General Jacobs in *UPA, ibid* n 61 at paras 38–48 and T–177/01 *Jégo-Quéré et Cie SA v Commission* [2002] 2 CMLR 44 at paras 44–45.

[63] Case 25/62 *Plaumann & Co v Commission* [1963] ECR 95.

[64] *UPA*, above n 63. Exceptions to this general rule have been made in relation to anti-dumping (C–358/89 *Extramet Industrie SA v Council* [1991] ECR I–2501), competition (Case 26/76 *Metro–SB–Gromβarkte GmbH & Co KG v Commission* [1977] ECR 1875) and state aids (Case 169/84 *COFAZ SA v Commission* [1980] ECR 391).

[65] [1997] 28 EHRR 361 discussed in HG Schermers, (1999) 36 *Common Market Law Review* 673 and I Canor, 'Primus inter pares: who is the ultimate guardian of fundamental rights in Europe? (2000) 25(1) *European Law Review* 3. See also *Cantoni v France* RJD. 1996–V 1614 in which the Court of Human Rights ruled that France's implementation of Directive 65/65 on medicinal products [1965] OJ L369 was not in breach of Article 7 ECHR.

[66] See further T King, 'Ensuring Human Rights Review of Inter-governmental Acts in Europe' (2000) 25(1) *European Law Review* 79.

and since the Decision and the Act constituted a Treaty, and therefore did not give rise to the possibility of a legal challenge before the Court of Justice, the Member States remained responsible for the protection of human rights. The United Kingdom was therefore liable for its breach of Protocol 1.

This possibility of intervention by the Court of Human Rights would appear to be limited to the Treaties because the Court of Justice has jurisdiction to review most secondary legislation, at least on the application of privileged applicants.[67] Judgments of the Court of Justice will not be reviewed by the Court of Human Rights since it assumes that the Court of Justice acts in accordance with the requirements of a fair trial under Article 6 ECHR.[68] This solution can therefore only be a partial one.

Fourth, secondary legislation adopted under Title IV EC (asylum and immigration) and Title VI EU (police and customs co-operation) is subject to review by the Court of Justice only in limited circumstances,[69] and the Court has no jurisdiction over the common foreign and security policy (Title V EU).[70]

Finally, access to the Community Courts is hampered by substantial delays in the hearing of cases.[71]

It is therefore submitted that the potential threats to fundamental rights, and the international credibility of the EU, necessitate greater protection than is currently available, given the difficulties in identifying and enforcing fundamental rights under EU law.

POSSIBLE IMPROVEMENTS

Enforcement of the Charter

The Member States agreed to address the status of the Charter on an ongoing basis,[72] and making it directly enforceable against the EU would

[67] Although a challenge to a Decision was brought before the Court of Human Rights (*DSR Senator Lines v the 15 Member States* App 56672/00), the case was cancelled (Press Release 508 of the Registrar of the Court of Human Rights, 16 October 2003) because the Court of First Instance had, in the meantime, annulled the contested elements of the Decision (T–191/98 & T–212–214/98 *Atlantic Container Line AB v Commission*, judgment of 30 September 2003, not yet reported).
[68] *M & Co* (1990) 64 DR 138 at 145.
[69] Article 68 EC limits Article 234 EC jurisdiction to final courts and Article 35 EU provides that the Court's only jurisdiction is under Article 234 EC, and then only if the Member State in question has accepted it. Both exclude any review of measures relating to law and order or national security.
[70] See further T Eicke, 'European Charter of Fundamental Rights — Unique Opportunity or Unwelcome Distraction' (2000) 3 *European Human Rights Law Review* 280 at 290–1.
[71] See further the 20th Annual Report of the Court of Justice and the Court of First Instance of the European Communities.
[72] Declaration 23 on the future of the Union, annexed to the Treaty of Nice 2001.

vastly improve rights protection. The Praesidium of the European Convention,[73] the Parliament,[74] ECOSOC[75] and the Committee of the Regions[76] proposed that it be integrated into the Treaty as a binding legal text, and indeed it was drafted 'as if' it were legally binding in order to allow for such a possibility.[77] Alternatively, it could have been made legally binding by incorporating a reference to it in the Treaty and putting it in an Annex or Protocol.[78]

Although such a radical development as incorporation seemed unlikely, the history of the Community Charter of Fundamental Social Rights of Workers 1989 indicated that it was not impossible in the longer term. This Charter subsequently formed the basis for the Social Policy Agreement annexed to the Social Policy Protocol to the EU Treaty 1992, and was eventually incorporated into the EC Treaty (Articles 136–45) by the Treaty of Amsterdam 1997. The draft Treaty establishing a constituion for europe[79] incorporates the Charter, but the impact of this development, if the Treaty is ratified, remains to be seen. For example, making the social and economic rights in the Charter fully effective would result in considerable expenditure by the EU, a possibility which the (successful) challenge to Commission expenditure on welfare programmes within the EU in *United Kingdom v Commission*[80] suggests could be unwelcome to at least some Member States.

A Human Rights Enforcement Body

A dedicated enforcement body could have a number of advantages, provided that it addresses internal human rights policies rather than only external policies,[81] is truly independent, and has an appropriate remit. A Human Rights Commissioner integrated into the existing Commission

[73] 'Draft of Articles 1–16 of the Constitutional Treaty' CONV 528/03, Brussels, 6 February 2003.
[74] Resolution B5, European Union Charter of Fundamental Rights, http://www2.europarl.eu.int/omk/sipade2? PUBREF=-//EP//TEXT+TA+P5-2000-0417+0+DOC+XML+V0//EN&L=EN&LEVEL= 3&NAV= S&LSTDOC=Y (Accessed 24 August 2004).
[75] ECOSOC Resolution 1005/2000, adopted on 20 September 2000.
[76] Committee of the Regions Resolution 140/2000, adopted on 20 September 2000.
[77] Commission Communication on the legal nature of the Charter of Fundamental Rights of the European Union, COM (2000) 644 final 11 Oct 2000 at paras 7–8.
[78] European Convention Working Group II, 'Draft Final Report on Incorporation of the Charter/Accession to the ECHR' WGII WD025 14 October 2002.
[79] CIG 87/04, Brussels, 6 August 2004.
[80] C–106/96 [1998] ECR I–2729.
[81] The European Parliament Committee on Foreign Affairs, Security and Defence Policy, 'Report on Setting up a Single Co-ordinating Structure Within the European Commission Responsible For Human Rights and democratisation' 4 December 1997, A4–0393/97 proposes that the remit of such a body be external rather than internal human rights.

structure[82] is unlikely to enthuse the citizens since he would lack independence from at least one of one (if not more) of the very bodies against which the rights are to be enforced.

Its remit must be wider than the collection and analysis of information entrusted to the Vienna Monitoring Centre on Racism and Xenophobia,[83] and could be based on the 'Paris Principles' produced by the United Nations as guidelines for national human rights institutions[84]: to produce proposals and reports to promote and protect human rights; to make recommendations to ensure that judicial, legislative and administrative provisions conform to human rights; to monitor human rights; to co-operate with national and international bodies on the promotion and protection of human rights; to promote education and research relating to human rights; and to publicise rights. It is submitted that it should also have standing to challenge legislation on the ground of incompatibility with human rights if it brings proceedings in the place of an identifiable victim or class of victims.[85]

However, this would require Treaty amendment and would not address the fact that few human rights are freestanding under EU law, the Court's restricted jurisdiction under Titles IV EC and VI EU and lack of jurisdiction under Title V EU, or the substantial delays in the Community Courts. Such a body would also be expensive to operate.

Accession to the ECHR

The Court of Justice has already ruled that the Community lacks competence to accede to the ECHR because this would be of constitutional significance and thus exceed the Community's powers under Article 308 EC.[86] While this ruling has been criticised on the grounds that accession is of

[82] Comité des Sages, *Leading by Example: A Human Rights Agenda for the European Union for the Year 2000* (Florence, EUI, 1998) at p7/para 19 and P Alston and JHH Weiler, *The European Union and Human Rights: Final Project Report on an Agenda for the Year 2000* (Florence, EUI, 1998), substantially reproduced in 'An "Ever Closer Union" in Need of a Human Rights Policy: The European Union and Human Rights' in P Alston with M Bustelo and J Heenan (eds), *The EU and Human Rights* (Oxford, OUP, 1999).

[83] Established by Regulation 1035/97 ([1997] OJ L151/1).

[84] 'Principles Relating to the Status of National Human Rights Institutions', UN Commission on Human Rights Resolution 1992/54 of 3 March 1992, Annex: UN General Assembly Resolution 48/134 of 20 December 1993, Annex. The Principles are not binding in international law.

[85] A similar proposal has been made for the Northern Ireland Human Rights Commission (Opinion 2/2002 of the Commissioner for Human Rights on Certain Aspects of the Review of Powers of the Northern Ireland Human Rights Commission, Strasbourg, 13 November 2002 Comm DH(2002) 16).

[86] Opinion 2/94 [1996] ECR I–1759 at para 35.

no greater constitutional importance than, for example, WTO membership,[87] the current position is nonetheless that Treaty amendment would be required and the new draft Treaty establishing a Constitution for Europe provides that the EU 'shall accede' to ECHR.[88]

The question is then whether accession would be of any more than symbolic importance. The Court of Justice has accepted that where the Community has competence to conclude international agreements, its institutions may submit to the courts established by such agreements.[89] However, the exact nature of the relationship between the Community Courts and the Court of Human Rights, which could determine the extent to which individuals could enforce the ECHR against the EU, would be a matter for negotiation.[90] The European Convention Working Group II argues that accession is 'a question of credibility, given that Member States have transferred substantial competence to the Union and that adherence to the ECHR has been made a condition for membership of new States in the Union',[91] and it is submitted that it would also remove some of the scope for conflict at Member State level between ECHR and EU human rights, since if EU law apparently obliged Member States to act in breach of the ECHR, an action could be taken directly against the EU.

Review of Art 230 EC

The restrictive *locus standi* applicable to natural and legal persons seeking to bring actions for annulment under Article 230 EC has been discussed above. In *Jégo-Quéré et Cie SA v Commission*[92] the Court of First Instance argued that these restrictions might deny an applicant any legal remedy and therefore that a person must be regarded as individually concerned by a Community measure of general application, and thus able to challenge it, if 'the measure in question affects his legal position, in a manner which is both definitive and immediate, by restricting this right or by imposing obligations on him'. In the earlier case of *Unión de Pequeños Agricultores (UPA) v Council*, Advocate General Jacobs made a similar argument and

[87] JHH Weiler and SC Fries, 'A Human Rights Policy of the European Community and Union: The Question of Competences' in P Alston with M Bustelo and J Heenan eds, *The EU and Human Rights*, above n 82 at p147.
[88] Article I-9 of the draft Treaty, above n 80.
[89] Opinion 1/91 [1991] ECR I–6049.
[90] See further the Secretariat of the European Convention, 'Modalities and Consequences of Incorporation into the Treaties of the Charter of Fundamental Rights and Accession of the Community/Union to the ECHR' CONV 116/02.
[91] 'Draft Final Report on Incorporation of the Charter/Accession to the ECHR' WGII WD025 14 October 2002.
[92] Above n 62.

suggested that a person should be regarded as individually concerned where 'by reason of his particular circumstances, the measure has, or is liable to have, a substantial adverse effect on his interests'.[93] Either test would improve access to the Community Courts by individuals seeking to enforce their fundamental rights, but in *UPA* the Court of Justice declined to extend the concept of individual concern.

The Court of Justice did note that an alternative system for judicial review could be adopted, but argued that it was for the Member States to do so. While it is true that amendments to the EC Treaty are a matter for the Member States, this argument is somewhat disingenuous given that the Court of Justice has in the past interpreted Article 230 EC so as to bring about a change to the *locus standi* requirements. In *Parliament v Council (Chernobyl)*[94] it permitted the Parliament to bring judicial review proceedings under Article 230 EC, despite the absence in that Article of any reference to the Parliament, and its own confirmation less than two years previously in *Parliament v Council (Comitology)*[95] that Parliament had no *locus standi* to bring such proceedings. The Court argued in *Chernobyl* that existing safeguards were inadequate to guarantee review of a measure adopted in disregard of the Parliament's rights and that granting Parliament *locus standi* under Article 230 EC was therefore essential. It is submitted that the existing safeguards in relation to individuals are equally inadequate to protect their fundamental rights. Widening the concept of individual concern would make it more likely that challenges on the ground of breach of fundamental rights would at least be heard.

Judicial Activism

A further possibility is for the Court of Justice to recognise human rights as freestanding. However, given that the Court has so far declined to do this, it is unlikely to do so while the Member States have recognised rights in the Charter but chosen not to make them legally binding, let alone freestanding. In any event, this would not solve the problems of access to the Court of Justice.

CONCLUSION

It is apparent that human rights protection at EU level is open to criticism. Rights are generally not freestanding, the Charter's legal status is

[93] Above n 61 at para 60.
[94] C–70/88 [1990] ECR I–2041.
[95] Case 302/87 [1988] ECR 5615.

uncertain, and enforcement is often hampered by the resulting lack of any simple way of identifying the existence or scope of the rights and by restrictions on the Court of Justice's jurisdiction and on *locus standi*.

However, while it is likely that most complaints will continue to be made against the national authorities, it is submitted that the right of redress against EU institutions will become increasingly important to EU citizens, particularly as the EU expands its competences in areas such as asylum, immigration and closer police and judicial cooperation.[96]

It is therefore essential that the nature and scope of rights under EU law, and its relationship with human rights protection at national level, are clarified. More importantly, rights under EU law must become readily enforceable, preferably by making the Charter legally binding, establishing a human rights commission and reforming the rules on *locus standi* under Article 230 EC, and through EU accession to the ECHR.

[96] See the Tindemans Report on the European Union Bull EC Supp 1/76 at pp 26–27.

7

Environmental Rights and Human Rights: The Final Enclosure Movement

LAURA WESTRA

INTRODUCTION: THE FINAL ENCLOSURES MOVEMENT

... environmental rights are human rights.
—CG Weeramantry, Dissenting Opinion, *Gabcikovo-Nagymaros* Case, Hungary/Slovakia, ICJ (1997)

MANY CENTURIES AGO, capitalism arose in agrarian England as the economic motive and competitiveness replaced traditional values in the 'enclosure movements'. The 'enclosures' provided 'the most famous redefinition of property rights': they eliminated the commons, with no regard for human rights.[1] Philosopher John Locke defended the right to property above all, although he predicated his defense upon ensuring that enough would be left to be held in common. But he also espoused the defense of 'improvements' as needed to impose value upon nature, an argument that supported the policies of his master, the Earl of Shaftsbury.

Through Locke's friendship with Jefferson, the Lockean arguments filtered into the American Declaration of Independence. But these enclosure movements, brutal though they were in their effects against the people, only started what eventually became known as the 'Tragedy of the Commons'.[2] What we encounter today, in the primacy of the economic motive over and above human rights including the right to a safe and healthy habitat, is the final 'enclosure movement': it is once again mostly the poor and dispossessed of the world who are shut out of the natural global commons.

[1] EM Wood, *The Origins of Capitalism* (New York, The Monthly Review Press, 1999) pp 67–94.
[2] G Hardin 'The Tragedy of the Commons' (1968) *Science* 162, pp 1243–48.

The benefits that would accrue to them are no longer available: whatever is left of the commons has become someone's property, and is used as such. Even the simplest 'natural goods' are no longer available freely: clean air, pure water, safe sunlight, safe foods, all are unavailable to the poor. Drinking water must be bought; sunscreen is needed to protect us against the sun; both travel to the few locations that can boast of 'clean air', and housing that is removed from hazardous industrial operations are expensive; food in areas of famine and safe, organically grown food are marginally more available, but often laced with toxic substances. All are commercial goods.

As Wood points out, the very notion of 'improvement' as originally conceived is problematic:

> ... we might like to think about the implications of a culture in which the world for "making better" is rooted in the word for making monetary profit.[3]

What was at stake then, as it is now, was first and foremost the existence of the most basic human rights — that of respect for human life, for human 'security and subsistence'[4] — long before questions of religious or sexual rights were at issue. Dispossessed farmer/tenants in 17th-century agrarian England had no way of supporting themselves or their families. Today many of us, especially in developed Western democracies can in fact support ourselves, but our life and health are under attack nevertheless.

The language of 'attacks' to describe the results of unsafe, unhealthy habitats upon us, is particularly apt as it emphasizes two main points connected to the law, one historical, the other moral. I have described the relation between what I term 'ecoviolence', that is violence perpetrated in and through the environment elsewhere.[5] Essentially, human rights law emerged from humanitarian law after the trials at Nuremberg. Its main object was to ensure that even in the case of armed conflicts between nations, some limits should be established on the harms that could be imposed, legally and morally on civilian populations and other protected groups, such as medical personnel or prisoners. Just war considerations appear far-fetched when the problem involved is ecological/environmental harm, especially in the realm of jus ad *bellum*, although it remains appropriate to point out that *any* form of violence can only be justified in response to an attack, and that is never the case with populations under environmental threats, be they in developing or developed countries, that

[3] EM Wood, *ibid*, p 81.
[4] H Shue, *Basic Rights: Subsistence, Affluence and American Foreign Policy* (Princeton, Princeton University Press, 1996).
[5] L Westra, *Ecoviolence and the Law* (Ardsley NY, Transnational Publishers, 2004) (forthcoming).

is, no one starts with attacks on industry or governments, before pollution is heaped upon them.

In addition, the presence of clear dividing lines between North and South where trade's impact on the life and safety of those in developing countries and the poor and people of colour even in developed countries needs to be emphasized. The very existence of rules of war represents a precedent for a clear dividing line between legitimate violence and violent crime. In the large existing literature on the just war, one may find the clearest possible answers about what might constitute a defensible justification for acts of violence, including the burden of proof that must be met by would-be attackers. Nuremberg trials were also intended to establish responsibility, hence we can apply similar arguments to the situation at hand, in order to discover where causality for environmental harms may also yield corporate or aggregate responsibility for those harms.

The harms that give rise to instruments for the protection of human rights indeed start with visible, evident physical harms, like the interference with the right to life, or to physical integrity, a right that persists even when we are characterized as 'the enemy' or the 'other', unless we offer harm in turn, and first. Of course, after recent political events, it is worth noting that pre-emptive strikes have no place in the law or morality of self-defense that is basic to just war theory.

When we consider environmental/ecological harms to life and health, we can therefore immediately eliminate the existence of 'threats', even potential ones, on the part of various targeted groups, like people of colour, both in North America and in developing countries,[6] thus eliminating the single universally accepted 'reason' for the infliction of harm on others. Thus we can conclude that there is no legitimate reason to 'wage war' by inflicting harm on any population or group, thus the responsibility for these harms rests with the corporate risk-imposers and the bureaucracies and governments who are complicit in their operations, and we will return to this topic in section 4.

UNIVERSAL PRINCIPLES AND HUMAN RIGHTS

For the most part, today's talk about human rights, outside the realm of armed conflicts, centres on religious or sexual rights, or the right to secede on the part of groups or to acquire national status. It seems that the most fundamental right, the basis of all others, has been quietly forgotten: the right to life has becomes, if not obsolete, at least politically incorrect, because of its possible conflict with other rights. Yet unless one returns to the defense of the most basic rights of all, as Shue terms them, it will not be

[6]Westra and Lawson, *Faces of Environmental Racism*, (2nd ed) (Lanham, MD Rowman Littlefield, 2001).

possible to protect humankind globally, and to indict those who breach those rights, and punish them with the severity appropriate to those crimes.

It is not my intention to view other right violations as unimportant, but simply to emphasize that our right to make any and all choices, be they political, religious or personal, start with our being not only alive, but in a condition that renders us capable of thinking, acting, and pursuing various goals:

> And part of what it means to be able to enjoy any other right is not to be prevented from exercising it by lack of security or subsistence. To claim to guarantee people a right that they are in fact unable to exercise is fraudulent, like furnishing people with meal tickets but providing no food.[7]

'Basic rights are the morality of the depths',[8] they represent 'everyone's minimum reasonable demands upon the rest of humanity'.[9] Subsistence rights include the bare necessities we all need, from our habitat's conditions of 'unpolluted air, unpolluted water, adequate food, adequate clothing, adequate shelter…'.[10] We note that although some of these subsistence rights are at least present in the language of the Universal Declaration of Human Rights[11] neither the International Covenant on Economic, Social and Cultural Rights (1966)[12] nor the International Covenant on Civil and Political Rights (1966), specifies that, beyond the right to life, the triad of air/water/food that is safe, hence supportive of life, is an actual right.

In addition, although we may tend to think of the two 1966 Covenants as needed to improve the life of developing countries' citizens, the 'triad' Shue names is emphatically not present as a right of citizens of affluent, technologically advanced democracies, any more than it is a clear right in the impoverished South. The role of poverty in depriving people of their rights and thus of basic justice worldwide is amply documented:

> … severe poverty has consequences: 790 million persons are not adequately nourished, while one billion are without safe water and 2.4 billion without basic sanitation (UNDP 2000: 30); more than 880 million lack access to basic health services (UNDP 1999: 22); about one billion are without adequate shelter and two billion without electricity (UNDP, 1998:49).[13]

[7] Shue, n 4, p 27.
[8] Shue, n 4, p 18.
[9] Shue, n 4, p 19.
[10] Shue, n 4, p 23.
[11] (UNGA Res. 217(LII),UN GAOR,3rd Sess., Supp. NO.13 @71, UN Doc.A/810 (1948), A.25.
[12] 993 U.N.T.S. 3, 1976 Can. T.S.No.46, 999 U.N.T.S. 171,1976 Can. T.S. No.47.
[13] TW Pogge, *Global Justice* (Oxford, Blackwell Pub1ishers, 2001).

Epidemiological data also exist about the lack of less than healthy air/water/food in the North/West, where particulates in the air, ozone layer depletion, unsanitary water and food laced with hormones, chemicals and other additives,[14] promote a wide range of disease including a 'cancer epidemic' [15] in citizens far removed from poverty.

In order to strengthen the principles that would sustain laws to protect basic rights, the first step is to leave behind any form of reasoning that is purely consequential, in favour of a deontological approach. We need the adoption of universal principles that impose the obligation to ensure respect for life's infinite value, in the Kantian sense. Respect for life, O'Neill contends, means rejecting not only the infliction of direct harms, but also that of 'indirect injury' to the 'natural world'.[16] She argues that such injury may be 'gratuitous', that is simply undertaken because it is 'convenient for the powerful', or it can be 'systematic', taken for granted as a normal way of conducting business or governing society[17].

In either case, there is a deep injustice in the destruction of natural environments:

> In the first place, their destruction is unjust because it is a further way by which others can be injured: systematic or gratuitous destruction of the means of life creates vulnerabilities, which facilitate direct injuries to individuals. Destroying (parts of) natural and man-made environments injures those whose lives depend on them. Secondly, the principle of destroying their reproductive and regenerative powers is not universalizable.[18]

Thus it is not an abstract cosmopolitanism that is advocated, but ensuring that justice should prevail globally in a practical sense, by 'identifying compatible institutions and practices'.[19] Note that although O'Neill does not clearly state this, *we all* depend on natural systems in various ways, and to be deprived of them is a severe attack on our life, health and natural function.[20] This attack extends to a plurality of others everywhere

14 D Fidler, *International Law and Public Health* (Ardsley NY, Transnational Publishers, 2001), L Westra, 'The Disvalue of Contingent Valuation and the Accounting Expectation Gap' *Environmental Values* (2000) 9, 153–71, A J McMichael, 'Global Environmental Change in the Coming Century: How Sustainable are Recent Health Gains?' in D Pimentel, L Westra and R Noss (eds) *Ecological Integrity: Integrating Environment, Conservation and Health* (Washington DC, Island Press, 2000).
15 S Epstein, *The Politics of Cancer* (San Francisco, Sierra Club Books, 1978).
16 O O'Neill, *Towards Justice and Virtue* (Cambridge, UK, Cambridge University Press, 1996).
17 O O'Neill, *ibid*, p 175.
18 O O'Neill, *ibid*, p 176.
19 O O'Neill, *ibid*, p 179.
20 C Soskolne and R Bertollini, 'Global Ecological Security and "Sustainable Development": Cornerstones of Public Health' (1999).<www.euro.who.int/globalchange/Publications/20020627 4>.

now, but also to future generations, whose ability to survive, thrive and have their rights protected must also be respected.[21] Our interconnectedness, not only to all living things and processes today but in the future, ensures that this dimension of our obligations cannot be avoided, and it represents the basis of ecological concern.[22]

Whoever the humans of the future might be, they will share our finiteness and vulnerability, hence in Kantian terms, 'inclusive principles of indifference to and neglect of others also cannot be universalized'.[23] Shue adds:

> The infant and the aged do not need to be assaulted in order to be deprived of health, life or the capacity to enjoy active rights. The classical liberal main prescription for the good life, do not interfere with thy neighbor, is the only poison they need.[24]

We can add all debilitated persons, malnourished, weakened adults, the infants and aged, and all of us who are exposed continually to unsafe living conditions.

GROUNDING HUMAN RIGHTS

The connection between environmental degradation and human life, health and normal function rests upon the inviolability of human rights. Although a detailed analysis of all existing arguments in their support is beyond the scope of this work, we will revisit briefly some of those arguments in support of our own thesis that human rights extend beyond the right of the human person, to the generic right to life, including our habitat. Our approach will be Kantian, in line with the previous arguments by O'Neill, Shue and Pogge.

The foundational arguments proposed by Alan Gewirth help to shed light on that basic connection between humans and their habitats. Gewirth argues that human rights are not based primarily on human dignity,[25] and that this Kantian principle is only partially right. He prefers to base 'human rights on the necessary conditions of human action',[26] as morality is intended to give rise to moral action. Gewirth adds that 'human rights are the equivalent to 'natural ' rights, in that they

[21] E Brown-Weiss, 'Intergenerational Equity' in *Environmenta1 Change and International Law*, E Brown-Weiss (ed), (New York, United Nations Press, 1992) pp 385–412.
[22] L Westra, P Miller, R Karr, WE Rees and RE Ulanowicz, 'Ecological Integrity and the Aims of the Global Ecological INTEGRITY Project' in *Ecological Integrity: Integrating Environment, Conservation and Health* (Washington DC, Island Press, 2000) pp 19–41.
[23] O'Neill, n 16, p 193.
[24] Shue, n 4, p 19.
[25] A Gewirth, *Human Rights Essays on Justification and Applications* (Chicago, University of Chicago Press, 1982).
[26] Gewirth *ibid* p 5.

pertain to all humans by virtue of their nature as actual or prospective agents'.[27] He cites five reasons in support of his claim: 1) 'the supreme importance, of the conditions of human actions' (and we will return to this point below); 2) action is 'the common subject matter of all moralities'; 3)'action' is more specific and less vague than 'dignity' or 'flourishing'; 4) thus 'action' ultimately secures 'fundamental moral status' for persons; 5) 'action's necessary conditions provide justification for human rights — as every agent must hold that he has a right to freedom and well-being as the necessary conditions of his actions'.[28]

Beyleveld and Brownsword argue that the 'basic' or 'generic needs' that represent the preconditions of all action including moral action are 'freedom or voluntariness' and 'well-being or purposiveness', where the former are procedural and the latter 'substantive',[29] and they view freedom as instrumental to well-being. I want to propose inverting this order. Life, health and the mental ability to comprehend and choose precede the exercise of voluntariness and are not only necessary for it, but sufficient, when all these conditions are in fact present.

In essence, this has been the argument of the previous section: 'basic rights'[30] represent the minimum all humans are entitled to, and they are prior to all other rights, both conceptually and temporally. For Gewirth as well, life and the capacities named above can be 'threatened or interfered with'.[31] Thus to say we have rights is to say equally that the preconditions of these rights represent something we are entitled to have not only in morality but also in the law. In other words any legal instrument that supports the existence of human rights, *ipso facto* ought to proclaim the requirement that their preconditions be equally supported and respected.

Some argue that the dignity of human beings is only partially the ground of human rights and that dignity itself is based on agency — still the argument allows the introduction of at least a further point in favour of extending human rights to life and health. The introduction of 'preconditions' means the introduction of conditions that are not only conceptually but temporally prior to agency, hence the protection of these pre-conditions entails the acceptance of potential consequences in the protection of agency.

Arguments about potentiality have been discussed rather cavalierly in the extensive literature on abortion, only to re-emerge more recently

[27] Gewirth *ibid* p 7.
[28] Gewirth *ibid* p 5.
[29] D Beyleveld and R Brownsword, *Human Dignity in Bioethics and Biolaw* (Oxford, Oxford University Press, 2001) at p 71.
[30] Shue n 4.
[31] Beyleveld and Brownsword, n 29, p 70; Gewirth, n 23, p 54.

because of the presence of the rights of the child (to be) while in utero. For instance, Deborah Mathieu says:

> Thus even if the foetus is not considered a person in the moral or legal sense, there are still important interests of a person which must be weighed against those of the pregnant woman: the interests of the future child. A pregnant woman should act for the sake of the child that the fetus will become. Her obligations, in other words, are to her future child, not to her fetus.[32]

Given that, the potential for developing certain genetic conditions has been used to explain or justify abortion, is hard to see why the future should be viewed as suspect when it is used to proscribe it instead, in cases where concern for the child's future health is not an issue.[33] Beyleveld and Brownsword argue that it is not necessary to support the presumed dignity of the embryo from conception:

> ... it is the consideration of the possibility that the zygote might be an agent (and have dignity) even though there is little evidence of this.[34]

The authors continue by citing the possible rights of the pregnant woman in this respect. To destroy the foetus by removing it from its first natural habitat, however, clearly violates the pre-conditions of its eventual agency, even if, with the authors, we accept 'the view that agency is the ground of human dignity'.[35]

Moving instead to consider Singer's position as foundational, thus grounding rights in sentience,[36] or even that of David De Grazia on 'nociception',[37] we have more than dignity, or even dignity-as-agency, where the Gewirthian 'Principle of Proportionality' maintains that agents have 'duties to all living creatures (human or non-human) on a proportional basis'.[38]

A discussion of the detailed arguments for and against abortion or the use of embryos would take us too far afield. Yet even this brief analysis indicates that the presence of life ought to be the most important category to render beings worthy of respect and consideration, aside from their present or possible mental states.

[32] D Mathieu, (2nd ed) *Preventing Prenatal Harm: Should the State Intervene?* (Washington DC, Georgetown University Press, 1996) p 28; see also Beyerveld and Brownsword, n 29, p 158.
[33] D Marquis, 'Why Abortion is Immoral' (1989) *The Journal of Philosophy* 86 183–202.
[34] Beylesveld and Brownsword, n 29, p 158.
[35] Beylesveld and Brownsword, n 29, p 112.
[36] P Singer, *Animal Rights and Human Obligations* (Englewood Cliffs NJ, Prentice Hall, 1976).
[37] D De Grazia, *Taking Animals Seriously* (New York, Cambridge University Press, 1995).
[38] Gewirth, n 25, p 112.

Kant defends the infinite value of life, as someone whose generic capacities to be human, with all that it might entail, is not eliminated by present adverse conditions, such as regular drunkenness, for instance. Non-human animals have also been deemed to have purposiveness,[39] so that the same could be said of foetuses, according to the comparable development of their nervous system at various stages, and they certainly do have nociception as an indication of the capacities they will possess later in their development.[40] If at least duties are owed to all beings capable of sentience and agency in various proportions, then the duty is not specific, but it can be owed to all life, and to its preconditions, that is to the habitats whose 'fittingness' supports our own. That is to say, by extending the meaning of dignity from its modern sense of *dignitas,* to its classical Greek sense of within the natural laws of the universe, one may be able to place Kant's imperatives within the more far-reaching imperatives of the 'principle of integrity'.[41] In this case, anything that conflicts with the 'dignity' of natural universal laws is *prima facie* suspect, hence — minimally — it requires serious justification, beyond 'preferences'[42] or economic advantages.

In fact these extended rights, or the pre-conditions of the rights themselves are everyone's entitlement, and those who deliberately or negligently impose the harms described in Section 2, should be considered to be guilty of crimes directly or indirectly, or of complicity in those crimes.

ECOVIOLENCE AND HUMAN RIGHTS: CAUSATION AND CONSPIRACY

The analysis of responsibility for crimes committed jointly or through a collective *body,* can also be found in war morality, particularly in the 'principles of Nuremberg', where the question of moral and legal complicity in regard to violence is discussed in detail.[43] A recent paper by Judith Lee Kissell analyses complicity as a multifaceted concept. Complicity includes 'encouraging', 'enticing', 'enabling', 'ordering' and 'failing to intervene', and one can cite examples from antiquity to the present that all fit loosely under the general heading of complicity.

[39] T Regan, *The Case for Animal Rights* (Berkely CA, University of California Press, 1983).
[40] D De Grazia, n 37.
[41] L Westra, *The Principles of Integrity: An Environmental Proposal for Ethics* (Lanham MD, Rowman Littlefield, 1994) pp 96–97.
[42] L Westra, 'The Disvalue of Contingent Valuation and the Accounting Expectation Gap', above n 14.
[43] R Wasserstrom, 'The Relevance of Nuremberg' in M Cohen, T Nagel and T Scanlon (eds), *War and Moral Responsibility* (New Jersey, Princeton University Press, 1974).

Kissell says:

> For example, we count as accomplices Aeschylus/Aegisthus, who *encourages* Clytemnestra to kill her husband, Agamemnon; Shakespeare's Jago, who *entices* Othello to kill his beloved Desdemona; the mother who *enables* her child to become an alcoholic; the gang leader who *orders* a beating of a victim; the Western powers who, according to Margaret Thatcher, were complicit for *failing to intervene* in the former Yugoslavia.[44]

These examples demonstrate the wide latitude we accord to the concept of complicity in a variety of settings, as Wasserstrom argues as well. With particular regard to complicity in the context of war, the Nuremburg Charter addresses both the substantive description of 'war crimes' or offences, as well as the conditions of individual responsibility. Thus Article Six provides:

a) Crimes against Peace: namely, planning, preparation, initiation or waging of a war of aggression, or a war in violation of international treaties, agreements or assurances, or participation in a common plan or conspiracy for the accomplishment of any of the foregoing.
b) War Crimes: namely violations of the laws or customs of war. Such violations shall include, but not be limited to, murder, ill-treatment or deportation to slave labor or for any other purpose of civilian population of or in an occupied territory, murder or ill-treatment of prisoners of war or persons on the seas, killing of hostages, plunder of public property, wanton destruction of cities, towns or villages, or devastation not justified by military necessity.
c) Crimes against Humanity: namely murder, extermination, enslavement, deportation, and other inhuman acts committed against any civilian population, before or during the war or persecutions on political, racial or religious grounds in execution of or in connection with any crime within the jurisdiction of the Tribunal, whether or not in violation of the domestic law of the country where perpetrated.

Many of the crimes described are easily translated into similar crimes of ecoviolence. Under 'War Crimes', 'murder' is not necessarily described as immediate, or evident at first sight. From the perspective of moral philosophy, murder is equally a crime if it is slow or delayed, as it invariably is when it is environmentally induced through cumulative

[44] JL Kissell, 'Causation — The Challenge of Complicity', (paper presented at the Eastern Meeting of the American Philosophical Association, Dec 27 1999).

small doses of chemicals or toxins. The 'wanton destruction' of cities, towns or villages can also be interpreted in an environmental sense. Consider for instance, 'devastation not justified by military necessity'. One could say that ecological devastation to which we are exposed has nothing to do, for the most part, with war. Yet this is precisely why 'devastation' as such (that is, as unconnected with war objectives) is termed a crime. 'Crimes against humanity' cover a lot of ground when defined (*inter alia*) as 'other inhuman acts committed against any civilian population'; it offers especially fruitful grounds for our environmental perspective as these crimes remain such 'whether or not in violation of the domestic law of the country where perpetrated'.

We can now turn to our main focus in this section: what constitutes a conspiracy where individual responsibility is present, even in collective actions? The first thing to note is that participation in a 'common plan' or 'conspiracy' are sufficient to ensure one's responsibility as an inividual. As Wasserstrom puts it:

'Conspiring to do certain things is itself a crime. But, even more than this, responsibility is derived from membership in a group'.[45] The language of culpable conspiracy, such as 'encouraging' 'enticing' or 'enabling' fits well within being part of a group membership.

Kissell defines conspiracy as: 'an offense in which one agent, the accomplice, becomes responsible for the acts of, and the harm caused by another agent, the perpetrator'. Following this definition she adds: 'complicity is an *offense* and not simply a collaborative action'.[46] Nevertheless it is clear that even 'planning', 'encouraging' or even 'enabling' are not in and of themselves harming anyone, when just two are involved, the accomplice and the perpetrator. It seems as though the situation is totally different when a group is involved. The one who delivers a hate speech to a group cannot claim innocence, when the inflamed group acts violently in consequence of hearing the encouragement to hate. The speaker cannot just claim he did not participate in the violence, and stood aside from it.

Speaking of the relation between accomplice and perpetrator, Kissell emphasizes their 'asymmetric relationship to the harm'; but when group complicity is at stake, the case is not so clear. It is not obvious that one can always distinguish between 'cause' and 'contributions' when a group conspiracy is at issue. Hitler at first 'encouraged', then 'planned', and finally 'ordered' and 'enabled' the killing of millions of Jews. He can certainly be seen as a perpetrator anyway, although he probably never personally, actively perpetrated a single violent crime, or killed a single Jew.

For all that, we can (and must) say that Hitler was indeed blameworthy and personally responsible for causing the atrocities he did not personally

[45] Wasserstrom, n 43, p 137.
[46] *Ibid*, p 2.

perpetrate. Nevertheless his causal agency is far more than a 'contributing factor'. Because of the authority he represented, his beliefs and his expressions, aside from the laws he enacted, were directly causative of the harms that ensued. In that case, it seems that *Kissell is mistaken* when she claims that 'causation' and 'complicit conduct' cannot be equated. She says:

> I can think of contribution as causal in the broad sense of being the object of inquiry that justifies censure. However, because it is not the same thing as a physical cause, it need not satisfy the necessity requirement, which in any case complicit conduct cannot do.[47]

Wasserstrom provides a clearer understanding of group dynamics in violent situations, so that the mere joining of certain groups when these are known to promote a specific, explicit agenda, is sufficient to ensure the personal responsibility of all who join, for the ensuing violence. An example might be joining the Ku Klux Klan in the US South, hence participating in its hate propaganda and its crimes.

For cases of institutionalised ecoviolence we have no centralised 'evil' authority we can point to, although, for instance, the demonstrators at the 1999 WTO protests had crystallised their movement against an organisation, at least, if not against a specific person. On the whole, groups and organisations are much harder to characterise as 'Evil, Inc': they usually have at least some favourable sides, or some tentative good intentions, or even a few decent people in their organisation, and all that might be to their credit. It is much easier in those cases, to be accused of belonging to a marginal group, or to be 'hysterical' or 'irrational', if one dares to protest against groups and organisations. That is a danger that all protestors incur. Yet, the principles of Nuremberg help to understand how those who belong to certain groups can be viewed as conspirators, in regard to environmental violence, at least in the moral sense.

CONCLUSIONS

The analysis of causality and conspiracy in the previous section should have raised — minimally — reasonable doubts about the legitimacy of 'business as usual' and its environmental effects on life and health. In addition, the connection between the right to life and that to health or 'biological integrity' is increasingly recognized by international and supranational courts.[48]

[47] Kissel, n 44, p 5.
[48] *Guerra v Italy* (1998) 26 EHRR 357; *Lopez Ostra v Spain* (1995) 20 EHRR 277 (ECHR).

Starting with a consideration of the import of the original 'enclosure movement', and the Lockean logic of 'improvements', we traced the reality of economic primacy, and the constant growth and legitimacy of that concern over the basic rights of humanity. There is a tendency to assume that perhaps there is no need to battle or even to argue for rights that are now, by-and-large, taken for granted, like the 'right to living',[49] and to normal physical function and basic health.[50]

A brief overview of humanitarian law indicates that life and physical integrity were, at least initially, the basis of all universal rights legislation. In contrast, although disregard for basic rights began in the seventeenth century, even beyond areas of armed conflict we can increasingly see the growing presence of the economic motive as causally related to the harms perpetrated against humankind.

In addition, we can appeal to the definition of both causality and complicity, as regulatory trade bodies like NAFTA, FTAA or the WTO, conspire with both industrial interests and governments to enshrine harmful institutions and regulations. Finally, by-passing utilitarian considerations and the enforcement of a liberalism incapable of providing principled guidance, we turn to a Kantian approach to a universal cosmopolitan rule. Some may accuse Kant of being too abstract, and too bound by formal rules. But we have seen that in practice, the prevailing Rawlsian liberalism has exacerbated North/South injustice, has supported the elimination of our habitat and attacks on all life without serious considerations of the effect of globalised policies on the basic rights of present and future generations to the universal commons. The greatest tragedy is that, unless some radical and immediate action is taken to reverse present trends, the very existence of the 'commons' will remain only a historic fact, not even a memory for future generations.

[49] FO Vicuna, 'State Responsibility, Liability and Remedial Measures under International Law: New Criteria for Environmental Protection' in E Brown-Weiss, (ed) *Environmental Change and International Law* (Tokyo, United Nations University Press, 1992) pp 124–158.
[50] L Westra, 'Institutionalized Environmental Violence and Human Rights', in D Pimentel L Westra and R Noss (eds), *Ecological Integrity: Integrating Environmental Conservation and Health* (Washington DC, Island Press, 2000).

8

International Rhetoric and the Real Global Agenda: Exploring the Tension between Interdependence and Globalisation

DUNCAN FRENCH

INTRODUCTION

THIS CHAPTER SEEKS to place globalisation within a broader normative framework and consider its implications for international governance, in particular the international community's stated goal of promoting international social justice through the elaboration of universal social welfare goals, such as the internationally agreed Millennium Development Goals (MDGs).[1] This notion of social justice is broader than many Northern States' traditional conceptions of human rights, though it finds clear expression in texts such as the 1966 International Covenant on Economic, Social and Cultural Rights[2] and more recent global declarations, such as the 1995 Copenhagen Declaration on Social Development.[3] However, to what extent is the continuing drive towards globalisation an impediment to the achievement of such universal

[1] Millennium Declaration, as adopted at the Millennium Summit of the United Nations (A/RES/55/2, 8 September 2000).

[2] (Adopted 16 December 1966, entered into force 23 March 1976) 999 UNTS 171 (ICCPR). See preamble: '*Recognizing* that, in accordance with the Universal Declaration of Human Rights, the ideal of free human beings enjoying freedom from fear and want can only be achieved if conditions are created whereby everyone may enjoy his economic, social and cultural rights, as well as his civil and political rights'.

[3] UN Doc. A/CONF.166/9 (19 April 1995), para 5: 'We share the conviction that social development and social justice are indispensable for the achievement and maintenance of peace and security within and among our nations'.

goals? Or phrased slightly differently, how far is universal goal-setting in the area of social welfare a largely idealistic and futile attempt to prescribe normative order to an international situation that is arguably unreceptive to welfare and right-oriented public policy concerns?

It would be wrong, of course, to suggest that all public policy is identical in terms of its reception by those affected by it. It is quite clear that there is a core of international regulation which all would recognise as fundamental to the well-ordering of international society, in the same way as there is acceptance of the need for certain minimum rules for well-ordered national systems. A discussion of what is required for well-ordered societies is beyond the scope of this chapter, though it obviously includes notions of economic and military security. However, the chapter will suggest that if the accepted 'core' becomes too focused on promoting private interests, whilst other societal concerns are marginalised and unsupported, international public law and policy will lose much of its potential normative impact. If this argument is correct, one might then be forced to question the value and purpose of the very attempt by the international community to establish social justice and universal social welfare goals. Is such 'rhetoric' simply a superficial gloss on what is ultimately the real global agenda?

In fact, seeking to address the relationship between globalisation and the promotion of social welfare and other public goods, brings into sharper focus the very nature of the international system itself. It is easy to characterise globalisation as a new — and distinct — phenomenon unrelated to, and separate from, previous epochs in the development of international politics. This is, however, a caricature that elevates globalisation to a point divorced from its origins and historical precedents. Nevertheless, the importance and impact of the current stage of globalisation should not be under-emphasised, and it is clear that the globalisation debate also raises some difficult structural questions. A central issue is the extent to which globalisation exacerbates pre-existing tensions within the current international system; for instance, the increasing uncertainty globalisation places upon sovereignty as the *locus* of political power within the global system.

In the final part of the chapter, I will seek to address some of these arguments with particular reference to the issue of corporate responsibility within the context of the 2002 Johannesburg World Summit on Sustainable Development (WSSD). How far do the processes and outcomes of the WSSD support my hypothesis that the establishment of social welfare objectives at the international level are frustrated by the imperatives of globalisation? The paper will conclude that whilst international approaches such as the WSSD are undoubtedly hindered by a narrowing global agenda and shifts in political power, global rhetoric remains an important aspect of the international debate. As noted in the conclusion, rhetoric is an inherent part of the political process and has a central purpose in allowing the international community to be idealistic, to set forward-looking objectives and to promote wider societal concerns. However, in equal measure, there is a need for a more balanced approach to globalisation. To achieve this, the — public — international community will have to move beyond mere rhetoric and seek a new consensus on structural and normative changes to the global order, both to reflect the changing nature of international society and to maintain the pre-eminence of the rule of law in international affairs.

GLOBALISATION, LAW AND INTERNATIONAL SOCIETY

The classic understanding of the political and legal position of the State is exemplified by the judgment of the Permanent Court of International Justice in the *Lotus* case (1927).[4] In its decision, the Permanent Court made the following general statement; '[t]he rules of law binding upon States therefore emanate from their own free will as expressed in conventions or by usages generally accepted as expressing principles of law…Restrictions upon the independence of States cannot therefore be presumed'. The *Lotus* case was the high point of the positivist theory of international law and, as the above quotation highlights, was based on two inter-related principles.

First, the notion that international law is based on the 'free will' of States, thus emphasising the consent-based nature of international law-making. States, as sovereign entities, have creative control over the law that they accept as binding. As one commentator notes, 'although international law controls sovereignty, in the sense that it sets a legal limit to a state's power, this power is not a delegation of international law…nothing is more repugnant to states than the idea that they are exercising a power conceded to them by the international order'.[5]

Second, there is a presumption that in the absence of internationally legally binding norms to the contrary, the independence and legal authority of States is largely without restriction. As the Permanent Court noted, States have a 'wide measure of discretion which is only limited in certain cases by prohibitive rules'.[6] This particular conception of sovereignty is based on the historical rejection of Papal control and the assertion of statehood following the Peace of Westphalia in 1648. Central to this development was the notion that the sovereignty of an independent State is the

[4] *The case of the SS Lotus* (*France v Turkey*) PCIJ Rep series A No 10.
[5] R Anand, *Confrontation or Cooperation? International Law and Developing Countries* (Dordrecht, Martinus Nijhoff Publishers, 1987) 87.
[6] See n 4.

source of its political power, both within its own territorial limits and in relation to other sovereign States internationally. Whilst many have, of course, rejected such an expansive account of sovereignty, it is nevertheless difficult to deny the influence that such a view has had on the development of international law and political thought.

The relationship between State and law in international politics has therefore always been a curious one. On the one hand, States as the 'founders' of the system use law as a tool to achieve their political and economic objectives. Law is but a mechanism through which States seek to assert their beliefs and consequently law, in and of itself, has no inherent normative purpose. On the other hand, there is a widely held conviction that the international legal system is not simply a formal mechanistic process, but it has the capability to reflect wider concerns and promote greater adherence to the *ideal* of international society.[7] This broader approach can be seen in many of the judgments of the International Court of Justice, and in particular its habit of placing its reasoning within a wider normative context. As one example, the International Court noted in its *Advisory Opinion on the Legality of the Threat or Use of Nuclear Weapons* (1996),

> [i]n the long run, international law, *and with it the stability of the international order which it is intended to govern*, are bound to suffer from the continuing difference of views with regard to the legal status of weapons as deadly as nuclear weapons. It is consequently important to put an end to this state of affairs ... .[8]

Underlying such reasoning is the view that the sovereign right of States to unilateral freedom of political action cannot be considered absolute, but should be constrained by the broader imperative of maintaining the fabric and purpose of the wider global society.

It is important to emphasise this duality in the nature of the international legal system to appreciate fully the transition in international law from its historical inception as a system of rules intended merely to regulate international order between sovereign States to a broader role in international dispute avoidance, problem-solving and international collaboration, often relying on new — and permanent — institutional frameworks, the archetype of which, of course, is the organization of the United Nations. As one commentator notes, '[t]he famous international lawyer... Wolfgang Friedman, described this new type of international

[7] P Allott, *Eunomia: New Order for a New World* (Oxford, Oxford University Press, 1990) 254: 'Through law society is able to organize the reality of its words and ideas and theories and values, to organize its struggle with the perennial dilemmas of all society'.
[8] [1996] ICJ Rep 226, para 98. Emphasis added.

law as "law of co-operation", thereby highlighting a new quality in the law, different from the ancient public international law'.[9] To what extent this 'law of co-operation' itself is being replaced by 'law in the age of globalisation', or any other such nomenclature one might wish to use, is of course presently debatable.

It is somewhat of a truism, therefore, to note that the international community has become increasingly interdependent. However, what might not be such an obvious remark is that traditionally international lawyers have accepted this interdependence as a sign of increasing *public* interaction between States at the level of regulation and policy. The conclusion of international agreements and the establishment of intergovernmental organisations are indications of the emerging interdependence at the level of the State. For a long time, private or corporate interaction at the transnational level was not considered as a distinct or separate phenomenon. What was regarded as more important was the inter-linkages between States, with little thought given to the nature, extent and influence of inter-linkages beyond the public sphere. This was partly due to the relatively limited nature of transnational corporate relations until quite recently, and also partly due to the political emphasis that was devoted to the public sphere, especially during the Cold War period.

The phenomenon of globalisation has forced a dramatic shift in focus. No longer is it feasible for international law — and the international lawyer — to be content to analyse international life through the lens of inter-governmental relations. Concurrently, concepts such as sovereignty, territory and jurisdiction, once considered fundamental to the workings of international law, now seem increasingly marginalised by developments that — particularly economically weaker — States seem relatively powerless to influence. In short, it would be easy to characterise globalisation as external to the traditional legal and political framework. Such a characterisation has elements of truth, but as already noted, is a caricature of the complexity of the real situation. As I have noted elsewhere, although the nation State is losing some of its influence, it is a mistake to view it as redundant. Far from it, the nation State continues to be a key player on the international stage because, quite simply, it remains the most complete nexus of relationships within the international order.[10]

Nevertheless, whilst the implications of globalisation are potentially universal, the benefits are not necessarily evenly distributed. Whilst certain pockets of humanity appear to be consistently progressing along a linear continuum of technological advance and economic

[9] S Hobe, 'The Era of Globalisation as a Challenge to International Law' 40 *Duquesne Law Review* (2002) 659.

[10] D French, 'The Role of the State and International Organizations in Reconciling Sustainable Development and Globalisation' 2 *International Environmental Agreements: Politics, Law and Economics* (2002) 140–141.

wealth, the vast majority struggles to maintain a reasonable — or even marginal — livelihood. It is this disparity which justifies many commentators to argue that human rights must be broadly construed to reflect also these severe economic and social differences. The extent of the variation between the perceived affluence of developed States ('the North') and the large-scale deprivation in many developing States ('the South') is, in statistical terms, quite staggering. It is estimated that whilst the richest 20% of the global population possess around 86% of the global GDP, the poorest 20% possess just 1%.[11] Numerous factors contribute to this general situation and it is impossible to provide a complete and comprehensive analysis of both the causes and the full extent of such global extremes. Nor, of course is it suggested that globalisation has caused such disparities. However, the impact of globalisation on an already inequitable situation remains disputed.

There is little debate that globalisation may offer benefits to humanity in terms of increased opportunities for international trade, foreign capital, technological investment and economic growth, in addition to the greater sense of transboundary, trans-regional, even cross-cultural discourse that globalisation will undoubtedly offer. What is less certain is how these benefits will be dispersed between rich and poor, and whether 'public goods' such as environmental protection, social development and the promotion of human rights are simultaneously promoted through the advance of globalisation. In other words, can globalisation provide a solution to these global imbalances, or will globalisation — as a new, and potentially more perverse, manifestation of global relations — further exacerbate existing disparities?

UNIVERSAL GOAL-SETTING IN THE SHADOW OF GLOBALISATION

A key feature of interdependence has been the attempt by the international community to develop political consensus on a range of issues of common concern. Such political consensus will often develop during international negotiations, often leading to the adoption of an international convention on the issue. However, whilst not in any way wanting to marginalise the role international agreements can play in international politics, this paper seeks to consider a rather different approach to international problems, *viz.*, the formulation of declarations and other non-binding documents promulgated by United Nations-organised global conferences. Many of these concerns are what one might term humanitarian

[11] United Nations Development Programme (UNDP), *1999 Human Development Report — Globalisation with a Human Face* (New York, Oxford University Press, 1999) 3.

or social-welfare orientated in nature. After briefly highlighting some of these events, this paper will consider their relevance in the age of globalisation.

The 1990s was the decade of the global conference, a trend that seems to be continuing into the early years of the twenty-first century. These UN-arranged conferences were all well-attended international jamborees on numerous issues including 'environment and development' (Rio de Janeiro, 1992), 'human rights' (Vienna, 1993), 'population' (Cairo, 1994), 'social development' (Copenhagen, 1995), 'women' (Beijing, 1995), 'food' (Rome, 1996 and 2002), 'least developed countries' (Brussels, 2001), 'racism' (Durban, 2001), 'financing for development' (Monterrey, 2002) and 'sustainable development' (Johannesburg, 2002). Along with these topic-specific conferences, one should also note the Millennium Summit of the United Nations, held in New York in 2000, at which the Millennium Development Goals (MDGs) were endorsed. Out of all of these conferences came grand political declarations, as well as, in many cases, more detailed plans of action setting out how the international community was going to take the issues forward.

Many of these documents are positive in tone and optimistic in content. They often consciously seek to set out a framework of action on which States politically — though not legally — commit themselves. On the other hand, the wording of such declarations is usually the result of painstaking negotiations and fudged compromises between different groupings of States, often between North and South. The difficulties in agreeing a text suggest that States take great care in international politicking, whether the text is intended to be legally binding or not. Consequently, these declarations are the epitome of diplomatic-speak, with all sides able to endorse the final result as reflective of their viewpoint. However, and probably more realistically, all States are aware of the compromise nature of such documents and are able to accept the final result as the best that could be achieved.

Nevertheless, it is easy to adopt too critical a view of such declarations. Supporters of such processes would suggest that it is worth asking why, if such declarations are inherently weakened by the compromises contained therein, do States — as a collective — continue to participate in their elaboration and, as importantly, continue to commit themselves to them politically? If it is accepted that, on the one hand, States are aware of the political difficulties inherent in such negotiations and that, on the other, it is a reasonable premise to suggest that States do not volunteer to engage in meaningless negotiation, one is led to the conclusion that States must consider that such events have some — if only limited — political virtue.

Global conferences are seen by some commentators as the closest that the international community has to the North American idea of a 'town hall meeting' or to other forms of community forum. It enables the international community to meet, often away from the ordinary venue of UN headquarters in New York, to consider in detail a particular topic. Much preparatory work is done before such conferences of course, but it is usually only at the conference itself that consensus is finally achieved. These conferences, however, have not only provided an opportunity for international debate amongst States, but often have contributed to wider societal involvement, though the extent to which non-State actors and civil society have been allowed to participate in the 'main event' rather than at its margins, remains both politically and doctrinally disputed.

The principal issue for this paper is to consider whether these international conferences — and the texts adopted by them — have largely failed to take into account the wider international reality, as coined by the concept of globalisation. In other words, are such texts simply idealised international rhetoric, not reflective of the true political situation? Do they maintain a false premise that the international community has the inclination and ability to promote public goods when in reality the actions of States, both in terms of their legitimacy and impact, are no longer as definitive as once they were?

This is not to suggest that such political declarations are devoid of any references to globalisation. As the 1995 Copenhagen Declaration on Social Development, for example, notes,

> [g]lobalisation, which is a consequence of increased human mobility, enhanced communications, greatly increased trade and capital flows, and technological developments, opens new opportunities for sustained economic growth and development of the world economy, particularly in developing countries. Globalisation also permits countries to share experiences and to learn from one another's achievements and difficulties, and promotes a cross-fertilization of ideals, cultural values and aspirations. At the same time, the rapid processes of change and adjustment have been accompanied by intensified poverty, unemployment and social disintegration. Threats to human well-being, such as environmental risks, have also been globalized. Furthermore, the global transformations of the world economy are profoundly changing the parameters of social development in all countries.[12]

However, the inclusion by this and other declarations of — some might say now clichéd — references to globalisation do not, of themselves, constitute an adequate response to the challenges posed by globalisation. It is what such conferences substantively achieve that matters and a failure to appreciate and reconcile fully the dynamics and implications of the changing global situation is likely to result in the international community setting goals that it cannot then achieve. The corporate ethic that exists

[12] Copenhagen Declaration, above n 3, para 14.

within globalisation has a strong influence on States to reorient their public sectors away from promoting social welfare and other public goods and towards narrowly construed commercial opportunities. A failure to recognise these pressures within such texts will militate against the development of effective international strategies.

It remains questionable, therefore, as to the extent global conferences can adequately respond to the varying pressures of globalisation. By their very nature, such conferences can — at most — develop 'soft' principles, rather than 'hard' legal regulation. However, more important than the legal status of any such declaration is the divergence that exists between the idealism of such gatherings and the reality of global politics — what one might colloquially refer to as the 'global agenda'. The reality is that whilst the concerns of individual communities remain clear (namely, issues of human rights, economic development, social progress, and environmental protection) the global political agenda is shrinking.

In recent years, the combined impact of aggressive free market philosophy and the existence of one superpower concerned almost exclusively with narrowly-defined security issues, has significantly hindered broader international cooperation. As Alston notes, '[t]he agenda that emerges seems remarkably consonant with one particular, rather narrow, vision of the role of the international community in response to the challenge of Globalisation'.[13] In particular, he argues that only where the developed world requires the assistance of others — in relation to 'drugs, corruption, weapons of mass destruction, terrorism, etc.' — is international co-operation likely to be effective. As regards social welfare and other related issues, the effectiveness of any action by the international community is thus limited, by comparison. If this assessment is accurate, one is left wondering what these global conferences can consequently achieve. In seeking to consider this issue still further, the final section of this paper concentrates upon the processes and outcomes of the World Summit on Sustainable Development, held in Johannesburg, 2002, with particular reference to the issue of corporate responsibility.

CORPORATE RESPONSIBILITY AND THE WSSD

The 2002 World Summit on Sustainable Development was attended by over 21,000 participants representing inter alia, States,[14] international organisations, non-governmental organisations (both political interest

[13] P Alston, 'The Myopia of the Handmaidens: International Lawyers and Globalisation' 8 *European Journal of International Law* (1997) 439.
[14] In many cases, not just representatives of the executive, but also the legislative and judicial branches of the State.

groups and business associations), scientific opinion and wider civil society. The technical purpose of the conference was to review progress on the implementation of Agenda 21, a plan of action adopted at the 1992 UN Conference on Environment and Development, held in Rio de Janeiro. In fact, as can be noted by the number of participants — both official and those at the margins of the conference — Johannesburg was much more than just an audit exercise.

The World Summit provided an opportunity under the umbrella of sustainable development to consider and debate issues of poverty, economic underdevelopment, national and international restrictions on social progress and environmental degradation. As the Political Declaration agreed at Johannesburg states, '[t]he deep fault line that divides human society between the rich and the poor and the ever-increasing gap between the developed and developing worlds pose a major threat to global prosperity, security and stability'.[15] However, despite negative prognoses of the current situation, as is usual with these events the perspective contained within the texts remains surprisingly positive and continues to be largely dependent upon the existence of effective public governance. As the same declaration notes, '[r]ecognizing that humankind is at a crossroads, we have united in a common resolve to make a determined effort to respond positively to the need to produce a practical and visible plan that should bring about poverty eradication and human development'.[16]

Nevertheless, and in line with the hypothesis set out in the previous section, how likely is it that the idealism and optimistic spirit of the World Summit is rendered largely ineffectual through pressures external to the international public community; pressures that the international community is unable either to change or fully influence? The inability of the international community — or perhaps, disinclination by its most influential members — to intervene effectively in the global market manifested itself quite clearly during the negotiations of the Johannesburg's Plan of Implementation. One particularly controversial issue concerned the responsibility of multinational enterprises (MNEs) for their policies and actions.

The topic of corporate responsibility, particularly of MNEs, in the areas of labour standards, human rights, and more recently environmental protection, has been on the political agenda for well over twenty years. It has been the subject of much political, academic and commercial discussion.[17]

[15] Report of the World Summit (UN Doc. A/CONF.199/20 (2002)) Political Declaration para 12.
[16] *Ibid* at para 7.
[17] See, for instance, E Westfield, 'Globalisation, Governance and Multinational Enterprise Responsibility: Corporate Codes of Conduct in the 21st Century' 42 *Virginia Journal of International Law* (2002) 1075–1108, which emphasises, in particular, labour standards.

As the number and influence of MNEs continues to grow, their importance in terms of *on the ground* impact is significant. For States to be able to promote social justice, being able to affect MNE behaviour — or hold MNEs to account when they undermine or damage community interests — is a fundamental part of the role of the State as regulator. However, as Fowler notes, MNEs 'operate in a vacuum between ineffective national laws and non-existent or unenforceable international laws'.[18] There have been numerous attempts both within the United Nations and elsewhere to fill this vacuum with 'soft' principles, such as codes of conduct, guidelines and recommendations. The success of such principles is, of course, difficult to gauge, though critics of such principles would argue that even if they appear to be successful they are no replacement for legally binding rules.

The most comprehensive set of principles promulgated by *States* is the OECD Guidelines for Multinational Enterprises, first adopted in 1976, amended in 1991 to take into account environmental considerations, and further updated in 2000.[19] Attempts by the UN to adopt a universal Code of Conduct for Transnational Corporations on similar lines have been less successful,[20] though the International Labour Organisation has had a Declaration of Principles concerning Multinational Enterprises and Social Policy since 1977.[21] Other compendia of guiding principles devised largely through non-State collaboration include the 1991 International Chamber of Commerce's Business Charter for Sustainable Development[22] and the 1999 Global Reporting Initiative (coordinated by the UN Environment Programme).[23] Another development has been the launch of the UN Global Compact Initiative by the UN Secretary-General Kofi Annan in 1999, which is not a code of conduct *per se*, but rather a list of nine principles (taken from areas of international human rights, labour and environmental law) which the Secretary General believes businesses should integrate into their commercial activities.[24] More recently, the Sub-Commission on the Promotion and Protection of Human Rights has drawn up — for further consideration — 'draft norms of the responsibilities of transnational corporations and other business enterprises with regard to human rights'.[25]

The issue raised at Johannesburg was the extent to which there was a need to supplement these various *ad hoc* — and voluntary — approaches

[18] R Fowler, 'International Environmental Standards for Transnational Corporations' 25 *Environmental Law* (1995) 3.
[19] See <http://www.oecd.org>. (Accessed on 23 August 2004).
[20] See B Frey, 'The Legal and Ethical Responsibilities of Transnational Corporations in the Protection of International Human Rights' 6 *Minnesota Journal of Global Trade* (1977) 153–188.
[21] See <http://www.ilo.org>. (Accessed on 23 August 2004).
[22] See <http://www.iccwbo.org/index.asp>. (Accessed on 23 August 2004).
[23] See <http://www.globalreporting.org/>. (Accessed on 23 August 2004).
[24] See <http://www.unglobalcompact.org/Portal/>. (Accessed on 23 August 2004).
[25] E/CN.4/Sub.2/2003/12/Rev.1 (30 May 2003).

with a legally binding international framework that would regulate MNEs internationally. The technical complexity and politically controversial nature of such a development meant that even a passing reference to such a possibility within the WSSD documents was impossible to achieve. The brevity of the final wording underlines this point. As paragraph 49 of the Plan of Implementation notes,

> Actively promote corporate responsibility and accountability, based on the Rio Principles, including through the full development and effective implementation of intergovernmental agreements and measures, international initiatives and public-private partnerships, and appropriate national regulations, and support continuous improvement in corporate practices in all countries.[26]

The wording is very clear that the possibility of negotiating a legally binding set of rules on corporate responsibility is not on the political agenda. This view is supported by an interpretative statement by the summit's contact group on globalisation noting that the issue of corporate responsibility was to be addressed within existing measures.[27] Moreover, in contrast to draft versions of the Plan of Implementation, there is not even explicit reference in the final version to the belief that corporate responsibility should be 'based on international agreements on human rights, environment and labour standards'.

To relate corporate responsibility so closely to sustainable development, which is the focus of the 1992 Rio Declaration, must be seen as a significant development in adopting a more integrated approach to corporate responsibility in terms of its social, environmental and developmental aspects. However, many of the Rio principles are expectant in tone, ambiguous in content and, importantly, not yet reflective of international legal norms. A reference in the Plan of Implementation to the Rio principles is therefore not as significant or as substantial as more explicit references to binding international treaties which would, in any event, provide a sounder basis for the elaboration of a more detailed framework of *legal*

[26] See also para 140(f), Plan of Implementation, above n 15: 'The international community should:...[p]romote corporate responsibility and accountability and the exchange of best practices in the context of sustainable development, including, as appropriate, through multi-stakeholder dialogue, such as through the Commission on Sustainable Development, and other initiatives'.

[27] See statement made by the United States, above n 15 at 145: 'During the conference, the Chairman of the Main Committee stated that it was "the collective understanding" of the contact group on means of implementation that paragraph 49 of the Plan of Implementation, regarding corporate responsibility and accountability, refers to existing intergovernmental agreements and international initiatives, and that this understanding should be reflected in the final report of the conference. The United States associates itself with this statement and notes that this understanding is of critical importance to the proper understanding and implementation of paragraph 49'.

oversight and regulation. Reliance on the Rio Declaration alone — a text focusing upon environment and development — also has the effect of marginalising human rights and labour standards.

The continued exclusion of MNEs from the remit of international regulation, which is confirmed by the negative wording of the Johannesburg Plan of Implementation on this point, is in sharp contrast to the rhetoric of much of the rest of the document as regards the promotion of social welfare-orientated goals. As the Plan comments elsewhere, States 'commit [them]selves to undertake concrete actions and measures at all levels' 'to further build on the achievements made since' the Rio Summit in 1992.[28] Taking into account the impact that the activities of MNEs can have on the sustainable development and social progress of, particularly developing, countries, it seems somewhat curious that the issue of corporate responsibility is dealt with so summarily within the text. For many, however, this merely reaffirms the divergence that now exists between the rhetoric that is an inherent part of how the *public* international community communicates and the reality of shifting patterns of power and influence.

MAINTAINING IDEALISM WITHIN INTERNATIONAL LAW

The conclusions that can be drawn from this short analysis of the changing global situation remain somewhat imprecise and uncertain. It is clear that momentous changes are happening in the way international society functions. The inter-State system as the sole and exclusive global system is no longer accurate. However, as we move away from a world simplistically characterised by inter-State relations, we are left with a situation where there is a need to maintain a balance between continuity and change, between the — former — almost exclusive intergovernmental approach to international affairs and the — present — far more complex nexus of international interactions. It is into this paradigmatic shift that the future direction of international law as a manifestation of public authority is to be considered. Of course, this is not to suggest naively that international law can provide the solutions to the world's ills. As noted above, international law is merely an elaboration of political will, and consequently, law may be as much an impediment to resolving global concerns as it is a solution. However, it is also quite clear that, where necessary, international regulation can operate as an effective check on the excesses of globalisation.

What then is one to make of the *desiderata* promised by global conferences, such as the World Summit on Sustainable Development? It is easy

[28] Plan of Implementation, above n 15, para 2.

to be cynical and consider them as nothing more than confused, vacuous and inherently idealistic statements of (non-)intent, constructed through political dialogue and compromise. The fact that there is not even the veneer of legality with these texts supports this negative assessment. However, to endorse this approach is to adopt the argument that international law is exclusively interested in outcomes. What does the final text of the treaty say? What did the International Court decide? How was the trade dispute finally settled? These are often interesting — and for the States involved, important — questions. However, the purpose of international law in establishing a normative framework is not simply to produce end-results.[29]

Law has as much to do with the debate generated, as it has to do with the result achieved. How did the international community get to this position? Which States had to give up what issues so as to accept the final compromise?[30] The existence, or lack, of effective legal rules must therefore be considered in context. It would be unfortunate to consider such issues solely in terms of 'success' or 'failure'. To do so would be a de facto return to an Austinian or Hartian perspective which views international law as the poor relation of — particularly Northern — municipal law. International law is, however, a formative process of action and reaction; attempts to take a snapshot of '*this is what the law is at this moment in time*' are therefore misguided. Legal knowledge and political choices are always in a state of flux. To consider international law simply as a contractual means of delimiting the legal rights and duties of States would be an unwelcome return to formalism.

Building on the previous point, international lawyers cannot escape from the natural law origins that continue to permeate the fundamental precepts of the international legal system. International lawyers like to think of themselves as having a more important role than simply interpreting and applying international law. To many, international law has a quality over-and-above that of the rules that comprise it. As regards sustainability and globalisation, one only needs to highlight the six guiding principles elaborated within the 1999 UNDP Report, *Globalisation with a Human Face* — *viz.*, ethics, equity, inclusion, human security, sustainability and development — to recognise the relevance of general principles to the politics and law of the international community.[31] Of course, it must be conceded that such principles may not be exterior to the will of States at all but, in fact, simply reflective of the longer-term strategy of the

[29] Cf M Koskenniemi, 'What is International Law for?' in M Evans (ed), *International Law* (Oxford, Oxford University Press, 2003), 111: 'There is a Messianic structure to international law, the announcement of something that remains eternally postponed'.
[30] Or alternatively, which States refused to accept a compromise, and why?
[31] Above n 11.

international community. Either way, such principles do seem to have a normative effect, however intangible that currently may be.

Such principles highlight the deep recognition felt by many in the international community that it is under a collective politico-moral obligation to achieve certain fundamental goals. 'Fundamental' in the sense that international law is not just the product of State consent, but that post-Second World War, post-UN Charter, post-Universal Declaration of Human Rights, international law has been imbued with certain underlying themes. This is not intended to be construed as an endorsement of a 'universal order of human dignity' of the New Haven approach to international law,[32] but simply to highlight the apparent moral underpinnings of much of what goes on within international forums. Texts such as the General Assembly's 2000 Millennium Declaration may be long on rhetoric and short on specifics, but its interweaving of moral precepts with political reality affirms the argument that the wider community believes in the existence of certain goals that States are under a collective obligation to strive to achieve. As it states,

> [w]e recognise that, in addition to our separate responsibilities to our individual societies, we have a collective responsibility to uphold the principles of human dignity, equality and equity at the global level. As leaders we have a duty therefore to all the world's people, especially the most vulnerable and, in particular, the children of the world, to whom the future belongs.[33]

Of course, such goals are idealistic, unsupported by State practice and may be of little practical consequence; yet, however superficial they may appear to be, their importance lies in the fact that they exist at all. Their influence — if only partial — over the international discourse is a pointer to the increasing socialisation of the international community as a society of States.

There will always be a divergence between the long-term idealism of international society and the shorter-term expectations of those possessing political power, as indicated by the debate over corporate responsibility at WSSD. However, as this paper has sought to highlight, rhetoric is an inherent part of much of what the *public* international community does, and it is important to recognise that the international community, through its normative manifestations, has a right — maybe even is under a corporate duty — to be idealistic, to set bold objectives, to promote wider societal concerns. However, idealism is only effective when

[32] See, as a classical exposition of the New Haven approach, M S McDougal and H D Lasswell, 'The Identification and Appraisal of Diverse Systems of Public Order' 53 *American Journal of International Law* (1959) 11.
[33] Millennium Declaration, above n 1, para 2.

complemented by a sense of political, social and commercial reality. Now that the actions of States are but one part of a much more complicated international situation, and the international community's inherent right to govern is increasingly questioned, it is more important than ever that the rule of law be maintained.

To continue to be relevant, therefore, the international community must endeavour to broaden the nature and scope of international law to reflect the changing nature of international society. In particular, it must be prepared to adopt structural and normative change, so as to maintain the legitimacy and role of the global order. Only then can the divide between rhetoric and reality begin to be tackled. Otherwise, the role of the international community of States — particularly when confronting the concerns and interests of its weakest members — will continue to drift somewhere between hypothetical idealism and ineffective politicking.

9

The International Criminal Court: Friend or Foe of International Criminal Justice?

CHRIS GALLAVIN*

THIS CHAPTER ADVANCES two principal contentions: first, that the establishment of the International Criminal Court (ICC) marks a significant ideological shift from international diplomacy to victim-centred enforcement of human rights; and, secondly, that this shift fails to achieve an acceptable equilibrium between the principled protection of human rights and the practical realities of international relations.

The chapter is in two parts. In Part I, the form of justice encapsulated within the provisions of the Rome Statute founding the ICC is analysed. Guided by victim orientated conceptions of universality, accountability, deterrence and punishment, it is suggested that the trajectory of ICC justice is strongly orientated towards investigation and prosecution. In Part II, consideration is given to the limited scope for prosecutorial discretion (as provided for by Article 53 of the statute). It is argued that, whilst the statute rightly seeks to exclude the politicisation of prosecutorial discretion, it lacks the flexibility that is essential if discretion is to be operated in a politically sensitive way.

If this chapter is correct in judging that the statute over-compensates against the ideology of international diplomacy, then there is a danger that the ICC not only will fail to maintain contact with reality but will also fail to operationalise the broader form of justice that is required if there is to be a workable respect for human rights.

JUSTICE: ICC STYLE

Justice is not inherently confined to a single and universal interpretation. Therefore, although justice forms the bedrock upon which the structure of

* I would like to thank Professor Roger Brownsword for looking at a draft of this chapter and his invaluable suggestions.

the ICC is built, it is important to examine the particular form of justice which is to be applied by the court. In principle the term is capable of two differing interpretations. Firstly, justice may be interpreted narrowly, in line with the immediate and subjective needs of victims. The application of this version will see an increased emphasis on securing accountability and satisfying a victim's desire for retribution. Secondly and more broadly, justice may be interpreted in light of the objective, long-term needs of the victims. This interpretation allows for a more flexible approach where issues of reconciliation and education predominate. While an equilibrium between these interpretations is necessary, the Rome Statute's reliance on the notions of universality, accountability (including the elimination of impunity), and deterrence and punishment, indicates that justice, ICC style, is firmly in the court of the narrow and inflexible.

Universality

The notion of universality acts as a narrowing influence within ICC justice. It operates to restrict the jurisdictional ambit of the court by ensuring that only the most extreme examples of criminal conduct are covered by the statute. Within the negotiation of the statute[1] it was implicit that the principle of universality demands concurrence at two levels, one *philosophical* the other *procedural*. At a *philosophical* level, the requirement is that it is agreed that in principle the general description of the offence is that of a universal crime; at a *procedural* level, the requirement is that it is agreed that the particular conduct is covered by the general description and thus constitutes a universal crime. Whilst meeting the requirement of universality at the philosophical level is necessary, it is not sufficient to give the court jurisdiction.

The offence of aggression illustrates these principles and their application. The offence of aggression is provided for pursuant to Article 5(1)(d). However, this provision is dormant, as no agreed definition could be arrived at by the negotiating parties.[2] Therefore, while *philosophical* universality as to the criminality of the offence was achieved, no *procedural* universality as to its specific interpretation could be reached. Likewise, the lack of concurrence between these elements resulted in the elimination of many 'treaty crimes' from the final form of the statute.[3] Consequently, the

[1] The United Nations Diplomatic Conference of Plenipotentiaries on the Establishment of an International Criminal Court was held over June and July of 1998 and resulted in establishment of the Rome Statute. The Statute was ultimately ratified by more than 60 States and therefore resulted in the establishment of the ICC on 1 July 2002 pursuant to Article 126.

[2] Pursuant to Article 5(2), Aggression is to come within the ambit of the court's jurisdiction once a definition of the crime has in fact been adopted under Articles 121 and 123 (the Rome Statute's review and amendment articles).

[3] For an initial draft of the court's statute compiled by the International Law Commission within which treaty crimes were included see 1994 ILC Draft Article 20(e). These 'treaty

requirement for strict *procedural* universality has resulted in a limited, tightly defined and inflexible jurisdiction whose elements and application are comparable to an exhaustive and binding list within the statute.

Accountability

Accountability through the elimination of impunity became a central theme leading up to the Rome Conference of 1998.[4] United Nations Secretary-General Kofi Annan acknowledged this in his speech at the inaugural meeting of the Rome Conference where he stated that in relation to the atrocities witnessed in Rwanda,[5]

> ... the United Nations and its Member States must summon the will to prevent such a catastrophe from being repeated anywhere in the world. And as part of that effort, we must show clearly that such crimes will not be left unpunished.

He continued by stating that,

> People all over the world want to know that humanity can strike back — that wherever and whenever genocide, war crimes or other such violations are committed, there is a court before which the criminal can be held to account; a court that puts an end to a global culture of impunity.

Additionally, the elimination of impunity is expressly referred to pursuant to paragraphs four and five of the preamble. Paragraph four states:

> That the most serious crimes of concern to the international community as a whole must not go unpunished and that their effective prosecution must be ensured by taking measures at the national level and by enhancing international co-operation.

crimes' included grave breaches of the Geneva Conventions, the Hague Convention for the Suppression of Unlawful Seizure of Aircraft of 16 December 1970, the Montreal Convention for the Suppression of Unlawful Acts against the Safety of Civil Aviation of 23 September 1971, the International Convention on the Suppression and Punishment of the Crime of Apartheid of 30 November 1973, the Convention on the Prevention and Punishment of Crimes against Internationally Protected Persons, including Diplomatic Agents of 14 December 1973, the International Convention against the Taking of Hostages of 17 December 1979, the Convention against Torture and Other Cruel, Inhuman or Degrading Treatment or Punishment of 10 December 1984, the Convention for the Suppression of Unlawful Acts against the Safety of Maritime Navigation of 10 March 1988, the Protocol for the Suppression of Unlawful Acts against the Safety of Fixed Platforms Located on the Continental Shelf of 10 March 1988, and finally the United Nations Convention against the Illicit Traffic in Narcotic Drugs and Psychotropic Substances of 20 December 1988. Refer Annex of the 1994 ILC Draft Statute.

[4] Above n 1.

[5] Press Release L/ROM/6.r1 15 June 1998 <http://www.un.org/icc/pressrel/1rom6r1.htm>, (31 March 2003). Such comments were echoed by the vast majority of countries

In paragraph five the State Parties proclaim that they are,

> Determined to put an end to impunity for the perpetrators of these crimes and thus to contribute to the prevention of such crimes.

In addition to these express provisions the statute implicitly refers to notions of accountability. The second paragraph reveals that the State Parties are,

> Mindful that during this century millions of children, women and men have been victims of unimaginable atrocities that deeply shock the conscience of humanity.

Clearly, the elimination of impunity is implicit in the wording of this provision.

The next paragraph of the preamble acknowledges not only the moral desirability of accountability, but the pragmatic necessity for it in order to maintain global stability. The paragraph states that State Parties recognise

> ... that such grave crimes threaten the peace, security and well-being of the world.

In addition to the preamble emphasising the moral obligation and pragmatic necessity for holding perpetrators of such crimes accountable, it continues in the sixth paragraph to state that,

> it is the duty of every State to exercise its criminal jurisdiction over those responsible for international crimes.

Finally, adding to the moral, pragmatic and legal duties of states, the eleventh paragraph of the preamble implores the reader to recognise the importance of ensuring accountability in order to

> ... guarantee lasting respect for and the enforcement of international justice.

represented at the June/July Conference of 1998. For further reading refer to the opening statements by Ms Hilde F Johnson, Minister for International Development and Human Rights, Norway, 15 June 1998, <http://www.un.org/icc/speeches/615nor.htm> (31 March 2003), The Honourable Ramesh Lawrence Maharaj, Attorney General of the Republic of Trinidad and Tobago, 15 June 1998, <http://www.un.org/icc/speeches/615tri.htm> (31 March 2003), the statement on behalf of the European Union delivered by Tony Lloyd MP, Minister of State, UK Foreign and Commonwealth Office, 15 June 1998, <http://www.un.org/icc/speeches/615uk.htm> (31 March 2003), and the statement by Mr. Wang Guangya, Head of the Chinese Delegation, 16 June 1998, <http://www.un.org/icc/speeches/616cpr.htm> (31 March 2003). Also refer to the hedged statement of the United States representative of 17 June 1998 <http://www.un.org/icc/speeches/617usa.htm> (31 March 2003), and the opening statement of the representative of Israel, 17 June 1998 <http://www.un.org/icc/speeches/617isr.htm> (31 March 2003). See, too, the closing statement of Judge Eli Nathan, speaking in relation to Israel's objection to the statute, who said that the court 'Mr. President, *inter alia,* [was] our idea'. He continued by questioning whether the statute and the court would be used and abused 'as one more political tool in the Middle East conflict?', 17 July 1998 <http://www.un.org/icc/speeches/717isr.htm> (31 March 2003).

Such wording implies an element of procedural pre-existence. This however, has clearly not been the case. While notions of philosophical universality have existed for perhaps an indeterminable period, these have only manifested themselves by way of a 'duty' within the context of the establishment of the ICC.[6]

As with the paragraphs of the preamble, the notion of accountability is reflected within many provisions of the statute itself. Perhaps the most significant relative to the legal duty of states to ensure accountability, are the provisions relating to complementarity. The doctrine of complementarity was formulated to ensure that primacy was given to domestic justice systems.[7] Unlike the operation of the ICTY and ICTR[8] the ICC must defer to a state investigation or prosecution. Only in the situation of a state's unwillingness or inability to investigate or prosecute an accused will the ICC's jurisdiction become operative.[9] The effect of this relationship is, for the first time, to place an obligation upon State Parties (at least the ratifying states) to ensure domestic legislative conformity with the Rome Statute. Provisions relating to the crimes within the Rome Statute must likewise exist within the domestic jurisprudence of these states. Conceivably non-complying states could be deemed to be 'unable' or perhaps 'unwilling' to prosecute, therefore invoking the jurisdiction of the ICC if the inability of a state to investigate or prosecute was based upon the lack of sufficient jurisdiction.[10]

Accountability is also manifest within the offences over which the court has jurisdiction. Beginning with the second paragraph of the preamble the reader is made aware of the jurisdictional limitations that are contained within the statute. By limiting the offences within the jurisdiction of the court, this paragraph impinges upon a universal application of

[6] So far as there can exist a legal duty under international law. This observation is made notwithstanding the possible condemnation that would ensue if a State were to fail to investigate crimes which may themselves (or correspondingly the duty itself) have matured into norms of customary international law.

[7] So as to preserve state sovereignty.

[8] The International Criminal Tribunal for the former Yugoslavia (ICTY) and the International Criminal Tribunal for Rwanda (ICTR). The jurisdiction of both these Tribunals takes precedence over that of domestic systems which must, if asked, defer to the jurisdiction of the Tribunals. Refer, Article 9(1) and (2) of the Statute of the International Tribunal for the Prosecution of Persons Responsible for Serious Violations of International Humanitarian Law Committed in the Territory of the Former Yugoslavia Since 1991, and Article 8(2) of the Statute of the International Criminal Tribunal for the Prosecution of Persons Responsible for Genocide and other Serious Violations of International Humanitarian Law Committed in the Territory of Rwanda and Rwandan Citizens Responsible for Genocide and Other Such Violations Committed in the Territory of Neighbouring States, between 1 January 1994 and 31 December 1994.

[9] Article 17(1)(a).

[10] Additionally, issues of retrospectivity would arise if such a state were to enact compliant legislation in an attempt to reclaim jurisdiction over such a case.

accountability, which would otherwise potentially require investigations and prosecutions in all cases of international crime.[11]

Finally, the articulation of accountability within the eleventh paragraph of the preamble is transmuted into the provisions of the statute which deal with the integrity of the court. These predominantly structural provisions provide for such things as the independence of the judiciary and the Prosecutor,[12] their appointment process,[13] and the structure of the judicial chambers.[14] The operational manifestation of accountability is apparent in the pre-investigative and prosecution procedures.[15]

Deterrence and Punishment

Like accountability, the statute's strong adherence to the notions of deterrence and punishment act to narrow the application of justice and consequently the court's discretion. Paragraph four of the preamble[16] in expressly referring to punishment and 'effective prosecution' gives significant support to the contention that the notions of deterrence and punishment are to be strictly applied. In addition to paragraphs ten[17] and eleven this provision emphasises the complementary relationship that is to exist between the court and domestic legislatures. However, it is clear from this paragraph that, notwithstanding the limit of severity that it reiterates, all cases which meet this criterion are to be investigated. This acknowledgement by the state parties as to their intention in establishing the ICC acts to limit the circumstances which the Prosecutor may legitimately consider when deciding whether to instigate an investigation.

Likewise, paragraph five of the preamble[18] clearly exhibits the importance the framers of the statute have placed upon the elements of deterrence and punishment. The paragraph acts as a further restriction upon the exercise of the Prosecutor's investigative and prosecutorial discretion. This discretion which is encapsulated under Article 53 'Initiation of investigation'[19] allows the Prosecutor to consider a number of factors in reaching a decision as to whether there ought to be an investigation or

[11] Also refer to Articles 5, 6, 7, 8, and 9 which detail the scope of the offences over which the court has jurisdiction. Also refer to the Report of the Preparatory Commission for the International Criminal Court 'Elements of Crimes'. <http://www.un.org/law/icc/>, (31 March 2003).

[12] Articles 40(1) and 42(1) respectively.

[13] Articles 36 and 42 respectively.

[14] Article 39.

[15] Articles 53, 54 and 56.

[16] Referred to under Accountability above.

[17] The paragraph states, '*Emphasizing* that the International Criminal Court established under this Statute shall be complementary to national criminal jurisdictions…' (Emphasis original).

[18] Referred to under Accountability above.

[19] Refer to 'Article 53 and the "Interests of Justice" provision' below.

prosecution.[20] Articles 53(1)(c) and 53(2)(c), which are similar provisions, dealing with investigations and prosecutions, encapsulate the widest discretion.[21] These provisions allow the Prosecutor to consider whether there are 'substantial reasons' in the 'interests of justice' not to instigate an investigation or prosecution. Notwithstanding this freedom, paragraph five of the preamble, strengthened by paragraph four, acts as a significant qualification over the words 'substantial reasons'. In such circumstances and in the absence of a Prosecutor's ability to consider issues of a purely political nature,[22] such factors appear limited to case specific issues only.

In the present context, we shall recall paragraph eleven of the preamble under which Member States resolve to ensure '... respect for and the enforcement of international justice'. As with paragraphs four and five, this paragraph while expressed via a number of provisions and Parts of the Rome Statute does act as a further limitation upon the Prosecutor's discretion under Article 53.

Turning to structural provisions, most obviously, we have the statute's allowance for penalties. Additionally, as with their relation to accountability, the statute's complementarity provisions aim to deter and punish. Acting as a type of 'big brother' over the domestic jurisdictions of State Parties, the court can police and if need be, instigate investigations and prosecutions in the place of any Member State which has not lived up to its primary responsibility. This will act as a particularly effective deterrent in that perpetrators will no longer be able to hide behind a state's inability, or unwillingness to prosecute. The fact that many offences within the limited jurisdiction of the ICC will and do occur in the situation of state collapse means that an offender's ability to go unpunished is severely limited.

To conclude, it is clear from both the philosophy and corresponding provisions of the Rome Statute that ICC justice is limited to the elements of philosophical and procedural universality, accountability and deterrence and punishment. However, it will be contended that within an international sphere, justice must incorporate significant elements of wider reconciliation. Consequently, the justice of the ICC's philosophy is grossly insufficient. Due to this limited philosophy and narrow perception of justice, the hands of the Prosecutor and the court are ultimately tied in what ought to be a wide discretion as to whether to instigate investigations and prosecutions. Dangerously, this may lead to prosecutions that have a destabilising effect within a region affected by the particular atrocity. This in turn may provide the quintessential opposite of

[20] Article 53(1)(a), (b), (c) and Article 53(2)(a), (b), (c).
[21] Refer to 'Article 53 and the "Interests of Justice" provision' below.
[22] An issue that will be elaborated on in Part 2 below.

justice, evoking retaliations, further or increased civil unrest, and an overall heightening of tensions. A form of justice must be incorporated which adheres to the fundamental tenets of the term as presently applied by the court, yet also reflects the unique nature of international justice and the stability of states within the global political environment by providing the Prosecutor with adequate flexibility. In order to give effective meaning to the concept of humanitarian protection and to allow for increased certainty in the law it is important to retain the fundamental elements of the current structure.[23] This is important in order not to allow reconciliation to become *the predominant* consideration within justice which would potentially lead to a reiteration of the arbitrary nature of the previous *ad hoc* system of trials under the guise of a permanent court. Therefore, what is required is flexibility within clearly defined parameters.

ARTICLE 53 AND THE 'INTERESTS OF JUSTICE' PROVISION

I have contended that the Rome Statute lacks flexibility in its philosophy and underlying methodology, its provisions focusing too much upon the immediate needs of victims. However, to describe the statute as 'too victim orientated yet not reconciliatory' may initially appear to be a contradiction in terms. Nevertheless, the Rome Statute caters overly for accountability and deterrence and only in a very limited way for victims' long term or objective requirements. This is once again manifest through the limited discretion availed to the court under Article 53 in deciding whether to instigate an investigation or prosecution.

Fundamentally, Article 53 is divided into two sections.[24] The first paragraph deals with the instigation of investigations, with the second tackling the instigation of prosecutions. The article as a whole acts as a guide to the Office of the Prosecutor (OTP) in exercising his or her duties under the statute. The conditions under which an investigation or prosecution may be instigated under paragraphs (1) and (2) ostensibly mirror one another.

Article 53(1)(c) states:

> Taking into account the gravity of the crime and the interests of victims, there are nonetheless substantial reasons to believe that an investigation would not serve the interests of Justice.

[23] Elements that ensure a move away from arbitrariness, frivolous point scoring political manoeuvring, and a relinquishing of responsibilities by states.

[24] I refer here to the substantive content of paragraphs (1) and (2), which provide the principal instruction for the OTP on the issue of instigating investigations and prosecutions. Paragraphs (3) and (4) of Article 53 merely deal with the review of decisions made pursuant to paras (1) and (2).

Article 53(2)(c) states:

> A prosecution is not in the interests of justice, taking into account all the circumstances, including the gravity of the crime, the interests of victims and the age or infirmity of the alleged perpetrator, and his or her role in the alleged crime.

For three interrelated reasons, it can be seen that these provisions do not allow for the consideration of the political repercussions of instigating an investigation or prosecution. Firstly, the philosophy of the court is opposed to the influence of politics upon the functioning of the court. Secondly, the structure of the court and its statute presents us with the clear expression of political independence. Thirdly, domestic systems upon which the court has been modelled support the separation of prosecution and politics. However, I contend that each of these reasons, which are likely to be argued to rebut any proposed reform of the current structure, is either ill-founded or inappropriately applied. I will begin with the philosophy of the court.

Indicators as to the philosophical underpinnings of the court are numerous. Firstly, there is the historical setting within which the court became a reality. The twentieth century is littered with non-avenged acts and campaigns of human rights injustices. From the failed Leipzig Trials of post-World War I to the establishment of a comprehensive but largely non-enforced international human rights infrastructure, inaction characterised the century. Even the Nuremberg, Tokyo, Yugoslav, and Rwandan Trials have been subject to numerous criticisms, from victor's justice[25] to political gesturing.[26] Political tools, such as a permanent member's right of veto within the Security Council, have resulted in a century of politically inspired inaction. It is before this backdrop therefore that the ICC has been established. Consequently, the structural safeguards within the Rome Statute which are to operate in isolating the court from issues of international diplomacy are clearly expressive of a more powerful underlying abhorrence of international political expediency.

More immediate indicators of the court's philosophy, other than its historical setting, include provisions such as paragraph five of the preamble

[25] See for example the comments of M Cherif Bassiouni who stated that while the, 'Nuremberg and Tokyo Charters were effective tools for individual enforcement of international criminal law. Their credibility, however, was undermined by the selective enforcement of their provisions and by not applying the same standards to those Allied personnel that committed some of the same atrocities.'

M Cherif Bassiouni, *Crimes Against Humanity in International Criminal Law* (Dordrecht, Martinus Nijhoff Publishers, 1992) p 206.

[26] Geoffrey Robertson speaking in relation to the establishment of the Yugoslav tribunal stated that the Security Council's actions were calculated to 'pretend to an anxious and appalled world that something was being done'. G Robertson QC, *Crimes Against Humanity; The Struggle for Global Justice* (London, Penguin, 2000), p 286.

which act as vivid illustrations of this philosophy.[27] Additionally, the associated media propaganda also acts to raise public awareness and expectations as to the role, abilities and effectiveness of the ICC. Likewise, criticisms of the court have provided an opportunity for commentators to express their 'reassurance' that the court does in fact herald a new age in international criminal prosecution. A vivid example exists within the troubling criticisms of the court from the United States. One of the express concerns of the United States is that the court will be used as a political tool by others to investigate and prosecute soldiers serving in the United States' Forces.[28] Notwithstanding the jurisdictional limitations that stand in the way of such a thing occurring,[29] such concerns have acted to raise awareness as to the court's intended political neutrality. It would appear that, short of a complete turnabout of the court's philosophical justification, coupled with the corruption of the entire ICC structural regime, politically motivated investigations and prosecutions will be an impossibility. However, any reiteration of the court's intended independent operation, directed at the freeing up of the OTP's discretion as advocated by this chapter, would be a misdirection.

Turning to the second possible criticism to the adoption of a more inclusive form of justice, the structure of the Rome Statute reinforces the philosophy of the court as expressed in the history of its establishment. Significant detail is included in the statute as to the independent operation of the judiciary and the OTP. These safeguards are clearly intended to insulate the court from the influence of international politics. Initial suggestions as to overt Security Council control over the court pursuant to the 1994 Draft Statute were rejected in favour of the less dominating influence of Article 16. Furthermore, effort has been made to insulate issues relating to financing and to amalgamate differing facets of competing international legal regimes.[30] However, as with the issue of the court's philosophy, the structural protections in place within the Rome Statute cannot be used in the debate against the liberalising of OTP discretion.

[27] Paragraph five of the preamble begins, '*Determined* to put an end to impunity…' Refer to 'Deterrence and Punishment' above for discussion. (Emphasis original).
[28] Statement of the United States representative of 17 June 1998 to the meeting of the United Nations Diplomatic Conference of Plenipotentiaries on the Establishment of an International Criminal Court <http://www.un.org/icc/speeches/617usa.htm.> (31 March 2003).
[29] The most significant of which are the complementarity provisions of the Rome Statute which give primacy to nation states in the instigation of investigations and possible prosecutions. Furthermore the pre-investigative procedures of the Prosecutor act to further cull politically motivated investigations which may have been prompted by a state referral pursuant to Articles 13(a) and 14. Additionally, the Pre-Trial Chamber procedure of Article 15, grafted from civil law jurisdictions, further operates to limit the possibility of such investigations occurring.
[30] ie the common law and civil or administrative systems as exhibited by the pre-trial procedures under Article 15 and 53(3)(b).

What is advocated here is not the restructuring of the court along partisan lines, but charging the court with the freedom that comes with the ability to consider its actions and the corresponding implications for justice.

Thirdly, domestic models, such as the prosecutorial system of England and Wales in which a strong relationship exists between 'interests of justice' and the 'public interest',[31] clearly exclude considerations of a political nature when deciding what constitutes the 'public interest'.[32]

Therefore, in the light of these considerations it is clear that the Prosecutor's discretion to find 'substantial reasons' pursuant to Article 53(1) and (2)(c) is limited to non-political occurrences. This observation is further reinforced by the fact that any finding of 'substantial reasons' in justification of not pursuing an investigation or prosecution by the Prosecutor is to be detailed before the Pre-Trial Chamber.[33] This, once again borrowing from the inquisitorial style of Administrative systems, insures structural integrity and transparency, all of which speak against the possibility of issues of political diplomacy falling within the ambit of 'interests of justice'.

What then, in the alternative, is required? Well, a number of things. Firstly, a clear distinction must be made between the abhorrence of a politically controlled (and therefore non-independent) court and a politically aware prosecution organ. The former must be repealed while the latter embraced. The fundamental point of distinction between a politicised court and a politically aware court lies in the element of control. Under the former, control is in the hands of extrinsic actors who by political manipulation may bend the court into conformity with a particular political goal. Under the latter the control is still firmly within the court itself, being in the hands of both the Prosecutor and the Pre-Trial Chamber. However, notwithstanding this distinction the philosophy, historical background, purposes and aims of the court both express and implicit alike must still be allowed to operate in order to ensure that as little political interference as possible occurs within the court. The most probable interpretation of the current provisions of the statute combined with the history, philosophy and purposes of the court is exemplified by the address of the Secretary-General of the United Nations Kofi Annan to the

[31] Speaking in relation to the Crown Prosecution Code and Article 53 of the Rome Statute Turone has stated that, '[i]f we compare the system of the ICC to the one of England and Wales, the similarities are significant'. Turone did not continue to explore the issues involved in any depth and certainly did not comment on the appropriateness of such a domestic styled system for operation in an international setting: G Turone, 'Powers and Duties of the Prosecutor' in A Cassese et al (eds) *The Rome Statute of the International Criminal Court: A Commentary* Vol II (Oxford, Oxford University Press, 2002) 1137 at pp 1174, 1175.

[32] Code for Crown Prosecutors, <http://www.cps.gov.uk/Home/CodeForCrown Prosecutors/index.htm> (10 April 2003).

[33] Article 53(1)(c) (second paragraph), and (2)(c) (second paragraph).

inaugural meeting of the United Nations Diplomatic Conference of Plenipotentiaries on the Establishment of an International Criminal Court where he stated:[34]

> But the overriding interest must be that of the victims, and of the international community as a whole. I trust you will not flinch from creating a court strong and independent enough to carry out its task. It must be an instrument of justice, not expediency. It must be able to protect the weak against the strong.

This statement, which was expressly and implicitly endorsed by the majority of states at that historic conference, shows a naivety as to the ambit of justice. The interest of the 'international community as a whole' may mean that justice is most appropriately served in a particular case through the application of an expedient resolution. The investigation and prosecution of offenders may not, in all cases be an unqualified good. Therefore, the Prosecutor under the supervision of the Pre-Trial Chamber ought not to be blindfolded as to the possible options available in seeking justice for the immediate victims, the nation[s] involved and the global community at large. The court does 'not operate in a political vacuum. Experience teaches us that we must carefully distinguish between what looks good on paper and what works in the real world'.[35]

In allowing the express consideration of political submissions by the Prosecutor and the Pre-Trial Chamber the court, however, does become exposed to at least the possibility of politicisation. Therefore, a strengthening of the appointment process for both the OTP and the judiciary (currently conducted by way of election by the Assembly of States Parties see, Articles 36 and 42) is required to eliminate the opportunity of political appointments. Additionally, an ability to appraise, analyse and assess issues of a purely political nature in addition to traditional 'legal' skills would be required of any judicial and prosecutorial nominees.

It is clear that allowing for the consideration of the political ramifications arising from the court's actions in order to assist in an Article 53 analysis would signal a move away from the rule of law as applied within the major domestic systems of the world. However, international law is inherently political and therefore different from domestic systems. Furthermore, it is contended that by developing a political awareness, partisan politicisation of either the OTP or the court would not necessarily occur. Additionally, such considerations would not give rise to a return of complete impunity as witnessed under the military and *ad hoc* tribunals of the twentieth century. These considerations would become one of a number of factors to be

[34] <http://www.un.org/icc/perssrel/1rom6r1.htm.> (31 March 2003).
[35] Statement by the Honourable Bill Richardson, United States Ambassador at the United Nations, <http://www.un.org/icc/speeches/617usa.htm> (31 March 2003).

considered in assessing what was in the 'interests of justice' for the purpose of Article 53(1)(c) and (2)(c).

CONCLUSION

The establishment of a permanent international court may be heralded as a victory for academic human rights scholars. However, for the victims of internationally significant crime the same may not necessarily be said. In supplanting the interests of international diplomacy for the goals of an unadulterated form of pure human rights ideology, cause for greater injustice has potentially occurred. The task of the United Nations Diplomatic Conference of Plenipotentiaries on the Establishment of an International Criminal Court was to bring together the competing ideologies into a coherent and workable, bricks and mortar structure. For the most part this has been achieved. However, international law and international diplomacy are interwoven to such an extent that to adopt an ideologically pure and narrow form of justice, as is exhibited within the Rome Statute, is ill founded. I believe that a wider form of justice must be encapsulated within the Rome Statute and consequently the operation of the ICC itself. Such a form of justice would allow for the Prosecutor (and subsequently the Pre-Trial Chamber) to consider the political ramifications in coming to a decision on whether an investigation or prosecution ought to be instigated. However, in allowing this broadening of the governing conception of justice, care must be taken not to compromise the political independence of the court. justice must always be the focus, however without the ability to consider the full scope of justice and those influences that may impinge upon its fulfilment, the ICC will always be out of touch with reality.

Part II: Competing Views of Fundamental Values — Law as a Mediator of Rival Conceptions of Human Rights and Human Dignity

10

Taking Human Rights Seriously: United Kingdom and New Zealand Perspectives on Judicial Interpretation and Ideologies

BEV CLUCAS AND SCOTT DAVIDSON

INTRODUCTION

THE MAJOR THRUST of this chapter is to examine the implementation of human rights norms at the domestic level. The underlying assumption is that if human rights are to have meaning and content and for the substantive rights contained within rights instruments to be of any practical value to those whose rights are to be protected, they must be implemented effectively within the domestic system. The responsibility for implementation and enforcement lies with all three branches of government — legislature, executive and judiciary, but our primary focus will be on judicial implementation of human rights.[1]

This chapter examines one of the main obstacles to substantive respect for human rights: interpretation. In the first half of the chapter, we focus on interpretation and application of existing applicable substantive human rights provisions, using the example of two cases concerned with, among other matters, Article 2 of the ECHR. The second half of our chapter will be an examination of interpretive issues and judicial activity in the

[1] As a point of interest, see K Starmer, 'Two Years of the Human Rights Act' (2003) *European Human Rights Law Review* 14–23 for a snapshot of the principal cases that were heard in the UK in the two years following the coming into force of the Human Rights Act 1998. Between October 2000 and April 2002 the ECHR was considered in 431 cases, compared with 316 cases from July 1975 to July 1996 (*ibid* 15). At the time of writing there had been 9 declarations of incompatibility under s 4 Human Rights Act, some of which were overturned on appeal, some of which were being appealed, and two declarations that stand (*ibid* 18–19).

face of gaps within human rights legislation, with a focus on the New Zealand (NZ) judiciary.

INTERPRETATION: LANGUAGE

Substantive compliance with human rights in implementation is dependent on effective interpretation of the rights guaranteed, as interpretation is logically prior to enforcement.

The first interpretive hurdle to be surmounted is that of the language itself: words and phrases may have a number of everyday meanings, and possibly also technical meanings.[2] This is true despite the best efforts of drafters striving for clarity in their provisions. As Richard Tur colourfully puts it:

> Even the most carefully drafted rules fail to achieve perfect fit. A rule may include some cases which morally should be excluded and it may exclude cases which morally should be included. Rules are either too wide and hard or too narrow and soft, frequently both and never, like the porridge or the bed in the fairy tale, 'just right'.[3]

Sometimes, ambiguity of phrasing may be intentional in order to allow for alternative interpretations. It is frequently said that courts and legislators ought to strike a balance between a sufficiently clear meaning of a provision and a rigidly explicit wording that may exclude application of the provision to deserving cases. What result is reached in such cases will depend on judicial approaches and ideologies, of which more below. However, difficulties of interpretation would not seem to be confined to instances of obscure or deliberately supple draftmanship. The recent cases *In Re A (Children) (Conjoined Twins: Surgical Separation)*[4] and the *Pretty* cases, *R (on the application of Pretty) v DPP*[5] and *Pretty v United Kingdom*,[6] illustrate the flexibility that can be found in even the most straightforward of phrases.

These cases are particularly instructive as examples because they are both concerned with the interpretation of the same provision: the right to life guaranteed in Article 2 of the European Convention on Human Rights and Fundamental Freedoms (ECHR):

> 1. Everyone's right to life shall be protected by law. No one shall be deprived of his life intentionally save in the execution of a sentence of a

[2] See for example Lord Parker CJ's consideration of 'offer for sale' in *Fisher v Bell* [1961] 1 QB 394.
[3] R Tur, 'Legislative Technique and Human Rights: the Sad Case of Assisted Suicide' (2003) *Criminal Law Review* 3–12.
[4] [2001] Fam 147.
[5] [2001] UKHL 61.
[6] (2346/02) [2002] 35 EHRR 1.

court following his conviction of a crime for which this penalty is provided by law.

2. Deprivation of life shall not be regarded as inflicted in contravention of this Article when it results from the use of force which is no more than absolutely necessary:
   a) in defence of any person from unlawful violence;
   b) in order to effect a lawful arrest or prevent the escape of a person lawfully detained;
   c) in action lawfully taken for the purpose of quelling a riot or insurrection.

Re A (children) (conjoined twins)

The conjoined twins, known as Jodie and Mary for the duration of the legal proceedings, were joined at the lower abdomen. They each had their own brain, heart, lungs, other vital organs, and their own arms and legs, but Mary's heart and lungs were inadequate to support her body. Had she been born a singleton, she would have died shortly after birth. Her life was being sustained by her sister. It was estimated that, if they remained conjoined, the twins would survive for 3–6 months before Jodie's heart would be unable to support the twins. The medical team in whose care they were thought it would be possible to separate the twins, and save Jodie. Separation would involve, among other things, the severing of a common artery, which would result in Mary's death. The hospital (St Mary's, Manchester) made an application to the High Court under the inherent jurisdiction of the court and the Children Act 1989 for a declaration that, where the children could not give valid consent and where the parents withheld their consent, it should be lawful and in the children's best interests to perform an elective procedure upon Jodie and Mary. The Human Rights Act 1998 had not quite come into force at the time of *Re A*, but the Court of Appeal acknowledged that they could not ignore any additional impact of direct incorporation of the ECHR into domestic law. In any event, the separation operation at issue would take place after incorporation, and the hospital performing the operation would be subject to the Act. The question with which we are concerned is whether a decision permitting separation would be a breach of Mary's right to life under Article 2(1).

In the Court of Appeal, Robert Walker LJ decided that:

> The Convention is to be construed as an autonomous text, without regard to any special rules of English law, and the word "intentionally" in article 2(1) must be given its natural and ordinary meaning. In my judgment the word, construed in that way, applies only to cases where the purpose of the prohibited action is to cause death. It does not import any prohibition of the

> proposed operation other than those which are to be found in the common law of England. The coming into force of the Human Rights Act 1998 on 2 October 2000 does not therefore alter my view of the case. The incorporation of the Convention into domestic law is a very important event but in this case its effect is to confirm, and not to alter, pre-existing law.[7]

His conclusion was that the proposed operation did not breach Article 2(1).

Brooke LJ[8] considered the domestic and Convention rights to be identical. He solved the matter by distinguishing from the present case *R v Woollin*,[9] the most recent authority to preclude the defence of necessity of circumstances to murder. He treated 'intentionally' in Article 2(1) as not necessarily having any effect on the concept of intention in the domestic law.

Ward LJ, in the leading judgment of the case, offered two possible interpretations of Article 2(1). The first is that the Convention requires the state to have adequate laws against murder. As applied to the hospital, he opined that the hospital's application to the court satisfied the requirement that there should be legal safeguards to protect patients' lives.[10] The second, literal interpretation, that life should be protected and preserved by law, caused more problems because of the 'impossibility of performance' — whatever decision was reached would offend against the right of one of the twins. In Ward LJ's words, 'I cannot believe that the court in Strasbourg would reach any other conclusion for solving the dilemma than we have done'.[11]

The Court of Appeal therefore concluded unanimously, for various reasons, that the separation that was to cause the death of Mary did not engage her Article 2 right to life.[12]

Diane Pretty

Mrs Pretty, at the age of 43, was in the advanced stages of Motor Neurone Disease. She remained mentally alert, but was paralysed from the neck down, and feared her increasing incapacity and death due to respiratory failure. She would have liked to commit suicide, but was unable to do so

[7] [2001] Fam 147, at 256–7.

[8] *Ibid* at 238.

[9] [1999] 1 AC 82.

[10] Even though he had admitted that no wrong would have been committed had the hospital and the parents agreed to separation without consulting the court.

[11] [2001] Fam 147, At 204.

[12] For more comprehensive discussion of some of the (non-human rights) issues raised by *Re A*, see B Clucas and K O'Donnell, 'Conjoined Twins: the Cutting Edge' (2002) 5 *Web Journal of Current Legal Issues*, <http://webjcli.ncl.ac.uk/2002/contents 5.html> (27 August 2004).

without help, specifically that of her husband. However, although the act of suicide had been decriminalised, s 2(1) of the Suicide Act made it an offence to aid and abet a suicide, which is punishable by up to 14 years imprisonment. Mr Pretty was willing to help his wife die, but not to risk prosecution and conviction for the s 2(1) offence.

Mrs Pretty wrote to the Director of Public Prosecutions (DPP), and asked for a written assurance that he would not prosecute her husband[13] if he helped her to die. The DPP refused. She applied for judicial review of the DPP's decision, arguing that the decision was unlawful or that the undertaking sought would not be unlawful; and requested a mandatory order requiring that the DPP give the undertaking sought, or a declaration that s 2 Suicide Act 1961 was incompatible with various Articles of the ECHR, including Article 2 (right to life). The case was appealed. We will be concerned with the House of Lords[14] and European Court of Human Rights (ECtHR) judgments.

Mrs Pretty's argument was essentially that Article 2 is a right to self-determination with respect to life and death, not a protection of life itself or an expression of the sanctity of life. The Article's aim, she claimed, is to protect individuals from the actions of third parties (the state and public authorities). On this interpretation, the right to die is the corollary of the right to life. Her disability prevented her from terminating her own life. The DPP's refusal to assure immunity to her husband should he act in her stead was a violation of Article 14, which prohibits discrimination against the enjoyment of Convention rights.

The courts' responses to Mrs Pretty's argument were clear. There was strong disagreement with her interpretation of Article 2. It was held that Article 2 does not protect the right to self-determination, but rather is a protection of the sanctity of human life.[15] The wording of the Article, the case law and the diverse religious views of the Member States were said to have supported this view. It was the unanimous view of the House of Lords and the European Court of Human Rights that Article 2 was not

[13] s 2(4) Suicide Act 1961: 'No proceedings shall be instituted for an offence under this section except by or with the consent of the Director of Public Prosecutions.' Tur's view is that s 2(4) is an attempt by the drafters to 'ameliorate the potential injustice of a widely stated blanket rule criminalizing assisted suicide [s 2(1)] in a statute decriminalizing suicide itself by empowering the Director to prevent prosecution by withholding consent' (Tur, n 3 above, p 9).

[14] At the time of *Pretty*, the Human Rights Act 1998 had come into force.

[15] See Tur, n 3 above, p 5 for a different point of view with respect to the Suicide Act 1961: 'There appears to be no way of determining from the wording of the Act or from the legislative history which is the principle underlying the Act. That a strong case can be made for either entails that a compelling case can be made for neither. Moreover, it appears that neither principle fully fits the legislative structure of the Suicide Act. It is as difficult to quadrate sanctity of life with section 1 and with subsection 2(4) as it is to square personal autonomy with subsection 2(1).' On balance, Tur prefers the better fit of the principle of self-determination (*ibid*, 10).

engaged.[16] The House of Lords also held unanimously that there was no violation of Articles 3, 8, 9, and 14. The ECtHR thought there may have been a breach of Article 8, but that this was justified under Article 8(2), and that any indirect discrimination that engaged Article 14 was justified.[17]

Interpretation of Article 2

The judges dealing with the cases of *Re A* and *Pretty* were all concerned with the interpretation of Article 2 ECHR. In *Re A*, the deliberate extinguishing of a life of a child unable to consent, whose parents did not consent, was held not to engage the right to life; in *Pretty*, the express wish of a competent adult to be assisted in her death was refused because to do so would violate the sanctity of life principle that was said to be the basis of the right to life.

Article 2 is written in straightforward language. There are clear exceptions in Article 2(2) that set out the circumstances in which the right to life shall not be regarded as violated. These exceptions, together with that of 2(1) ('save in the execution of a sentence of a court following conviction of a crime for which this penalty is provided by law') would appear to be exhaustive, and not merely examples.

It seems likely that the judges in *Re A* did not consider the difference between a positive right to life (guarantee of life) and a negative right to life (licence to be alive). If this had been recognised by Ward LJ, he would not have been troubled by the 'impossibility of performance'. If the correct interpretation of Article 2 is that it preserves life itself, then any circumstance where the state or a public body intentionally deprives a person of his or her life or permits that deprivation (as in *Re A*), is in contravention of Article 2. The fact that Jodie's proximate death would be inevitable would not violate Article 2, as this Article does not confer a positive right to life. However, if the correct interpretation of Article 2 is something other than the preservation of life — which is what is suggested by *Re A* — then Mrs Pretty's case may well have been wrongly decided.

Given the clarity of draftmanship in Article 2, it seems absurd that, although one case, *Pretty*, should recognise the principle of the sanctity of

[16] But see D Morris, 'Assisted suicide under the European Convention on Human Rights: a critique' (2003) *European Human Rights Law Review* 65–91, who argues that it is possible under the ECHR to make a case for assisted suicide in restricted circumstances.

[17] See J Allen, 'Rights, Paternalism, Constitutions and Judges' in G Huscroft and P Rishworth (eds), *Litigating Rights: Perspectives from Domestic and International Law* (Oxford, Hart Publishing, 2002) pp 29–46 for discussion of paternalistic defence of another's rights. Though he is not referring to a *Pretty*-type conflict of interpretation, his words (*ibid*, p 40) are apt: 'For [someone] to know what is best for us *better than we do ourselves*, is to assume a situation analogous to the one in which the paternalistic defender of constitutional rights is the normal adult and all the rest of us are, or will be, children, insane or severely inebriated.' (Emphasis Original).

life enshrined in Article 2, in *Re A*, decided a few months earlier, quite the opposite conclusion was reached. It may be thought then that the main obstacle to proper interpretation of human rights provisions and substantive respect for human rights is not necessarily the clarity or lack of clarity of language, but of something else: judicial motivation, approaches and ideologies.

JUDICIAL APPROACHES

The second hurdle to be overcome in pursuit of human rights compliance is that of different judicial approaches to interpretation. There are the traditional canons of statutory interpretation: the literal, mischief and golden rules.[18] Adams and Brownsword have elaborated the distinction between the general adjudicative ideologies of formalism and realism, and present a fourfold typology of judicial approaches. Textual and purposive formalists regard fidelity to precedents or statute as paramount, either the text (former) or purpose (latter) of the provision. Realists, both weak and strong depending on the relative importance given to precedent or statute, do not regard fidelity to the provision as their primary goal.[19]

The type of case at issue adds another layer of complexity. There are clear cases, where the law is plain and the judge has no reservations about applying it; difficult cases, where the law is unclear,[20] and hard cases, where the law is clear but the judge has reservations about its application to the facts of the case.[21]

The Court of Appeal in *Re A* can be viewed as taking a very narrow literal or textual formalist approach to the phrase 'no one shall be deprived of his life intentionally', importing a technical meaning of 'intention' that divorces what is desired and what is foreseen, and incidentally moving away from the purpose behind the drafting of Article 2. Alternatively, it could be thought that the Lord Justices were acting as realists: that they had decided that it was better to save Jodie at the more immediate expense of Mary's life, rather than let them both die[22] and that they manipulated their interpretation of the law accordingly. Both the House of Lords and the European Court in *Pretty* seem to have taken a 'mischief' or purposive formalist tack in regard to the right to life, but could also be

[18] J Adams and R Brownsword, *Understanding Law* (London, Sweet & Maxwell, 2003), Chapter 4.
[19] *Ibid*, Chapters 4 and 5.
[20] Dworkinian hard cases: see R Dworkin, *Law's Empire* (Oxford, Hart Publishing, 1986).
[21] J Adams and R Brownsword, n 14 above, pp 97–9.
[22] This could be seen as an espousal of a utilitarian moral principle over a deontological, rights-based moral principle.

viewed as realists who have decided for whatever reason to present the sanctity of life as being the inevitable interpretation of Article 2 when it is not in fact inevitable.

Unpredictability in interpretation can result in decisions that are viewed as substantively morally wrong. However, we should be concerned not only with the moral respectability of individual cases, but also with the profile of judicial interpretation as a whole. There is disparity of interpretive approach at a local level, within the UK, between the UK and different national jurisdictions, and between national jurisdictions and the purposive interpretation of the ECtHR. Inconsistency of interpretation offends at a procedural level, against principles of distributive justice, of treating like cases alike, as well as against the substantive rights of individual complainants.

The solution to this problem must be found in standardisation of approaches and focus on effecting substantive respect for human rights. From this first part of the paper, it ought to be evident that uniformity of interpretive approaches is a necessary element of respect for human rights. To ensure substantive compliance with existing human rights provisions, the particular interpretive approach ought to be that of purposive formalism, fidelity to the purpose of the provision, of protecting human rights.

JUDICIAL IDEOLOGIES OF LAW

Thus far we have been concerned with the interpretation of existing human rights provisions, and of the crucial role of judicial approaches (reflecting adjudicative ideologies) in this enterprise. However, judicial approaches to interpretation are premised on something else: judicial ideologies of law itself.

By 'judicial ideologies of law' we are referring specifically to a judge's stance on the concept of law debate, upon which legal reasoning is parasitic. The two positions most relevant to this point are legal positivism, the position that law is not necessarily conceptually connected to morality,[23] and legal idealism, the position that law is necessarily conceptually connected to (some form of) morality.[24]

Judicial ideologies influence and explain a judge's attitude towards clear and difficult or hard cases (no reservations in the former case; reservations in the latter), and can provide a guide to the outcome of a difficult or hard case. For example, if a judge believes there to be a necessary conceptual connection between law and morality, she will be content with a

[23] See generally HLA Hart, *The Concept of Law*, 2nd Edn (Oxford, Clarendon, 1994).
[24] See n 25 below.

clear case whose result is not immoral; will be troubled by application of the law that will result in an immoral outcome, and may use moral principles to guide her interpretation of a difficult or Dworkinian hard case where the application of the law to the facts is not straightforward. When judicial approaches are factored into interpretation of a provision, the outcome can never be foretold with confidence, even in cases where the law is apparently clear (as with Article 2 ECHR).

Where existing human rights provisions are interpreted, there is a great deal of overlap between a purposive formalist approach and an ideological stance of legal idealism focused on the protection of rights[25]: the former is the logical legislative and judicial expression of the latter. But sometimes, the rules to be applied, although ostensibly promoting and protecting human rights, may be deficient in either substance or compass, and a rigid emphasis on giving effect to the rule would be counter-productive to human rights. A rule that is deficient in substance would fail to protect — or violate — human rights. To interpret this rule purposively would be to perpetuate the violation.

Where rules purporting to respect human rights leave significant lacunae, much greater than our understanding of the hard case, such as a failure to protect at all the rights of children, the effect of rights violation is the same. These two defects of substance and scope can only be remedied where a judge has a conception of law as an enterprise that (at least) must not violate human rights. Such a conception could enable a judge to strike out substantively deficient rules (*lex injustia non est lex*), and to create law that respects rights where regulation has been silent.[26]

There is no guarantee that standardization of judicial approach and ideology will result in the correct outcome in each case, for judges are fallible, but we contend that these are necessary steps towards the goal of substantive compliance with human rights.

IMPLEMENTATION AND APPLICATION OF HUMAN RIGHTS IN NEW ZEALAND

In the first part of this chapter, the problems of interpretation and application of human rights standards in Britain were examined through an

[25] See R Dworkin, n 19 for one version; for a morally objective version of legal idealism, see D Beyleveld and R Brownsword, *Law as a Moral Judgment* (Sheffield, Sheffield Academic Press, 1994).

[26] An illustration that steps outside the bounds of traditional judicial activity and could be viewed as either purposive formalism to legislative aims in a broad sense, or as exhibiting a legal idealist conception of adjudication, is 'social action legislation', found in its most striking form in the Indian Supreme Court. 'Social action legislation' is the use of the legal system to ensure constitutionally guaranteed rights, even where the substantive rules do not do so (S Goonesekere, *Children, Law and Justice: a South Asian Perspective* (New Delhi/London,

analysis of the *Conjoined Twins* and *Diane Pretty* cases. Our conclusion is that to ensure substantive compliance with human rights in cases of existing human rights legislation, the preferred mode of interpretation ought to be that of purposive formalism; that is, judges should be faithful both to the text and the spirit of the instrument to be interpreted. Here, we are concerned with judicial rectification of gaps in human rights legislation, rather than the substantive application of human rights themselves. We examine here how judges of another common law jurisdiction (New Zealand) have dealt with such issues of interpretation. Attention is devoted to the crafting of remedies where none previously existed through the application of interpretative method. It is contended that in the absence of specific remedy provisions in legislation, compliance with human rights is best achieved by a rights-oriented judicial ideology — a form of legal idealism. It is not claimed that all New Zealand judges are legal idealists, but that where remedies fall to be devised by the judiciary, those judges who view their legitimate role as being focused on rights rather than having traditional (positivist) concerns about trespassing onto Parliament's territory, are more successful in respecting human rights.[27]

New Zealand is an interesting case study in this field both because of its constitutional similarities to and differences from Britain. It differs from Britain in having a single chamber Parliament which is elected by proportional representation based on the additional member system for a period of three years.[28] Like the Westminster Parliament, however, it is legislatively supreme and substantially mirrors Westminster practice and procedure in legislative matters.[29] New Zealand also maintains a separation of powers but the head of the judiciary, the Minister for Justice, and the Attorney General are, as in the Britain, political appointments with the latter having particular responsibility under the New Zealand Bill of Rights Act 1990 (NZBORA) for alerting Parliament to legislation which might be in conflict with the rights protected therein.[30]

Sage Publications, 1998), pp 64–73). Judicial activism in this sense is much more than law-applying: it includes the creation and modification of concepts and remedies. Examples from India given by Goonesekere are the development of the concept of 'epistolatory jurisdiction' in the Supreme Court, a means of addressing the court via non-standard procedures, alleging rights violations (*ibid*, p 64); the same court's modification of the English law-based concept of standing (*ibid*, pp 64–5); the court's unorthodox use of judicial review to curtail violation of fundamental rights by the executive, state and its organs (*ibid*, p 65); and court decisions as an influence and even as a directive force concerning legislative provisions.

[27] Paul Rishworth has some interesting observations on the judges as guardians of fundamental rights principles within the common law framework: P Rishworth, 'The Rule of International Law' in G Huscroft and P Rishworth, *Litigating Rights* (Oxford, Hart Publishing, 2002) pp 267–72.

[28] Electoral Act 1993.

[29] See generally PA Joseph, *Constitutional and Administrative Law in New Zealand*, 2nd Edn (Wellington NZ, Brookers, 2001).

[30] Section 7 NZBORA.

HUMAN RIGHTS IN NEW ZEALAND

The Framework for Protection

As a former British colony with a common law system, New Zealand inherited an approach to human rights based on notions of civil liberties; in other words, a negative premise based on the assumption that that which was not forbidden was permitted.[31] As in Britain, this retarded the development of a rights culture and produced vigorous arguments for and against a Bill of Rights during the 1970s and 1980s.[32] The fourth Labour government led by David Lange and latterly by Geoffrey Palmer, a convert to the Bill of Rights cause, eventually promoted and passed NZBORA as an ordinary statute.[33]

The International Dimension

New Zealand has maintained a longstanding commitment to international human rights having initially played an important role in the development, drafting and final adoption of the Universal Declaration of Human Rights.[34] It has also usually been quick to sign and ratify human rights agreements, although it did take twelve years to accede to the Optional Protocol (OP) to the International Covenant on Civil and Political Rights (ICCPR).[35] In addition to the ICCPR, New Zealand is also party to ICESCR, CEDAW, CERD, UNCAT and UNCROC all of which require steps to be taken in domestic law for their implementation. Elizabeth Evatt, a former Human Rights Committee (HRC) member, states that the preferred means of rights implementation recognised in the ICCPR is through incorporation of the ICCPR in the domestic legislation of the state.[36] The HRC has

[31] For discussion of this in a broader context see G Leane, 'Rights Discourse: Are We all in This Alone?' (2002) 8 *Canterbury Law Review* 187. See also T McBride, *New Zealand Civil Rights Handbook* (Auckland NZ, Legal Information Service, 2001). It is interesting to note that the 1973 edition of this book was entitled *New Zealand Handbook of Civil Liberties* (Wellington NZ, Price Milburn, 1973). The difference in title reflects the shift from a liberties to a rights culture in New Zealand in the intervening years.
[32] P Rishworth, 'The Birth and Rebirth of the Bill of Rights' in G Huscroft and P Rishworth, *Rights and Freedoms* (Wellington NZ, Brookers, 1995) 1.
[33] Palmer's initial opposition to a Bill of Rights for New Zealand can be found in G Palmer, 'A Bill of Rights for New Zealand' in K Keith, (ed) *Essays on Human Rights* (Wellington NZ, Sweet & Maxwell, 1968) 106.
[34] M Bell, 'New Zealand's Contribution to the Early Post-War Development of International Human Rights', (1998) 4 *Human Rights Law and Practice* 1; New Zealand Ministry of Foreign Affairs and Trade, *New Zealand Handbook on International Human Rights* (Wellington NZ, Ministry of Foreign Affairs and Trade, 1998) pp 14–15.
[35] J Elkind, 'The Optional Protocol: A Bill of Rights for New Zealand' [1997] *New Zealand Law Journal* 96.
[36] E Evatt, 'The Impact of International Human Rights on Domestic Law' in G Huscroft and P Rishworth, *Litigating Rights* (Oxford, Hart Publishing, 2002) p 281 at 288.

criticised New Zealand in its concluding observations on the latter's ICCPR periodic reports for failing to entrench the NZBORA,[37] but as New Zealand has made clear this would be contrary to its constitution.

The international instruments to which New Zealand is party not only require domestic implementation, but they also create international supervision mechanisms. They all require states to submit periodic reports on the measures taken to promote enjoyment of human rights, while the ICCPR, CERD, CEDAW and UNCAT provide for individual communication procedures. Of these, the OP to the ICCPR is probably the most important since individuals can petition the HRC if a violation of their rights has occurred and they have been denied a domestic remedy. Significantly, the final views of the HRC have also been utilised as an aid to interpretation by New Zealand judges when evaluating the scope of the NZBORA.

INTERNATIONAL HUMAN RIGHTS INSTRUMENTS AND THE JUDICIARY: MATTERS OF INTERPRETATION

The New Zealand courts are often perceived as the last bastion of human rights protection.[38] By interpreting the indeterminate language of human rights the courts are able to define the content, limits and effects of particular rights.[39] As a general observation, a court which adopts a strong realist approach will maximise the application of human rights, while that which approaches the task on the basis of textual formalism will tend to limit those rights. Similarly, an activist (realist) court is more likely to control the actions of the Executive in the field of human rights through a robust application of judicial review, while a more conservative (formalist) court will, again, tend to give the benefit of the doubt to the Government. In New Zealand, the Court of Appeal's record in this area has been mixed with Cooke P and Thomas J standing out as legal idealists in a Court of Appeal which, in recent years under Richardson P, has become more conservative.

In New Zealand the courts have used international agreements to interpret the legislation which implemented them into domestic law.[40]

[37] Concluding observations of the Human Rights Committee: New Zealand 07/08/2002 CCPR/CO/75/NZL, para 8.

[38] See Rishworth, above note 32.

[39] As Rishworth puts it the NZBORA is 'lofty and majestic in tone, it is deliberately general — and hence unavoidably vague — in its scope'. P Rishworth, 'Affirming Fundamental Values' in G Huscroft and P Rishworth, *Rights and Freedoms* (Wellington NZ, Brooker's, 1995) p 71 at 73.

[40] P Hunt and M Bedggood, 'The International Dimension of Human Rights Law' in Huscroft and Rishworth, *ibid*, p 37 at 53. See also, A Conte, 'From Treaty to Translation: The Use of International Human Rights Instruments in the Application and Enforcement of Civil and Political Rights in New Zealand' (2001) 8 *Canterbury Law Review* 54.

The use of international agreements as an aid to interpretation is unexceptional, and the principle that Parliament does not intend to legislate in a manner contrary to the state's international obligations is well accepted.[41] If, however, legislation is clear, the courts must apply it, regardless of whether it violates international law, this being the presumed intent of the legislature. In *Ashby v Minister for Immigration*[42] Richardson J said that 'if the terms of the domestic legislation are clear and unambiguous they must be given effect in our courts whether or not they carry out New Zealand's international obligations'. If this were the case, however, the state would then incur responsibility under international law and it would also allow individuals to vindicate rights violations should an international instrument so permit.[43] Given the number of safeguards in New Zealand law under NZBORA and the processes under which both the executive and the legislature must act, it might be thought that this scenario would be unlikely to arise. In *R v Barlow*,[44] however, Richardson J noted that since NZBORA did not contain a general affirmation of the right to liberty and security of the person, as was the case in the ICCPR, this must have been the intention of Parliament and as a consequence he refused to give an extended meaning to NZBORA.[45]

NZBORA is designed to implement New Zealand's international human rights obligations and its long title states that it is an Act:

> (a) To affirm, protect and promote human rights and fundamental freedoms in New Zealand; and
> (b) To affirm New Zealand's commitment to the International Covenant on Civil and Political Rights.

It is apparent therefore, that an interpretation or application of the Act might involve reference to the ICCPR.[46] Judicial policy concerning the interpretation of human rights standards in the New Zealand courts shows a diversity of approaches. In *R v Noort*[47] Cooke P appeared to set

[41] See the *Tangiora Case* below n 52.
[42] [1981] 1 New Zealand Law Reports 222, 229. For commentary see J Elkind and A Shaw, 'The Municipal Enforcement of the Prohibition against Racial Discrimination: A Case Study on New Zealand and the 1981 Springbok Tour' (1984) 55 *British Yearbook of International Law* 189.
[43] On the requirements a petitioner must satisfy in order to lodge a successful communication with the HRC see JS Davidson, 'Individual Communications to the United Nations Human Rights Committee: A New Zealand Perspective' [1997] *New Zealand Law Review* 374.
[44] (1995) 2 Human Rights of New Zealand 635.
[45] For further discussion see P Rishworth, 'Affirming the Fundamental Values of the Nation: How the Bill of Rights and the Human Rights Act affect New Zealand Law' in Huscroft and Rishworth, *Rights and Freedoms*, n 39 above, 71.
[46] Because the text of the ICCPR is not fully reproduced in the NZBORA recourse to the original text of the ICCPR is necessary for interpretative purposes. Rishworth, 'The Rule of International Law', *Litigating Rights*, n 36 above, p 267 at 272–4.
[47] [1992] 3 New Zealand Law Reports 260.

the benchmark. Here, Noort, who had been arrested for drink-driving complained that he had not been given access to a lawyer in accordance with s 23(1)(b) NZBORA. In identifying the mode of interpretation which ought to be adopted in respect of NZBORA, Cooke P cited Lord Wilberforce's dictum in *Minister of Home Affairs v Fisher*[48] where he said that interpretation of constitutional human rights provisions called for:

> A generous interpretation avoiding what has been called the 'austerity of tabulated legalism', suitable to give individuals the full measure of the fundamental rights and freedoms referred to.

Following this and s 5(j) of the New Zealand Acts Interpretation Act 1924, Cooke P said that NZBORA ought to be given:

> Such fair, large and liberal construction and interpretation as will best ensure the attainment of its object according to its true intent meaning and spirit.

Following the Adams and Brownsword taxonomy of interpretative approaches it would seem that Cooke P was advocating purposive formalism for the human rights provisions of NZBORA. Indeed, the former Court of Appeal President has gone further suggesting that the affirmation of the rights and freedoms contained in NZBORA might require the development of the law, especially given the general recognition that certain human rights were fundamental and anterior to domestic law. In *Baigent's Case*[49] he reiterated a statement made in *Noort* saying:

> The long title shows that, in affirming the rights and freedoms contained in the Bill of Rights, the Act requires the development of the law when necessary. Such a measure is not to be approached as if it did no more than preserve the status quo.

In a number of cases the courts have resorted to the ICCPR and the final views of the HRC as an aid to interpreting or confirming the meaning of NZBORA. In *R v Bain, Application by TVNZ*[50] Television New Zealand applied for a suppression order relating to certain hearsay evidence in Bain's murder trial to be lifted. The Court of Appeal concurred with the view of the trial judge that the order should be maintained until the criminal process had been concluded with an appeal to the Privy Council. It was held that the maintenance of the suppression order was justified on the grounds of proper administration of justice and protection of the

[48] [1980] AC 319.
[49] *Simpson v Attorney-General (Baigent's Case)* [1994] 3 New Zealand Law Reports 647.
[50] 22/7/96 (CA 255/95).

public interest. Keith J relying on s 25(a) NZBORA and Article 14(1) ICCPR held that while these demanded the openness of the justice system, this was nonetheless subject to limitations in the public interest. In a paper to the Commonwealth Judicial Colloquium Sir Kenneth observed that the domestic provisions and their international counterparts were congruous.[51] There have also been other cases where such congruity has been evident or where the ICCPR and final views of the HRC have been used to interpret NZBORA provisions. In *Wellington District Legal Services Committee v Tangiora*[52] the Court affirmed the presumption of statutory interpretation that, so far as its wording allows, legislation should be read in a way which is consistent with New Zealand's international obligations. This presumption applies whether or not the legislation was specifically enacted for the purpose of implementing the international instrument in question.[53] This principle was further exemplified by the Court of Appeal in *Quilter et al v Attorney-General*[54] where the Court in determining the meaning of discrimination under s 19 NZBORA, referred to the relevant international human rights instruments including the Covenant. Again, in *Manga v Attorney-General*[55] reference to Article 9 ICCPR and the final views of the HRC was made when deciding the meaning of 'arbitrary' in s 22 NZBORA.

FILLING THE GAPS: INTERPRETATION AND THE CREATION OF REMEDIES

A significant area where interpretative method has been used to resolve lacunae in the NZBORA has been in the area of remedies.[56] Early in the life of NZBORA the courts were confronted with the problem of how best to provide remedies for breach of the rights protected by the Act. In the field of criminal evidence where the issue first arose, the response was to adapt exclusionary remedies which had been available under the pre-NZBORA common law. In *Simpson v Attorney-General (Baigent's Case)*[57] and *Auckland Unemployed Workers' Rights Centre v Attorney-General*,[58] however, the Court of Appeal confronted situations which could not be

[51] Sir Kenneth Keith, 'Application of International Human Rights Law in New Zealand', Judicial Colloquium on the Domestic Application of International Human Rights Norms, (Georgetown, Guyana, 3–5 September 1996) p 13.
[52] (1998) 4 Human Rights Reports of New Zealand 136 (CA).
[53] See Davidson above n 43 at 387–90.
[54] (1998) 4 Human Rights Reports of New Zealand 170 (CA).
[55] (1999) 5 Human Rights Reports of New Zealand 177, 185 (HC).
[56] R Harrison, 'The Remedial Jurisdiction for Breach of the Bill of Rights' in Huscroft and Rishworth, *Rights and Freedoms*, n 39 above, p 401. See also A Conte, 'International Reflections on Civil and Political Rights' (2002) 8 *Canterbury Law Review* 480 at 489.
[57] [1994] 3 New Zealand Law Reports 667.
[58] [1994] 3 New Zealand Law Reports 720.

addressed by an application of pre-existing remedies but instead had to craft new remedies. This was done by interpreting NZBORA and its antecedent international instrument, the ICCPR. In *Baigent's Case* the breach arose from the fact that Simpson's premises had been wrongly identified as those of a drug dealer and she claimed compensation for breach of s 21 NZBORA which prohibits unreasonable search and seizure. In the *Auckland Case*, the plaintiffs claimed that the police had relied on an illegal search warrant to search their premises, again in breach of s 21. Although the Crown argued that it was immune from process for wrongful police action under s 6(5) of the Crown Proceedings Act 1950, the Court of Appeal rejected this argument and held that a cause of action lay directly against the Crown for breach of its obligations under NZBORA. The Crown further argued that the absence of a remedies provision in NZBORA meant that the Parliament had intended to exclude any remedy for breach of the Act. This too was rejected by the Court of Appeal emphasising New Zealand's international obligations, particularly Article 2(3) ICCPR which provides:

> Each State Party to the present Covenant undertakes:
>
> To ensure that any person whose rights or freedoms as herein recognised are violated shall have an effective remedy, notwithstanding that the violation has been committed by persons acting in an official capacity;
>
> To ensure that any person claiming such a remedy shall have his right thereto determined by competent judicial, administrative or legislative authorities, or by any other competent authority provided for by the legal system of the State, and to develop the possibilities of judicial remedy;
>
> To ensure that the competent authorities shall enforce such remedies when granted.

Following reference to Article 2(3) ICCPR and s 3 NZBORA Lord Cooke stated:

> Section 3 ... makes it clear that the Bill of Rights applies to acts done by the courts. The Act is binding on us, and we would fail in our duty if we did not give an effective remedy to a person whose legislatively affirmed rights have been infringed. In a case such as the present the only effective remedy is compensation. A mere declaration would be toothless. In other cases a mandatory remedy such as an injunction or an order for return of property might be appropriate: Compare *Magana v Zaire* (1983) ... [59]

Casey J also adopted a similar approach to interpretation saying:

> The rights and freedoms affirmed are fundamental to a civilised society and justify a liberal purposive interpretation of the Act, even though it has

[59] Above n 57, at 676.

> not been constitutionally entrenched and has the same status as ordinary legislation.[60]

He went on to say:

> By its accession to the First Optional Protocol to the Covenant ... New Zealand accepted individual access by its citizens to the [UNHRC] for violation of rights under the Covenant where they have been unable to obtain a domestic remedy. The Act reflects Covenant right, and it would be a strange thing if Parliament, which passed it one year later, must be taken as contemplating that New Zealand citizens could go to the United Nations Committee in New York for appropriate redress, but could not obtain [it] from our own Courts.[61]

The only member of the Court to dissent from this broad purposive approach was Gault J who took the view that the obligation in Article 2(3) ICCPR could be met by giving effect to 'traditional' common law remedies. This was very much a minority view and the subsequent history of remedies forged in *Baigent's Case* for breach of NZBORA has been confirmed in other cases.[62]

The 'declaration of incompatibility' is a new 'remedy' first considered in *Moonen v Film and Literature Board of Review*[63] where the defendant was accused of publishing objectionable material. If the court finds in a case that an enactment conflicts with NZBORA, cannot be interpreted consistently with NZBORA, cannot be justified as a reasonable limitation in a free and democratic society and must therefore on this interpretation take priority over a right contained in NZBORA, it will declare that the enactment must be applied, but declare that it is inconsistent with the rights and freedoms contained in NZBORA. It seems clear that such a declaration will have no legal effect on the Crown, but it suggests a strong indication by the courts that it is likely to be in breach of domestic legislation and international obligations. As Tipping J observed:

> Such judicial indication will be of value should the matter come to be examined by the [HRC]. It may also be of assistance to Parliament if the subject arises in that forum. In the light of the presence of s5 in the Bill of Rights, New Zealand society as a whole can rightly expect that on appropriate occasions the Courts will indicate whether a particular legislative provision is or is not justified thereunder.[64]

[60] *Ibid* at 691.
[61] *Ibid.*
[62] See *Upton v Green* (1996) 3 Human Rights Reports of New Zealand 179 (breach of the right to natural justice); *Dunlea v Attorney-General* [2000] New Zealand Law Reports 136 (unreasonable search).
[63] [2000] 2 New Zealand Law Reports 9.
[64] *Ibid* at 18.

Although this 'remedy' has yet to be used, the Court of Appeal signalled clearly that it was prepared to hold Parliament to account where its legislation fell short of the standards required by NZBORA. While NZBORA is not entrenched and the courts do not have the power to overturn statutes as unconstitutional, none the less a declaration of incompatibility by the courts will prove a powerful antidote to a Parliament which legislates against human rights standards either by design or accident.

A further major role of the judiciary in protecting human rights is through judicial review. In a number of cases the question of whether New Zealand's international obligations might be counted as relevant factors in the exercise of ministerial discretion has been considered. In *Ashby v Minister of Immigration*,[65] the plaintiff claimed that by granting entry visas to the Springbok rugby team the Minister for Immigration had erred in not taking into account New Zealand's obligations under CERD. Although the Chief Justice dismissed the plaintiff's application, he did accept that CERD was a relevant consideration which the Minister was bound to take into account. He found as a matter of fact, however, that the Minister had adverted to CERD when making his decision.

In *Tavita v Minister of Immigration*[66] the Minister had dismissed an appeal by an overstayer against the execution of a warrant for his removal from New Zealand. Tavita argued that he should not be removed because of changed circumstances in his family situation, particularly the birth of his child who by virtue of being born in New Zealand was a New Zealand citizen. It was further argued that Article 9(1) UNCROC guaranteeing the right of a child to be together with his or her parents and 23(1) ICCPR guaranteeing the right to family life were relevant factors which the Minister should have considered. The Minister's decision was referred back to afford him the opportunity to consider such international aspects in reviewing the exercise of his discretion under the legislation. In response to the Crown's contention that it was not obliged to have regard to New Zealand's international obligations under UNCROC and the ICCPR, the Court observed that they were 'distinctly relevant' and must be considered by the Minister. Cooke P further commented that he found the Crown's argument 'unattractive ... apparently implying that New Zealand's adherence to the international instruments has been at least partly window-dressing'.[67] It should be stressed, however that although Ministers are to have regard to international human rights instruments to which New Zealand has voluntarily consented to be bound, they are not obliged to follow them if they consider other factors more decisive. This was the case in *Rajan v Minister of Immigration*[68] in which the Court of

[65] [1981] 1 New Zealand Law Reports 222.
[66] [1994] 2 New Zealand Law Reports 257.
[67] *Ibid* at 266.
[68] [1996] 3 New Zealand Law Reports 543.

Appeal reaffirmed the traditional doctrine. Here, the Minister of Immigration had taken the relevant provisions of the ICCPR into account when making his decision but had decided that other factors were more compelling. The decision, as a consequence of this, could not be challenged.[69]

CONCLUSION

This chapter began with the premise that the interpretation of human rights is logically prior to their effective implementation. If human rights are to have substance, and if they are to be protected effectively, then they must have meaning. However, the meaning and thus the substance of human rights depends upon judicial interpretation, and above all, judicial ideologies of law since it is the courts which are called upon to undertake the first step of interpretation and then convert that interpretation into practical application. While the courts of Britain and New Zealand are both located within similar common law traditions, there are also notable differences in terms of the political and broader legal contexts within which they operate. Despite these differences, it is significant that the judicial techniques employed in the realm of interpreting human rights bear conspicuous similarities. The cases considered in the first part of the chapter relate to the most fundamental of all human rights: the right to life, and it is significant that the divergent judicial decisions in these cases can be justified by recourse to traditional modes of statutory interpretation. The cases considered in the New Zealand context are rather different since they deal with lacunae in the system of human rights protection and not substantive rights per se. While these might be difficult cases, they are not hard cases, but they do tell us something about judicial philosophy in that the techniques of purposive formalism (ie, fidelity to the text and to the spirit of human rights instruments) and the ideological position of legal idealism can result not only in the consistent and effective implementation of human rights, but also in the filling of gaps in the mechanisms for their protection.

[69] The effect of not giving more weight to New Zealand's international obligations has been to open New Zealand's immigration policy to challenge before the HRC under the ICCPR.

11

Globalisation of Justice: for Better or Worse?

CHANDRA LEKHA SRIRAM*

INTRODUCTION

JUSTICE IS BECOMING increasingly globalised. Crimes anywhere in the globe may be subject to prosecution in faraway nations, whether through the occasional *ad hoc* tribunal or through the exercise of universal jurisdiction. This globalisation might be viewed in another way, as externalisation of justice, precisely because of the distance from the original locus of the crime at which judicial proceedings may occur. Such external proceedings often take place because domestic ones are unlikely to occur. I argue that while the increasingly global reach of judicial mechanisms is in many instances a positive development, there is reason for caution, particularly in the exercise of universal jurisdiction.[1] These observations proceed from a theoretical inquiry as well as initial investigations into the exercise of universal jurisdiction, but the lessons drawn here have more wide-ranging implications for externalised justice such as that to be dispensed by the International Criminal Court.[2] I argue that

*Completion of this chapter was enabled by funding from the Ford and MacArthur Foundations to the International Peace Academy's Peacebuilding: Issues and Responses research project. The author is grateful for excellent comments from Brad R Roth, Jamie Mayerfeld, and Amy Ross.

[1] C L Sriram, 'Externalizing justice through universal jurisdiction — problems and prospects' (2001) 12 *Finnish Yearbook of International Law* 47; C L Sriram, 'Contemporary practice of universal jurisdiction: disjointed and disparate, yet developing,' (2002) 6 *International Journal of Human Rights* 49; J Mayerfeld, 'The Mutual Dependence of External and Internal Justice: Understanding the role of the International Criminal Court' (2000) 12 *Finnish Yearbook of International Law* 71; See S Macedo, (ed), *Universal Jurisdiction: National Courts and the Prosecution of Serious Crimes* (Philadelphia, University of Pennsylvania Press, 2003). See also *The Princeton Principles on Universal Jurisdiction* (Princeton, Princeton University Program in Law and Public Affairs, 2001); A Cassese, 'Reflections on International Criminal Justice' (1998) 68 *Modern Law Review* 1.

[2] M Morris, 'The Disturbing Democratic Defect of the International Criminal Court,' (2000) 12 *Finnish Yearbook of International Law* 109, and M Morris, 'High Crimes and Misconceptions: The ICC and Non-Party States,'(2001) 64 *Law and Contemporary Problems* 13.

such justice may not take sufficient account of local needs, and that by taking place at a great distance from the locus of the crimes, it may fail to serve many of the putative purposes of prosecution.

This chapter proceeds with three lines of inquiry. I first turn to three key strands of political theory to shed light upon what key goals might be sought in political transitions including, but not limited to, accountability for past crimes. I then examine the implications of these broad normative goals for nations and societies in transition themselves. Finally, I examine the degree to which externalised justice can truly address these local needs, and find it often wanting.

I do not argue that it is never appropriate to do justice 'elsewhere' or to exercise universal jurisdiction.[3] Externalising prosecution may at times be the only solution where a state or society is unwilling or unable to come to terms with the past; amnesties may have precluded legal action domestically, or the state may lack the technical capacity to act.[4] However, there is a serious risk that solutions that speak first to the interests of the international community at large will fail to take account of the goals articulated above.

WHAT IS AT STAKE AFTER TRANSITION? THREE NORMATIVE PERSPECTIVES

I have argued elsewhere that what is needed before engaging in debates about what modes of response to atrocities are appropriate — amnesty, truth commission, lustration, prosecution — is a consideration of what is at stake normatively in choices about transition. Such an examination makes clear the importance of *national* decisions with regard to what is best for society. By this I mean not simply elite pacts, in which choices are made *for* the society, often by perpetrators, but a serious consideration *by* a given society with regard to what is best for it. In the heat of discussions about accountability, such considerations may be lost; when decisions are taken from afar, they may be ignored altogether. Drawing on three strands of political theory — utilitarianism, deontological liberalism, and communitarianism, I draw out key normative concerns of transitional societies.[5]

[3] See H Kissinger, 'The Pitfalls of Universal Jurisdiction,' (2001) 80 *Foreign Affairs*, but compare K Roth, 'The Case for Universal Jurisdiction,' (2001) 80 *Foreign Affairs* 150.
[4] See B Simma and A L Paulus, 'The Responsibility of Individuals for Human Rights Abuses in Internal Conflicts: a Positivist View,' (1999) 93 *American Journal of International Law* 314; J Widner, 'Courts and Democracy in Postconflict Transitions: A Social Scientist's Perspective on the African Case,' (2001) 95 *American Journal of International Law* 64.
[5] C Sriram, 'Truth Commissions and Political Theory: Tough Moral Choices in Transitional Situations,' (2001) 18 *Netherlands Quarterly of Human Rights* 471.

Implicit in the tension between justice and peace is the battle between a form of the categorical imperative and consequentialism. We may seek, for the sake of some 'greater good' such as peace, to limit prosecutions, but this comes at a cost; alternatively, in pursuit of the greater good of reconciliation and social peace, there may be a need to pursue accountability, but at a price. It is worth spelling out more clearly what is at stake in each choice about accountability for a society. I present here very brief accounts of each philosophical position, and the implications of each for accountability.

Utilitarianism

Utilitarianism often underpins many arguments for lesser accountability, suggesting that in order to prevent the greater harm of an unstable polity or renewed fighting, the quest for an unattainable justice should be abandoned; there are more rarely utilitarian claims about deterrence, or satisfaction for victims in seeing justice done.

Utilitarianism, variously formulated, rates more highly that which tends to increase the aggregate well-being.[6] This makes punishment difficult to justify: its utility is minimal unless it acts as a deterrent, or unless the satisfaction felt by the victim in revenge is sufficiently large.[7] Thus, there may be utilitarian support for pardons where prosecutions or other mechanisms for accountability would be likely to do more harm. In the transitional context, the greater good of reconciliation and social peace may require the abandonment of prosecutions.[8]

Deontological Theories and Rights-Centred Theories

Deontological liberalism,[9] from Immanuel Kant through John Rawls and Ronald Dworkin, prioritises the right over the good.[10] Kant's categorical imperative insists that one must act according to principle, regardless of the consequences.[11] Thus moral judgment should be made not with

[6] See M Warnock, J S Mill (ed), *Utilitarianism and other Writings* (Meridian, New York, 1962): J Austin, 'The Province of Jurisprudence Determined,' pp 322–42; J Bentham, 'An Introduction to the Principles of Morals and Legislation,' pp 33–77.
[7] K D Moore, *Pardons: Justice, Mercy, and the Public Interest* (New York, Oxford University Press, 1989) p 37.
[8] A Heller, 'The Limits to Natural Law and the Paradox of Good and Evil,' in S Shute and S Hurley, (eds), *On Human Rights: The Oxford Amnesty Lectures 1993* (New York, Basic Books, 1993) pp 149–74.
[9] The term is Sandel's term for both Rawls and Ronald Dworkin. M J Sandel, *Liberalism and the Limits of Justice*, (Cambridge, Cambridge University Press, 1982) p 9.
[10] See S Freeman, 'Utilitarianism, Deontology, and the Priority of Right,' (1994) 23 *Philosophy and Public Affairs* 312.
[11] I Kant, *Grounding for the Metaphysics of Morals*, trans. J W Ellington (Indianapolis, IN, Hackett, 1981) pp 25–6.

reference to some collective utility, but on the basis of right principles.[12] For deontological liberalism, then, simply balancing harms and goods is insufficient. Rather, one must examine underlying principles, and act according to what is just. Kant's writings, in directing people to treat others as ends rather than means, have other important implications for punishment: he famously argued for the 'right' of the criminal to be punished.[13] The focus on rights and on individuals as ends in themselves means that individuals cannot be aggregated: one cannot offer a group account of the good.[14] Acting thus, one is likely to emphasise the importance of punishing wrongdoers, and vindicating the rights of victims, over an amorphous greater good.[15]

Communitarianism

I can only summarise a few strains of the diverse array of communitarian thought here.[16] Rather than emphasising 'the right' or rights of persons in the abstract, communitarianism holds that morality is achieved in a community, which provides the 'social preconditions that enable individuals to maintain their psychological integrity, civility, and ability to reason.'[17]

The community builds on tradition, and values are generated by the community rather than imposed from outside or by an elite. [18] Individual claims

[12] See generally J Rawls, *A Theory of Justice*, (Harvard University Press, Cambridge MA, 1971); See also J Rawls, *Political Liberalism* (New York, Columbia University Press, 1993) pp 190–200.
[13] Kant, *The Metaphysics of Morals* in H Reiss, (ed), *Kant: Political Writings* (Cambridge, Cambridge University Press, 2001) pp 154–60. K D Moore, *Pardons: Justice, Mercy, and the Public Interest* (New York, Cambridge University Press, 1989) pp 28–34.
[14] G Doppelt, 'Beyond Liberalism and Communitarianism: Towards a Critical Theory of Social Justice,' and C Mouffe, 'Rawls: Political Philosophy Without Politics,' in D Rasmussen, (ed), *Universalism vs. Communitarianism: Contemporary Debates in Ethics* (Cambridge MA, The MIT Press, 1990). See also Rawls, *Theory* at 22–7; R Dworkin, *Taking Rights Seriously*, (Cambridge MA, Harvard University Press, 1977) pp xii, 96 ff, and 169.
[15] See M Drumbl, 'Are there Limits to Globalizing International Criminal Law?' paper presented at the annual conference of the Law and Society Association (Budapest, 2001).
[16] See D Rasmussen (ed), *Universalism vs. Communitarianism*, n 14 above; A Etzioni (ed), *New Communitarian Thinking: Persons, Virtues, Institutions, and Communities* (Charlottesville VA University of Virginia Press, 1995); A McIntyre, 'The Virtues', and C Taylor, 'Hegel' in MJ Sandel (ed), *Liberalism and Its Critics* (New York, New York University Press, 1984); see also MJ Sandel, *Liberalism and the Limits of Justice*; n 9 above; M Walzer, *Spheres of Justice: A Defense of Pluralism and Equality* (United States, Basic Books, 1983); and P Selznick, *The Moral Commonwealth: Social Theory and the Promise of Community* (Berkeley, University of California Press, 1992).
[17] A Etzioni, 'Old Chestnuts and New Spurs,' in A Etzioni, (ed), *New Communitarian Thinking* n 16 above, p 16.
[18] See especially MacIntyre, 'The Virtues,' and Taylor, 'Hegel,' in Sandel, (ed), *Liberalism and Its Critics*, n 16 above. See also A Ferrara, 'Universalisms: Procedural, Contextualist, and Prudential,' p 28 and A Honneth, 'Atomism and Ethical Life: On Hegel's Critique of the French Revolution,' p 132 in Rasmussen, (ed), *Universalism vs. Communitarianism*, n 14 above.

are limited, however: individual rights should not trump community solidarity when the community would be worse off as a result. The implications for responding to atrocities are complex, and depend upon what the community determines to be most important. This may well be reconciliation or stability, it may be re-establishing justice and the rule of law, etc, but it will involve a decision by the community whether to seek prosecution or some lesser form of accountability, or no accountability at all.

Moving from Theory to Practice

Moral absolutes are quite difficult to define or pursue in transitional situations. Accountability for violations is not the only important 'good' to be pursued, although it is important. Many times, a tainted peace is achieved through sacrificing some degree of accountability. Other moral goods that might also reasonably be pursued; what is appropriate may be, so to speak, in the eye of the beholder (victim, nation, people, or international community).[19] I do not follow any one of the theories above, but propose to use them to identify key needs and goals of societies after conflict, and consider the degree to which local or distant justice will have a positive impact on these.

JUSTICE AFTER TRANSITION — LOCAL NEEDS

The needs of societies after transition are variegated, and may militate for or against punishment; the relevant considerations include not only the culpability of the criminal, but also other societal needs. These include stability, democratisation and the rule of law, reconciliation, and social learning, all of which require local actions to be addressed thoroughly.[20] Doing justice elsewhere may serve retributive purposes, may speak to the culpability of the criminal, might serve deterrent purposes and certainly is part of a process of reinforcing and elaborating upon global human rights norms, but it is far less clear that it will have positive effects upon the needs of the society itself.[21]

[19] J E Alvarez, 'Crimes of State/Crimes of Hate: Lessons from Rwanda,' (1999) 24 *Yale Journal of International Law* 365.
[20] I offer a more extended account of possible goals in C L Sriram, *Confronting past human rights violations: justice vs. peace in times of transition* (London, Frank Cass, 2004). See generally, C Hesse and R Post, (eds), *Human Rights in Political Transitions: Gettysburg to Bosnia* (New York, Zone Books, 1999); R I Rotberg and D Thompson, (eds), *Truth v. Justice: The Morality of Truth Commissions*, (Princeton, Princeton University Press, 2000).
[21] See E Lutz and K Sikkink, 'The Justice Cascade: The Evolution and Impact of Foreign Human Rights Trials in Latin America,' (2001) 2 *Chicago Journal of International Law* 19. See, in contrast, B Roth, 'Anti-Sovereigntism, Liberal Messianism, and Excesses in the Drive against Impunity,' (2001) 12 *Finnish Yearbook of International Law* 17, and R Paris, 'Peacebuilding and the Limits of Liberal Internationalism,' (1997) 22 *International Security* 54.

What, then, are those needs? I next address those needs and the appropriateness of internal trials to address them, and reflect briefly on the relative likely impact of external trials; the subsequent section will address the merits of external justice in more detail.

Stability, Democratisation and the Rule of Law

Transitional societies have numerous urgent needs, key among them stability and the enhancement of the rule of law.[22] What is most likely to aid in the achievement of these goals is frequently less clear.[23] Punishment domestically might prove counterproductive if it provokes a response from elements of the old regime that undermines the nascent democracy, weakening its legitimacy or undermining its authority over the security forces.[24] Such unrest could easily end the democratic experiment, and democratic stability and the goods it protects may be viewed as moral goods themselves.[25] Thus democratisers frequently choose to trade away some degree of accountability in the hope of entrenching the rule of law. Reformers will recognise that the chances of a handover are slim where members of the current regime fear future retribution, and may accept amnesties or other compromises to avoid a backlash.[26] Moreover, the large number of potential defendants may render prosecution of all of them unrealistic, resulting in limited or tiered prosecutions.

There is thus reason for scepticism as to the utility of domestic trials, though they also may have benefits: they may in some cases contribute to the reinforcement of the rule of law, human rights, and democratic processes.[27] However, external trials take place precisely because the rule of law and democracy have not been restored, or because they have but

[22] See R Teitel, 'Transitional Jurisprudence: The Role of Law in Political Transformations,' (1997) 106 *Yale Law Journal* 2009. S H Barnes, 'The Contribution of Democracy to Rebuilding Postconflict Societies,' (2001) 96 *American Journal of International Law* 86. See also H Strohmeyer, 'Collapse and Reconstruction of a Judicial System: The United Nations Missions in Kosovo and East Timor,' (2001) 94 *American Journal of International Law* 46.

[23] See J E Mendez, 'National Reconciliation, Transnational Justice, and the International Criminal Court,' and B R Roth, 'Peaceful Transition and Retrospective Justice: Some Reservations. A Response to Juan E Mendez,' (2001) 15 *Ethics and International Affairs* 25 and 45, respectively.

[24] L Berat and Y Shain, 'Retribution or Truth-Telling? Legacies of the Transitional Phase,' (1995) 20 *Law and Social Inquiry* 166.

[25] J Benomar, 'Justice After Transitions,' *Journal of Democracy* 4. See also D Orentlicher, 'Settling Accounts,' in N J Kritz, (ed), *Transitional Justice, How Emerging Democracies Reckon with Former Regimes* (Washington DC, United State Institute of Peace Press, 1995) Vol I, p 379; N Roht-Arriaza, 'Conclusion: Combating Impunity,' in N Roht-Arriaza, (ed), *Impunity and Human Rights in International Law and Practice* (New York, Oxford University Press, 1995) p 296.

[26] J M Van Dyke and G W Berkley, 'Redressing Human Rights Abuses,' (1992) 20 *Denver Journal of International Law and Policy* 246.

[27] See R J Rychlak, 'Society's Moral Right to Punish: A Further Exploration of the Denunciation Theory of Punishment,' (1990) 65 *Tulane Law Review* 299.

the state is not willing to act; they do little to aid in the strengthening of nascent democracies. It may also prove to be the case that external trials may actually serve to destabilise democratising societies by re-opening partially healed wounds or by offering a focus for hardliners seeking to regain power.

The Needs of Victims

Prosecutions may also be pursued as a way of addressing the needs of the victims. Victims of violence in general tend to lose their sense of control and autonomy, and often feel isolated. After state-sponsored human rights abuses, victims may feel especially isolated, as others in the community may distance themselves from victims.[28] Procedures must be installed that recognise their needs; however prosecutions are not the only viable alternative: truth commissions may also address these needs.[29]

Trials may serve certain needs of victims, such as public acknowledgement, but may also serve to re-traumatise them, particularly where interrogation of the victims may be particularly invasive or public proceedings are extensive. If domestic trials only address some of the needs of victims, external trials may address even fewer; they provide for acknowledgment, but by outsiders rather than by the actors implicated in the abuses. Further, given the distance of proceedings, the victims may achieve little sense of satisfaction; they may not even be aware of the proceedings, much less able to participate.

National Reconciliation

Post-conflict or transitional societies face difficulties in reconciliation, as victims and perpetrators may live in close proximity. Amnesty is often putatively offered to support national reconciliation, though this claim is often cynical. Alternatively, it may be the case that only trials, which allow an airing of grievances, can contribute to long-term social healing. They might also have a broader educative impact on the society, providing for the creation of public discourse and memory regarding events which might have been concealed for some time.[30] However, trials may also

[28] See generally J Malamud-Goti, *Game Without End: State Terror and the Politics of Justice* (Norman OK, University of Oklahoma Press, 1996); M Minow, *Between Vengeance and Forgiveness: Facing History after Genocide and Mass Violence* (Boston, Beacon Press, 1998) p 21.
[29] See M Popkin and N Roht-Arriaza, 'Truth as Justice: Investigatory Commissions in Latin America,' (1995) 20 *Law and Social Inquiry* 105. See D A Crocker, 'Reckoning with Past Wrongs: A Normative Framework,' (1999) 13 *Ethics and International Affairs* 47.
[30] M Osiel, *Mass Atrocity, Collective Memory, and the Law* (New Brunswick, Transaction Publishers, 1997).

have the reverse effect, and may perpetuate an unhealthy cycle of blame and scapegoating. In countries where massive abuses have occurred, mistrust of fellow citizens and the justice system is widespread, so any prosecutions might be suspect.[31]

Thus while trials may aid social reconciliation, there is cause for doubt. This doubt becomes greater where trials take place at great remove. Distant trials have less to offer to reconciliation, much as they may have less to offer for social learning: they may either fail to permeate society, or be interpreted in ways that actually undermine reconciliation.

DISTANT JUSTICE — WHAT DOES IT OFFER?

The putative advantages to domestic justice, already limited, appear to be more limited for externalised justice processes such as universal jurisdiction. However, there are some advantages of doing justice 'elsewhere' when it seems unlikely to be done at home. Where there are legitimate processes in place at home that will conduct genuine examinations of past atrocities, there ought to be no need for outsiders to step in, no need for judicial proceedings abroad to supersede local processes. In the absence of such local action, what can external judicial action offer?

Bringing Perpetrators to Justice

Perhaps the most obvious virtue of the exercise of universal jurisdiction, and the one most frequently invoked, is that it leaves perpetrators of atrocities with 'no place to hide'. There is at a minimum a certain symbolic effect: no longer can former dictators continue to live off the benefits of despotic rule, travelling abroad to seek expensive medical attention or even living abroad, far from the complaints of their victims. Such global reach serves at least one key normative goal, and one political goal, as outlined above. First, it serves the need to preference 'the right,' and to ensure that perpetrators get their due. Second, it might well have a demonstration effect, acting as a deterrent to other would-be offenders.

Retributivism

Retributivism requires that past abusers be punished for one simple reason: their actions were reprehensible. Selective prosecutions and

[31] On Rwanda, see M A Drumbl, 'Sclerosis: Retributive justice and the Rwandan genocide,' (2000) 2 *Punishment and Society* 287; see also M A Drumbl, 'Punishment, Postgenocide: From Guilt to Shame to *Civis* in Rwanda,' (2000) 75 *New York University Law Review* 1221.

domestic amnesties are thus unacceptable.[32] Some putatively retributive approaches may demand punishment not just because of the atrocious nature of the crime (that goes without saying), but also because failure to punish invites repetition though this is in truth a deterrence argument.[33]

Deterrence

Prosecution at home might deter potential individual violators, and strengthen societal respect for the rule of law and new democratic institutions. Failure to punish perpetrators will weaken the new state by raising serious doubts about the legitimacy and efficacy of the judicial system.[34] Successful punishment will not only enhance the credibility of the new regime, but also aid its consolidation and reform efforts.[35] While not every crime must be punished, at least some exemplary punishments are necessary for deterrent purposes.[36] When prosecution cannot take place where the crime occurred, it might be hoped that the spectre of prosecutions taking place anywhere in the world would serve as a powerful deterrent.

However, there is a practical problem with the hope that prosecution will deter future abuses: it is based on the assumption that the perpetrator believed herself to be acting wrongly, and had some expectation that such wrongdoing would result in negative consequences. Unfortunately, many leaders and active participants in authoritarian and abusive regimes have by all accounts not believed themselves to be doing something wrong. If this is indeed the case, then such abuses are un-deterrable, since potential abusers will see such punishments as unjustifiable, or simply as punishment of behaviour not analogous to their own.[37] Such deterrent

[32] R Rychlak, 'Society's Moral Right to Punish,' n 27 above pp 325–31. C S Nino, 'A Consensual Theory of Punishment,' (1983) 12 *Philosophy and Public Affairs* 289. A Neier, *War Crimes: Brutality, Genocide, Terror, and the Struggle for Justice* (New York, Random House/Times Books, 1998) pp 83–4.

[33] But see J L Mackie, 'Morality and the Retributive Emotions,' (1982) 1 *Criminal Justice Ethics* 4; J Murphy, 'The Retributive Emotions,' pp 1–9, and 'Forgiveness and Resentment,' pp 14–34, in J G Murphy and J Hampton, *Forgiveness and Mercy* (Cambridge, Cambridge University Press, 1988); compare Hampton, 'Forgiveness, resentment, and hatred,' pp 35–87 in the same volume. See W Sadurski, 'Distributive Justice and the Theory of Punishment,' (1985) 5 *Oxford Journal of Legal Studies* 47. See generally M Minow, *Between Vengeance and Forgiveness* n 28 above.

[34] See J Malamud-Goti, 'Punishment and a Rights-Based Democracy,'(1991) 10 *Criminal Justice Ethics* 1.

[35] See remarks of J Malamud-Goti in 'Symposium: Transitions to Democracy and the Rule of Law,' (1990) 5 *American University Journal of International Law and Policy* 1040.

[36] See P Akhavan, 'Justice in the Hague, Peace in the Former Yugoslavia?' (1999) 20 *Human Rights Quarterly* 737. See also P Akhavan, 'Beyond Impunity: Can International Criminal Tribunals Prevent Further Atrocities,' *American Journal of International Law* 7; See also J Malamud-Goti, 'Transitional Governments in the Breach: Why Punish State Criminals?' in N J Kritz (ed), *Transitional Justice*, Vol I, pp 189–93 n 25 above.

[37] N Roht-Arriaza, 'The Legal Setting,' in N Roht-Arriaza, (ed), *Impunity and Human Rights*, p 14 n 25 above; Rychlak, 'Society's Moral Right to Punish,' pp 309–10 n 27 above.

effects, it is to be feared, may be further attenuated where the punishment is carried out far from home; it is likely to be viewed as illegitimate, sporadic and thus unlikely to recur, or simply have little impact at all.[38] There is not strong evidence that international trials have a deterrent effect; some evidence demonstrates the reverse.[39] There is little reason to believe that prosecutions effected at a distance would be a greater deterrent.

CONCLUSION — A CALL FOR CAUTION

In many instances, resort to externalised justice might well be appropriate where local action is barred. At the moment, the fear that there will be a vast outbreak of politically motivated prosecutions through universal jurisdiction or international tribunals appears to be mere speculation. We have not seen frivolous or harassing prosecutions as yet, and the majority of jurisdictions that have heard, or are likely to hear such cases, have sufficiently embedded standards of rule of law and due process that it seems unlikely for the moment that they would allow such actions to go forward. It seems more plausible that in the near term we can expect that prosecutions will continue to be motivated by a genuine desire to defend fundamental human rights norms. However, it is not at all clear that doing justice at a distance serves its intended purposes.[40] It is also unclear that well-meaning external actors on the opposite side of the globe (or even in a neighbouring country) will take sufficient account of the balance that may already have been struck locally in coming to terms with the past. Taking action after a society has implemented an agonising set of choices may upset nascent stability and reconciliation.[41]

I have not meant to argue that pursuing war criminals and human rights abusers elsewhere is never appropriate, and never serves the needs of the societies where the crimes took place. I rather strike a note of caution. While limitations do not formally exist on the exercise of universal jurisdiction, the use of the principle of complementarity would be most appropriate. There is currently nothing to prevent external

[38] J E Mendez, 'National Reconciliation, Transnational Justice, and the International Criminal Court,' pp 30–1 n 23 above.

[39] D Wippman, 'Atrocities, Deterrence, and the Limits of International Justice,' (1999) 23 *Fordham International Law Journal* 473. See also C Rudolph, 'Constructing an Atrocities Regime: The Politics of War Crimes Tribunals,' (2001) 55 *International Organization* 655; see C Gustafson, 'International Criminal Courts: Some Dissident Views on the Continuation of War by Penal Means,' (1998) 21 *Houston Journal of International Law* 52.

[40] See generally G J Bass, *Stay the Hand of Vengeance* (Princeton, Princeton University Press, 2000). D Wippman, 'Symbolic Justice: The Past and Future of War Crimes Prosecutions,' (2001) 6 *International Journal of Human Rights* 1.

[41] See B R Roth, 'Peaceful Transition and Retrospective Justice,' pp 49–50 n 23 above. See also M Drumbl, 'Are There Limits'.

national courts from asserting primacy over local national courts, with the ramifications for the home society detailed above, though limits do exist upon the jurisdiction of internationally-constituted tribunals. [42] Care should be exercised in pursuing justice at a distance, particularly through universal jurisdiction, where the least constraints currently exist.[43] Otherwise, there is a risk that increasingly, resources will flow to external procedures that do not address some of the most salient needs of transitional societies, or even tend to undermine them.

[42] See Rome Statute of the International Criminal Court, UN Doc A/Conf 183/9 (1999), and Statute of the ICTR, UN Doc S/Res/955 (1994).

[43] The ICJ has indicated one limitation, that of foreign minister immunity, in the *DRC v Belgium* case: *Case Concerning the Arrest Warrant of 11 April 2000 (Democratic Republic of the Congo v Belgium)* (14 February 2002), ICJ, General List no 121 <www.icj-cij.org> (accessed 23 August 2004).

12

Globalisation and Human Dignity: Some Effects and Implications for the Creation and Use of Embryos

DERYCK BEYLEVELD AND SHAUN D PATTINSON

OUR LIFESTYLES DISPLAY the reality of globalisation. The bananas in our fruit bowls in the UK could have been growing in Ecuador just three days ago. Television and newspapers display images of people we have never met from places that we might never visit. Globalised trade, travel, and communication form the context in which attempts to regulate all human activities must now operate. The creation and use of human embryos is no exception. Global opportunities create many regulatory pressures. Pressures are generated by *patients'* demands and by patients travelling abroad for assisted reproduction services. Pressures are also created by *researchers'* demands and researchers travelling to other jurisdictions to take advantage of greater resources or a more favourable regulatory climate. In addition, pressures are created by the demands and economic power of potential *investors*. Combined, these pressures can distort attempts to create principled regulatory approaches to the creation and use of embryos. This chapter explores the impact of globalisation on the ability of states to adopt and maintain a consistent approach to the dignity of the human embryo.

We will start by examining competing conceptions of human dignity as they apply to the human embryo or fetus. After outlining the potential for creating and using functional embryos we will then examine the impact of globalisation on attempts to uphold a consistent regulatory position on the dignity of the embryo. We will argue that globalisation creates pressures for the adoption of one particular view on the dignity of the embryo, but this view itself poses regulatory challenges.

HUMAN DIGNITY AND THE *IN VITRO* EMBRYO

In practice, pure moral positions on the status and value of the human embryo are inevitably distorted by the political process. From a moral point of view, however, the status of the embryo is easy to map according to whether and to what extent the embryo or fetus is thought to possess human dignity. At one extreme, are moral positions holding that the embryo deserves the same level of protection as an adult human being. According to what may be called the *full dignity* position, full moral status is to be granted to the embryo from the moment of its creation. At the other extreme, is what may be called the *no dignity* position, which holds that the embryo itself has no intrinsic value or status, until at least birth. According to this position, an *in vitro* embryo is no more than a bunch of cells whose intrinsic features grant it no special protection. Between these two extremes are *limited dignity* positions, which hold that the embryo has a status resting somewhere between full and none. The most popular limited position is the *proportional dignity* position, which holds that the moral status of the embryo increases with gestational development until it obtains full moral status at birth or beyond. In short, the embryo can be recognised as having full dignity, no dignity, proportional dignity, or a fixed level of dignity below full dignity.

A consistent, principled approach to the dignity of the embryo requires that all human embryos be granted at least the level of protection required by the underlying conception of human dignity. To put it another way, if embryos, by virtue of their intrinsic properties, are to be granted dignity *to any degree*, then all entities possessing those properties must be granted that degree of dignity. It follows that philosophical stances on the dignity of the embryo have implications for political and regulatory policy. Those adopting the full dignity position cannot regard the intentional destruction of embryos as anything but impermissible. All non-therapeutic research on embryos (see below) must be held to be intrinsically wrong and equivalent to murder. Consequently, non-therapeutic embryo research must be prohibited and those who conduct such research must be thought of as murderers. At the other extreme, the no dignity position must hold that no intrinsic wrong is committed by the intentional destruction of an embryo. Any constraints on what may be done to an *in vitro* embryo must derive from the need to protect the dignity and interests of others. Between these two extremes, a limited dignity position cannot allow embryos to be treated as if they were adult humans or mere collections of cells. It follows that embryo research cannot be left as a free-for-all or prohibited in its entirety.

We have argued elsewhere that the existing regulatory approaches and policies in Europe are dominated by positions that suggest adherence to a limited dignity position.[1] For some countries, where the level of protection granted to the embryo and fetus increases with gestation age, the regulatory approach suggests adherence to a proportional dignity position.[2] In contrast, some countries adopt approaches suggesting adherence to the full dignity position. Prohibition of destructive research on embryos — as in Austria, Germany, and Ireland — suggests adherence to such a position. The political reality is, however, that the only way to view most regulatory approaches as principled is to view them as attempts to implement the no or a limited dignity position. Where, for example, the creation of embryos by research is prohibited but research is permitted on embryos left over from IVF treatment (surplus embryos), a coherent way of explaining this distinction needs to be found within a no or a limited dignity position.

In this chapter we argue that the pressures of globalisation pose a practical and ethical threat to the full dignity position, which render existing attempts to uphold this position morally incoherent. This is because globalisation creates pressures for the adoption of the no dignity or a limited dignity position. However, attempts to regulate coherently from a limited dignity position also pose regulatory challenges. One such challenge is presented by the need to interpret legislation so that subsequent scientific developments, particularly developments that produce additional means of creating functional embryos, are regulated in a way consistent with the underpinning conception of dignity.

USING, CREATING, AND EXPERIMENTING ON *IN VITRO* EMBRYOS

It is now over twenty-five years since the first child was born following the implantation of an embryo created outside the body. This technique, known as *in vitro* fertilisation (IVF), is permitted in all the developed countries of the world. Until the creation of Dolly, the most famous sheep in history, there were only two techniques known to be capable of creating a human embryo. The first, *standard fertilisation*, involves the fertilisation of the human egg with human sperm. The second, *embryo splitting*, involves splitting an existing embryo to create two separate

[1] See D Beyleveld and S Pattinson, 'Legal Regulation of Assisted Procreation, Genetic Diagnosis, and Gene Therapy' in H Haker and D Beyleveld, (eds), *The Ethics of Genetics in Human Procreation* (Aldershot, Ashgate, 2000) 215; and D Beyleveld and S Pattinson, 'Embryo Research in the UK: Is Harmonisation in the EU Needed or Possible?' in M B Friele, (ed), *Embryo Experimentation in Europe* (Bad Neuenahr-Ahrweiler, European Academy, 2001) 58.

[2] We suggest, below, that the UK position can be mapped onto a proportional dignity approach. Similarly, the three trimester framework adopted by the US Supreme Court in *Roe v Wade* 410 US 113, 93 SCt 705 suggests an underlying proportional dignity position.

embryos. Other methods of creating a functional embryo have now become feasible. Dolly was the result of replacing the nucleus of an egg with a somatic (body) cell nucleus.[3] This technique should also work with human cells.[4] More recently, a group of Chinese scientists have claimed that they have created a functional embryo by replacing the nucleus of a rabbit egg with a human somatic cell nucleus.[5] Thus, the Dolly technique has potential for both intra and inter-species application. Other means of creating a functional embryo are future possibilities. It might, perhaps, one day become possible to create a functional embryo without using gamete cells at all, by causing a somatic cell to develop into a functional embryo.

There are many potential uses of *in vitro* embryos and their functional equivalents. In particular, embryos created outside the body can be used for research, implantation, or as sources of tissue. Where embryos are used for research purposes, those purposes can be therapeutic, in the sense of intended to benefit the embryo itself, or non-therapeutic, in the sense of not intending to benefit the embryo. For convenience, in this paper, we use the term 'embryo research' to refer to non-therapeutic research, and use the term 'experimental treatment' to refer to innovative procedures carried out on embryos intended for the benefit of that embryo.

Embryo research has, and is likely to continue to have, a vast impact on the development and use of assisted reproduction techniques. In particular, research involving the creation and/or use of *in vitro* embryos has the potential to

(a) improve basic scientific knowledge;
(b) improve the selection of suitable gametes or embryos for assisted reproduction purposes;
(c) increase the possibilities for creating functional *in vitro* embryos and the understanding of those possibilities (eg, research into new fertilisation and cloning techniques);
(d) improve the development of *in vitro* embryos (eg, research directed towards improving the quality of the culture media);
(e) improve the quality of *in vitro* embryos (by, eg, genetic manipulation techniques); and
(f) lead to the therapeutic use of embryonic cells, particularly embryonic stem cells.

[3] See I Wilmut et al, 'Viable Offspring Derived from Fetal and Adult Mammalian Cells' (1997) 385 *Nature* 810.
[4] A few scientists claim to have created cloned human beings, but none of these claims have yet been substantiated.
[5] See C Dennis, 'Chinese Fusion Method Promises Fresh Route to Human Stem Cells' (2003) 424 *Nature* 711.

An individual research project might have multiple aims. Also, scientific research often produces unexpected results, which means that research initially performed with one set of aims might actually achieve or facilitate the achievement of other aims.

Embryo research conducted to develop therapeutic products for existing humans is proving to be particularly challenging for regulators. In 1998, a US research team successfully isolated human embryonic stem cells (ES cells). Whereas ordinary stem cells have potential as sources of new cells (blood stem cells could, eg, become blood cells), embryonic stem cells are pluripotent and thereby have the potential to become any one of hundreds of human cell-types. If it becomes possible to control the mechanism that causes pluripotent stem cells to become particular types of cells, then ES cells could be the source of many future cell-based transplantation therapies for serious diseases, such as Alzheimer's disease, Parkinson's disease, and diabetes. If this research proves successful, it might be possible to derive ES cells from cloned embryos (produced using the Dolly technique utilising human ova and cells from the prospective patient) so as to render the tissue produced immunologically compatible with the potential recipient. ES stem cell research, therefore, has greater potential for future tissue transplantation therapies. It is possible that artificially produced neural tissue could be created for the treatment of Parkinson's disease, muscle tissue for the treatment of heart defects, and so forth.

MAINTAINING A CONSISTENT FULL DIGNITY POSITION IN THE FACE OF GLOBALISATION

As we have seen, the full dignity position requires the prohibition of *in vitro* embryo research, which it regards as unethical and equivalent to murder. In Europe, Austria, Germany, and Ireland have prohibited embryo research and, on the face of it, appear to have adopted this position. The question that the full dignity position raises is whether and to what extent it is permissible for supporters of this position to utilise the results of embryo research conducted by those adopting other views on the dignity of the embryo. Some countries permit embryo research (subject to conditions) and others do not.[6] Yet those countries prohibiting embryo research must, in order to protect the full dignity of the embryo, regard embryo research conducted in other countries as illegal and unethical.

[6] See S Pattinson, *Influencing Traits Before Birth* (Aldershot, Ashgate, 2002) Appendix 3; and D Solter, D Beyleveld et al, *Embryo Research in Pluralistic Europe* (London, Springer-Verlaa, 2003).

Globalisation introduces many practical difficulties for the full dignity position. *First*, global communication and the movement of persons renders it inevitable that clinicians who deal with *in vitro* embryos in countries that prohibit embryo research will be aware of the results of embryo research conducted elsewhere. *Second*, embryo research conducted elsewhere will sometimes lead to improvements in the safety and efficacy of existing techniques and the development of new treatment options. *Third*, in practice, it will sometimes be difficult, if not impossible, to separate knowledge derived from embryo research from knowledge derived from non-research directed manipulation of human gametes and embryos. *Fourth*, unless heavy restrictions are put on the movement of persons, some clinicians and patients will travel to more permissive jurisdictions to obtain the benefits of embryo research, usually with the intention of returning to their home country afterwards. Insofar as research experience can improve the knowledge and technique of clinicians, patients are likely to seek out such clinicians, which in turn is likely to encourage clinicians to seek research experience. Indeed, we have argued elsewhere that the economic and prestige advantage generated by embryo research places considerable pressure on countries to weaken their regulatory stance against embryo research.[7]

This poses an intractable difficulty for states seeking to maintain a regulatory position tracking the full dignity view in an age of globalisation. On the one hand, the full dignity position must regard using the results of embryo research as even more problematic than the issue raised by use of the results of historically unethical experiments such as those conducted by the Nazis. To use the results of embryo research is to facilitate and encourage its continuance. Is it not hypocritical to hold a view of the moral status of the embryo that requires embryo research to be prohibited, yet to utilise the results of embryo research conducted elsewhere? If the intentional destruction of embryos is murder, then to encourage embryo research is to encourage murder! On the other hand, we have seen that globalisation makes rejecting embryo research and its results extremely difficult. This difficulty is exacerbated by the potential for ES cell research to produce therapeutic benefits. The upshot is that globalisation creates pressures for the adoption of regulatory positions that are not compatible with the full dignity view of the dignity of the embryo.

Are the practical effects of permitting IVF and other forms of assisted reproduction incompatible with a strict full dignity position? In practice, IVF produces more eggs penetrated by sperm than can survive if implanted and in no country prohibiting embryo research is it a requirement that they all be implanted so that they can develop into children. If these entities are embryos possessing full dignity, then a strict full dignity position

[7] D Beyleveld and S Pattinson, 'Embryo Research in the UK', n 1 above.

must require that they all be offered to someone who is willing to gestate them or not be created in the first place.[8] Moreover, as we have already indicated, in practice, the benefits of embryo research (particularly with regard to the safety and efficacy of existing techniques, and the development of new techniques) will be utilised by IVF clinics. To take just one example, the recent development of Intracytoplasmic Sperm Injection (ICSI), a variant of IVF now commonly used where the man's sperm cannot penetrate the egg unaided, was the product of embryo research. Failure to utilise advances achieved with the benefit of embryo research is practically impossible in a context where patients demand best practice and can travel elsewhere for treatment.

Many countries prohibiting embryo research allow IVF and other related forms of assisted reproduction. Consider the Irish position. The Eighth Amendment to the Irish Constitution (which forms Article 40.3.3) states that,

> The State acknowledges the right to life of the unborn and, with due regard to the equal right to life of the mother, guarantees in its laws to respect, and, as far as practicable, by its laws to defend and vindicate that right.

This is a clear and unequivocal adoption of the full dignity position. In addition to its effects on the legality of abortion,[9] this provision is thought to prohibit *in vitro* embryo research, and a number of reproduction practices (such as preimplantation genetic diagnosis). Additionally, the Medical Council's ethical guidelines declare that certain activities (such as creating embryos for research) constitute professional misconduct, thereby indicating that the Council will revoke the licence to practise of any medical practitioner who performs the prohibited activities.[10] Nonetheless, IVF is legal and practised in Ireland.

The German and Austrian legislation[11] seek to reconcile allowing IVF with the prohibition of embryo research. Both prohibit all embryo research (though both countries allow experimental treatment on embryos). Similarly, though allowing IVF, both countries limit the number of eggs that may be fertilised in one treatment cycle to a number that

[8] See below for the German approach to this difficulty.

[9] See, eg, *Attorney General v X* [1992] 1 IR 1. A proposed amendment to the constitution, which would have removed the threat of suicide as a sufficient ground for legal abortion, was recently rejected by a narrow majority in a referendum: see R Cowan, 'Irish Reject Tougher Law on Abortion', *The Guardian*, Friday 8 March 2002, 2.

[10] Section F of these guidelines is devoted to 'Reproductive Medicine'. The prohibition of creating embryos for 'experimental purposes' is in para 26.2: see Medical Council (Ireland), *A Guide to Ethical Conduct and Behaviour* 5th ed (Dublin, Medical Council, 1998) 39.

[11] Law No 275 of 1 July 1992, s 2 (Austria), and the Embryo Protection Law 1990, ss 1(1), 1(2), and 2 (Germany). For English translations see 'Austria. Federal Law of 1992' (1993) 44(2) *International Digest of Health Legislation* 247; and 'German Law Protects Embryos' (1990) *Bulletin of Medical Ethics*, 9 December.

may be implanted.[12] However, neither prohibits the destruction of all the eggs that have been penetrated by sperm left over from IVF treatment. Can the full dignity position, suggested by the prohibition of embryo research, be reconciled with the destruction of the surplus products of IVF? In this regard it is important to appreciate that the German legislation defines an embryo as coming into existence only from the time of fusion of the nuclei (syngamy) (s 8(1)), and the general practice in German clinics is to freeze the surplus material before this stage.[13] This enables them to claim that they are not freezing and storing embryos and, consequently, not destroying embryos if and when the frozen material is destroyed.[14] This is certainly a coherent full dignity position. However, it surely adopts an arbitrary view on when an entity becomes an embryo possessing full dignity, as it raises the question as to why the entity has no status before the fusion of the pronuclei (at which point it acquires full status). If the entity is assumed to gain whatever metaphysical property justifies possession of human dignity at this point, this presents the problem that possession of metaphysical properties cannot be identified scientifically. We have argued elsewhere that where possession of a metaphysical property is taken to determine possession of dignity, reliance on assumptions over whether a particular entity has this property needs to be restrained by a precautionary approach.[15] That is to say, since treating an entity that has full dignity as if it has no dignity is morally atrocious, we must treat all entities that might *possibly* have dignity as having dignity insofar as we can without violating our duties to entities that are more likely to have dignity. No matter how unlikely it is that an egg in the process of fertilisation has whatever metaphysical property embryos are thought to possess, if it is logically possible that fertilised eggs have this property, then they must be accorded some status. Depending on what the relevant metaphysical property is, this status must be either proportionally less status or the same status as that of a zygote at syngamy. In short, attempts to uphold the full dignity possession by relying on an idiosyncratic definition of an embryo cannot justify treating entities just short of satisfying this definition as worthless.

[12] The Austrian legislation prohibits the creation of more fertilised eggs than necessary, taking account of the current state of medical science, within a single menstrual cycle for 'promising and reasonable' assisted reproduction (s 9(1)). The German legislation prohibits attempts to fertilise more eggs than may be transferred into a woman within one treatment cycle and restricts that number to three (ss 1(iv) and (iii), respectively).

[13] See the Parliamentary Commission Report: Bericht der Enquete-Kommission, 'Recht und Ethik der modernen Medizin', 67–9.

[14] S 2(1) of the Act renders it a criminal offence to do anything to an embryo 'for a purpose not serving its preservation'. This seems to suggest that if all the viable products of IVF were embryos, then these entities could not lawfully be treated as if they were surplus.

[15] D Beyleveld and S Pattinson, 'Precautionary Reasoning as a Link to Moral Action', in M Boylan (ed), *Medical Ethics* (Upper Saddle River New Jersey, Prentice-Hall, 2000) 39.

This is not the only problem faced by attempts to identify the German position as being underpinned by the full dignity view. More strikingly, the recently enacted Stem Cell Act 2002[16] allows human ES cells to be imported for research under strict controls. Embryo research and deriving ES cells from embryos in Germany remain illegal (under the Embryo Protection Act 1990), but the products of embryo destruction conducted elsewhere can be imported! Presumably to prevent accusations of encouraging further embryo destruction, one of the conditions imposed by the 2002 Act is that the ES cells must have been derived before 1 January 2002 (s 4(1)(a)). In our view, this *ad hoc* political compromise is best saved from moral incoherence if it is viewed as a rejection of the full dignity position in favour of a restrictive limited dignity position, whereby many of the restrictions derive from concerns other than protecting the dignity of the embryo.[17] Indeed, the Austrian and German prohibition of embryo research is partly explained by a societal need to disassociate from historical acts done in the name of eugenics.

The potential of ES cell research has forced many similar political compromises that are difficult to reconcile with what are ostensibly full dignity positions. The President of the US, George Bush, announced in late 2001 that US federal funds would not be used to create new ES cell lines but could be used to fund research on ES cell lines already derived from embryos at the time of his announcement.[18] President Bush then estimated that 'more than 60 genetically diverse stem cell lines already exist'.[19] Only a month later the US government admitted that there were probably only 25 useable ES cell lines created before Bush's announcement, and this figure has itself been questioned as 'optimistic'.[20] Whatever the correct figure, this decision attempts to adhere to the full dignity position by seeking to obtain the benefits of past unethical conduct without directly encouraging future unethical conduct. This precursor to the German position raises the same tension: although the products of future embryo destruction cannot be used directly, the results of that research will no doubt influence the research on the products of past embryo destruction.

Contrast the Bush position with a recent European Commission proposal on the use of EU funds for research involving the derivation of ES cells.

[16] For an English translation see L Matthiessen-Guyader, (ed) *Survey on opinions from National Ethics Committees or similar bodies, public debate and national legislation in relation to human embryonic stem cell research and use: Volume I in EU Member States* (European Commission, September 2003).

[17] The German Justice Minister has in fact indicated that she wishes to liberalise the German law on use of ES cells (see <http://www.dw-world.de/ english/0,3367, 1430_A_1016499_1_A,00 .html>, downloaded 24 November 2003).

[18] 'Bush's Stem Cell Decision: Full Text', Friday 10 August 2001, *BBC News* (<http://news.bbc.co.uk/1/hi/sci/tech/1483579.stm>, downloaded 24 November 2003).

[19] *Ibid.*

[20] 'US Revises Stem Cell Estimate', Friday 7 September 2001, *BBC News* (<http://news.bbc.co.uk/1/hi/sci/tech/1530874.stm>, downloaded 24 November 2003).

The sixth framework programme of the EU left open the conditions for community funding of ES cell research conducted on cells derived from embryos left over from IVF treatment, and the Council and the Commission agreed to establish policies on this issue by 31 December 2003. Until this date, the Commission agreed to fund ES cell research only on banked or isolated ES cells in culture — an interim measure that is very similar to the Bush position. In July 2003 the Commission released a proposed funding policy to replace the interim decision.[21] This proposal was to allow EU funding for such research where the ES cells are derived from surplus embryos (ie embryos originally created for the purpose of IVF) *created before 27 June 2002*. This was the date that the sixth framework programme was adopted by the European Parliament and Council. This proposal is difficult to reconcile with a principled dignity position, because the full dignity position is against the intentional destruction of embryos no matter when those embryos were created, the no dignity position is incompatible with constraints designed to protect the interests of embryos, and the proportional dignity position rests the status of the embryo on its development, not the date of its creation. Fortunately, the recent vote of the European Parliament to allow EU money to be spent on ES cell research has rejected reliance on such a date.[22]

MAINTAINING A CONSISTENT PROPORTIONAL DIGNITY POSITION

Maintaining a consistent *proportional dignity* position simply requires that the state grant some protection to *in vitro* embryos, where this protection increases with gestational age but remains less than that of an adult human. The flexibility of this position renders it more adaptable than the full dignity position to global pressures created by patient, researcher, and investor tourism, and the economic and prestige pressures created by the potential benefits of embryo research. Nonetheless, the adoption of a morally coherent *proportional dignity* position (as with other limited dignity positions) does place limitations on the regulatory position of a state.

Consider the UK Human Fertilisation and Embryology Act 1990. In our view, this Act is incompatible with the view that the embryo has full or no dignity. The Warnock Report, which formed the basis of the 1990 Act, makes it clear that the underlying view is that 'the embryo of the human species ought to have a special status' albeit less than that of a living child

[21] COM (2003) 390 final.

[22] This vote took place on 19 November 03. For the text adopted by the European Parliament see: <http://www3.europarl.eu.int/omk/omnsapir.so/pv2?LISTING=AfficheTout&PRG=CALDOC&FILE=20031119&LANGUE=EN&TPV=PROV>, downloaded 24 November 2003.

or adult.[23] The long title of the Act states that its purpose is to 'make provision in connection with human embryos and any subsequent development of such embryos'. Moreover, since the embryo before 14 days is given less protection by the 1990 Act than the embryo after 14 days[24] and different gestational periods are used for the purposes of abortion,[25] this special status appears to be proportional to its development. The underlying conception of human dignity is, therefore, best viewed as one of *proportional dignity.* If we are right about this, this Act must be interpreted in the light of this conception of human dignity insofar as it is possible to do so without rendering the Act incoherent on other grounds.

In recent litigation the courts were faced with the question as to whether the 1990 Act encompassed the application of the Dolly technique to human cells. The 1990 Act unequivocally regulates both standard fertilisation and embryo splitting, because it imposes a licensing requirement on the creation, storage, and use of live human embryos *outside of the body* (ss 3(1) & 1(2)). However, 'embryo' is defined to mean 'a live human embryo where fertilisation is complete' (s 1(1)(a), including 'an egg in the process of fertilisation' (s 1(1)(b)) and many scientists take the view that the Dolly technique does not involve an act of fertilisation.[26] Our early view was that

> in practice, it is very likely that the term 'fertilisation' will be judicially construed to include the nuclear substitution of an egg, especially since the HFEA seems to be acting according to this construction of the term.[27]

This issue was the subject of a judicial review action taken by Bruno Quintavalle on behalf of the Prolife Alliance. At first instance, Crane J held that the Dolly technique did not involve the creation of an embryo, because it did not involve an act of fertilisation: *R (on application of Quintavalle) v Secretary of State for Health*.[28] The Court of Appeal reversed

[23] *Report of the Committee of Inquiry into Human Fertilisation and Embryology* (London, HMSO, 1984) (Cm 9314) (Report of the Warnock Committee) para 11.7.
[24] Under the 1990 Act, research on embryos is permitted under licence up to the appearance of the primitive streak or up to 14 days after fertilisation, whichever is the earliest (ss 3(3)(a) and 3(4).
[25] The Abortion Act 1967, which was amended by s 37 of the Human Fertilisation and Embryology Act 1990, created defences to the offences created by s 58 of the Offences Against the Person Act 1861 and the Infant (Life Preservation) Act 1929. For some purposes abortion is permitted up to 24 weeks, whereas for other (more pressing circumstances) it is permitted up to birth.
[26] See eg, I Wilmut and G Bulfield as quoted in Science and Technology Committee, *Fifth Report: The Cloning of Animals from Adult Cells. Session 1996–97* (London, HMSO, 1997) xii.
[27] D Beyleveld and S Pattinson, 'Legal Regulation of Assisted Procreation, Genetic Diagnosis, and Gene Therapy', n 1 above, 233. For slight misinterpretations of our position see 375 HC Deb 1144 (29 November 2001), and A Plomer, 'Beyond the HFE Act 1990: The Regulation of Stem Cell Research in the UK' (2002) 10 *Medical Law Review* 132, fn 61.
[28] [2001] EWHC 918.

the decision of the High Court by adopting a purposive construction implying a phrase into the relevant sub-section, so that it is read as defining an embryo as 'a live human embryo where [*if it is produced by fertilisation*] fertilisation is complete'.[29] The House of Lords agreed that the Dolly technique did not involve an act of fertilisation[30] and that the 1990 Act was to be interpreted purposively in the light of subsequent developments. This purpose was, their Lordships held, to provide for the regulation of live human embryos created outside the body, rather than to regulate only those embryos created by fertilisation. How, then, is s 1(1) to be read? According to Lord Bingham (with whose speech Lord Hoffmann and Lord Scott agreed),

> the four words ['where fertilisation is complete'] were not intended to form an integral part of the definition of embryo but were directed to the time at which it should be treated as such.... The essential thrust of section 1(1)(a) was directed to such embryos, not to the manner of their creation ... [31]

Lord Steyn was prepared to accept the Court of Appeal's attempt to read the words 'if produced by fertilisation' into s 1(1)(a), but preferred to treat the restrictive wording of s 1(1) 'as merely illustrative of the legislative purpose'.[32] Lord Millet held that the words of s 1(1) were *not* intended to define 'the word "embryo" but rather to limit it to an embryo which is (i) live and (ii) human' (para 45). Their Lordships' reading of s 1(1)(a) effectively means that the 1990 Act applies to any entity that is *functionally* a human embryo.

Some commentators have questioned the reasoning of the appeal courts. Plomer has argued that Crane J's reasoning is to be preferred, as the Court of Appeal's reasoning 'crosses the boundaries between statutory construction and judicial legislation'.[33] Grubb has argued that Crane J's decision was 'correct', and that, 'The clear wording of s 1(1) left a lacuna in the law but that was for Parliament rather than the courts to fill'.[34] In our view, Crane J's reasoning was flawed. As we will argue below, a consistent view on the dignity of the embryo requires a purposive construction bringing the creation of an embryo by the Dolly technique within the regulatory ambit of the Act, but there is a preferable construction to the specific construction adopted by the appeal courts.

[29] [2002] EWCA Civ 29, para 45.
[30] See [2003] UKHL 13, paras 14 (Lord Bingham), 20 (Lord Steyn), and 37 (Lord Millet).
[31] *Ibid*, para 14.
[32] *Ibid*, see para 26.
[33] Plomer, n 27 above, 158.
[34] A Grubb, 'Regulating Cloned Embryos?' (2002) 118 *Law Quarterly Review* 358, 361 and 362, respectively. See also his commentary on the decision of the House of Lords: A Grubb, 'Cloning (Cell Nuclear Replacement)' (2003) 11 *Medical Law Review* 135, especially 138.

Whether the appeal court decisions are unacceptable acts of judicial legislation must turn on whether they adhered to, or frustrated, the will of Parliament. According to the Act's long title, the purpose of the 1990 Act was to regulate 'human embryos and any subsequent development of such embryos' and to 'prohibit certain practices in connection with embryos and gametes'. Parliament had anticipated only two cloning techniques: the replacement of the nucleus of an embryo with the nucleus of a human cell or embryo (which was prohibited: s 3(3)(d)) and embryo splitting (which was regulated, as it involves the use of an existing embryo created by *standard fertilisation*).[35] Parliament had not, then, displayed an intention to prohibit the creation of *all cloned embryos*. It had, however, displayed an intention to regulate the creation and use of *in vitro* embryos. Some activities were licensed and some were prohibited, but no means of creating or using an *in vitro* embryo known at the time was left unregulated. Embryos were to be treated as possessing dignity, albeit less dignity than an adult human being. A human embryo created by the Dolly technique is no less a human embryo than one created by standard fertilisation; both are capable of developing into a human child. Whatever Parliament's specific intentions were with regard to embryos created by nuclear transplantation, their intentions would surely be frustrated if such embryos were not captured by the regulatory ambit of the 1990 Act. Parliament had, after all, regulated (by prohibition) the only nuclear transfer technique considered at the time.

Plomer warns that,

> The danger is that judicial creativity in such cases becomes a licence for the judge to import moral principles or policies into the law which turn out to be no more than a reflection of the judge's own individual moral views.[36]

While we recognise this danger, the moral principles in question are derived from the 1990 Act and the underpinning view on the dignity of the embryo. It is, therefore, submitted that it was right for the appeal courts to interpret the 1990 Act so as to regulate the creation of embryos using the Dolly technique *if at all possible.* This approach to the interpretation of the 1990 Act is analogous to the effect of s 3(1) of the Human Rights Act 1998 on the interpretation of legislation. S 3(1) requires all legislation to be to be interpreted as compatible with rights of the European Convention on Human Rights and Fundamental Freedoms given effect by the Human Rights Act *if it is possible to do so*. Similarly, we submit that

[35] The licensing authority has prohibited embryo splitting for treatment purposes. Para 9.11 of the current Code of Practice states: 'Centres should not attempt to produce embryos *in vitro* by embryo splitting for treatment purposes'. Failure to comply with the Code of Practice will expose the clinic to the risk of losing its licence: s 25(6).
[36] A Plomer, n 27 above, 159.

the correct reading of the 1990 Act requires its provisions to be read so as to give effect to the special status of the human embryo *if it is possible to do so*. To be clear, our use of s 3(1) is merely analogical, we do not claim that the Human Rights Act itself has extended the boundaries of purposive interpretation generally (a position rejected by Lord Steyn in the *Quintavalle* case).[37]

Could Parliament be taken to have had a more specific and prohibitive regulatory intention towards the creation of embryos by nuclear substitution? The Prolife Alliance argued that s 3(3)(d) demonstrates an intention to prohibit cell nuclear substitution *as such*.[38] This section renders it a criminal offence to replace 'a nucleus of a cell of an embryo with a nucleus taken from a cell of any person, embryo or subsequent development of an embryo'. If Parliament's intention was to prohibit nuclear substitution *as such*, then words would have to be read into s 3(3)(d) to fulfil this intention. On a literal reading, this section only prohibits replacing the nucleus of an *embryo*. The word 'embryo' cannot be interpreted to apply to an unfertilised egg, as this would render the rest of the Act — which has different provisions for gametes than for embryos — incoherent. Words could, however, be read into this section so that it has the effect of prohibiting the replacement of the nucleus of an embryo 'or any other cell' with another nucleus for the purpose of creating a functional embryo.[39] Why, however, must the Act be assumed to have the purpose of prohibiting the creation of an embryo by nuclear substitution *as such*? The only suggestion of any such purpose in the Act derives from s 3(3)(d) itself. Is it not a little odd to read words into a section to fulfil the purpose of that section when that purpose itself is said to derive from that very section? Interpreting the purpose of s 3(3)(d) in this way raises a more pressing problem: there is an alternative explanation of the purpose of s 3(3)(d) suggested by the underpinning conception of dignity. If it is a *prima facie* wrong to destroy or otherwise harm an embryo, and the version of proportional dignity underpinning the Act implies that it is, then replacing the nucleus of an embryo must be at least a *prima facie* invasion of that embryo's dignity.[40] There is no inconsistency in allowing some destructive use of embryos but not others, at least where the permitted

[37] [2003] UKHL 13, para 21.
[38] More precisely, the Prolife Alliance argued that s 3(3)(d) *successfully* prohibited the application of the Dolly technique to humans. Their Lordships unanimously rejected this argument: para 18 (Lord Bingham), para 28 (Lord Steyn), paras 34–5 (Lord Hoffmann); and paras 50–1 (Lord Millet). Lord Scott agreed with Lord Bingham and Lord Steyn.
[39] Their Lordships did not even consider the possibility of such a reading of s 3(3)(d).
[40] Lord Bingham notes that the White Paper (paragraph 36) referred to 'techniques aimed at modifying the genetic constitution of an embryo', and proposed that legislation 'should clearly prohibit all such activities, but with a power for Parliament itself, by affirmative resolution, to make exceptions to these prohibitions if new developments made that appropriate'. Section 3(3)(d) was, I infer, enacted to give effect to this recommendation (para 18).

destructive use is held to track the more important moral interests of beings with higher moral status. S 3(3)(d) prohibits embryo destruction as a result of nuclear substitution, it does not *by itself* imply a prohibitive attitude towards the creation of embryos by replacing the nucleus of an egg. Creating embryos using the Dolly techniques does not involve the destruction of embryos. In short, the existence of s 3(3)(d) can be coherently explained by reference to the dignity of the embryo without implying any secondary purpose with regard to nuclear substitution *as such*.[41] Thus, while Plomer is right to assert that the Act does not explicitly 'adopt moral principles endorsing the use of cloning techniques in embryo-research',[42] neither does the Act explicitly adopt any moral principles *requiring* embryos created by the Dolly technique to be treated differently from embryos created by fertilisation.

What the moral principles implied by the Act do require is that functional embryos be regulated *insofar as possible*, and there are less restrictive ways to achieve that purpose. However, as Plomer and Grubb point out, the appeal court decisions create certain 'anomalies'.[43] There are gaps with regard to the consent provisions, the time limit for which a cloned embryo can be kept or used, and the use of stem cells once they have been derived from embryos. The Act requires the written consent of gamete providers for the creation and use of an embryo (s 12(c) and Sch 3, para 6). Since a cloned embryo will be genetically almost identical to the donor of the somatic cell from which the nucleus is derived, Plomer and Grubb object that it is appropriate for that donor's consent be obtained. The House of Lords made short shift of this and related objections by noting that the licensing authority could attach conditions to licences. It could, for example, make it a condition of the licence that the somatic cell donor's consent be obtained.[44] In our view, this issue could have been avoided altogether by the adoption of a purposive interpretation capable of retaining the existing controls. Rather than reading words into s 1(1) or reading the provision as something other than an exclusive definition of a human embryo, the word 'fertilisation' could have been read purposively. Fertilisation, understood purposively, is the creation of an embryo by the joining of genetic material. The creation of Dolly the sheep merely showed that standard fertilisation was not the only means of creating an embryo by the joining of genetic material. Similarly, 'gamete' can be interpreted purposively by reference to the process in which a gamete is to be used. Use of gametes is regulated because of their potential to join with

[41] A Plomer, n 27 above, 156.
[42] *Ibid* at 160.
[43] *Ibid* 157. See also A Grubb, 'Regulating Cloned Embryos?', n 34 above, 362–4; A Grubb 'Cloning (Cell Nuclear Replacement)', n 34 above, 138.
[44] See, eg, para 16 (Lord Bingham).

other gametes to form embryos. The creation of Dolly has shown that an ordinary body cell can be rendered functionally equivalent to naturally occurring gametes. Thus, when body cells are taken for this purpose, they are functionally progenitors of future embryos in the same way that sperm are. This interpretation of gamete is consistent with the Act. See, for example, s 1(4), which states,

> References in this Act to gametes, eggs or sperm, except where otherwise stated, are to live human gametes, eggs or sperm but references below in this Act to gametes or eggs do not include eggs in the process of fertilisation.

This provision can be interpreted in a way compatible with a purposive approach derived from the proportional dignity position.

Our suggestion also avoids the implications that the appeal courts' interpretation has for the Act's time limit for keeping or using embryos defined under s 3(3)(a) as 'the appearance of the primitive streak'. S 3(4) states that 'the primitive streak is to be taken to have appeared in an embryo not later than the end of the period of 14 days beginning with the day when the gametes are mixed'. The appeal courts' reasoning renders this section inapplicable as no gametes are mixed, so the Act sets no limits on the time for which an embryo produced using the Dolly technique can be kept or used. Under our preferred interpretation, the 14 days begins when the cloned embryo is created as it is then that what are functionally gametes are mixed.

Our suggestion does, however, call for an explanation of the Human Reproductive Cloning Act 2001. This Act, passed between the decision of Crane J and that of the Court of Appeal, declares in s 1(1) that: 'A person who places in a woman a human embryo which has been created otherwise than by fertilisation is guilty of an offence'. This Act was intended to prohibit the implantation of an embryo created using the Dolly technique. It was intended that the Dolly technique be treated as creating an embryo by a means other than fertilisation. If fertilisation is defined consistently between the two Acts, then successful use of the Dolly technique cannot be treated as an act of fertilisation. Although the 2001 Act does not mention the 1990 Act, it was clearly passed to fill a gap in it. Historically, the courts have often been willing to interpret legislation so as to render it seamlessly compatible with subsequent legislation in the same area. In *R v Bourne*,[45] for example, MacNaghten J interpreted the word 'unlawfully' in s 58 of the Offences Against the Person Act (OAPA) 1861 to import related concepts from the later Infant Life (Preservation) Act 1929. The Infant Life (Preservation) Act, however, makes reference to the OAPA, and neither the 1990 Act nor the 2001 Act makes any claims about the wider application of

[45] [1939] 1 KB 687.

the definitions used. In principle, there is no reason why stipulative definitions cannot differ from one Act to another and Parliament has not explicitly foreclosed this possibility. Words always need to be read in the light of their underlying purpose, which is here inescapably moral, and here the proportional dignity view must provide an interpretative backdrop to the 1990 Act. Competing interpretative approaches to the 1990 Act render it less morally coherent. We submit that a consistent approach to the dignity of the embryo is better served by utilising different stipulative definitions for the two Acts. Unfortunately, this approach was rejected by the House of Lords in *Quintavalle*, as their Lordships clearly held that the Dolly technique does not involve an act of fertilisation for the purposes of the 1990 Act.[46]

CONCLUSION

We have argued that global pressures have produced political compromises that threaten the coherence of attempts to implement the full dignity position. If the intentional destruction of embryos is to be regarded as murder, then utilising the benefits of embryo research (especially where this is likely to encourage and facilitate its continuance) must be regarded as supporting and encouraging acts of murder. The realities of globalisation mean that in practice it is difficult, if not impossible, to consistently adopt a full dignity position while allowing IVF and related forms of assisted reproduction. Moreover, the full dignity position is being undermined by global pressures pushing for permissive approaches to ES cell research. States currently prohibiting embryo research, therefore, need to

[46] Another gap in the 1990 legislation, highlighted rather than created by the *Quintavalle* decision, concerns the use of ES cells. The 1990 Act regulates the creation, storage, and use of embryos, and derivation of stem cells from any embryo will involve the use of an embryo within s 3(1)(b) of the 1990 Act. It has, however, been suggested that use of stems cells derived from embryos falls outside its jurisdiction (see above Grubb 'Regulating Cloned Embryos?', n 34 above, 363–4). Unfortunately, the conception of human dignity in play here does not automatically imply a gap-filling solution. However, the Medical Research Council has established an oversight committee for the UK's new national stem cell bank, which is preparing a code of practice for use of isolated ES cell lines.

In our view, the *Quintavalle* decision has wider implications, because it means that the Chinese experiments — involving the insertion of a human somatic cell nucleus into a rabbit egg — would fall within the ambit of the 1990 Act if conducted in the UK. Neither the 1990 Act nor the *Quintavalle* case explicitly address this activity, but a purposive interpretation of the 1990 Act must treat the resultant entities as human embryos. Like the approach to embryo replacement, the 1990 Act takes a prohibitive approach towards interspecies conception involving human gametes (the mixing of human gametes with those of an animal is prohibited, s 4(1)(c), with one exception: Sch 2, para 1(1)(f)). The creation of these entities must either be subject to a licensing requirement (viewed functionally they are human embryos because they are capable of creating human children) or prohibited (viewed functionally the human somatic cells are used as gametes and the mixing of human and animal gametes is prohibited). The former approach is suggested by the *Quintavalle* decision.

consider whether they intend to adhere to the full dignity position and, if so, accept that globalisation requires more restrictive approaches than have been enacted hitherto. In short, globalisation is pushing states towards positions only reconcilable with the *no* or *limited dignity* positions.

Although globalisation poses little threat to states adopting the *proportional (or other limited) dignity* position, consistent adoption of this position also has regulatory implications. We have argued, using the UK legislation as an example, that the proportional dignity position has logical implications for statutory construction.

Regulatory adoption of a particular view on the dignity of the human embryo can create problems for individual citizens who adopt a conflicting view. While globalisation enables those who disagree with the regulatory policy of their own country to travel to a country whose policy adheres more closely to their view, to what extent can a citizen remain in a country with a regulatory policy that they consider to be immoral? This question poses particular difficulties for adherents of the full dignity position living in societies permitting research on embryos. While regulatory approaches produced by democratic societies carry the procedural legitimacy of that process, the intentional destruction of the embryo is held to be equivalent to murder. Similarly, can a state consistently hold the view that other states are actively encouraging the worst possible moral abomination while continuing to operate close economic links with those states? These questions will have to be left for a future paper.

It is easy to underestimate the effects and implications of globalisation on attempts to regulate the creation and use of embryos. Globalisation is in many ways antithetical to the maintenance of full moral pluralism.

13

What the World Needs Now: Techno-Regulation, Human Rights and Human Dignity

ROGER BROWNSWORD*

INTRODUCTION

THE STORY CURRENTLY being told about globalisation is one about the removal of barriers, about a deeper connectedness and interdependence, and about shifting spheres of influence.[1] In this story, it is trade rather than technology that acts as the principal driver. Nevertheless, modern technologies are far from marginal.[2] In particular, with the rapid development of communications and information technologies, especially the Internet, our connectedness is represented by our membership of a global information society.[3] Biotechnology, too, speaks to our connectedness but also to a number of our concerns — for example, to concerns about exposure to genetically modified organisms, about bio-prospecting and bio-piracy in the Third World, and about patent practice that privileges First World commercial interests. When we set these

*I am indebted to Mark Taylor and Natasha Semmens for reactions to a very early draft of the ideas in this chapter; and to the Leverhulme Trust, whose support enabled me to complete my work on this chapter.

[1] See eg, J Stiglitz, *Globalization and its Discontents* (London, Penguin/Allen Lane, 2002). For an account that is less focused on the economy, see B de Sousa Santos, *Toward a New Legal Common Sense* (2nd ed) (London, Butterworths, 2002).

[2] See eg, D Held and A McGrew, 'Introduction' in D Held and A McGrew (eds), *Governing Globalization* (Cambridge, Polity Press, 2002) 1 at 6; and cf, J Habermas, *The Future of Human Nature* (Cambridge, Polity Press, 2003) at 21 for a rather different analysis of the significance of the 'explosive' conjunction between 'globalized neoliberalism' and Darwinian-inspired biotechnological application.

[3] See eg, C T Marsden, 'Introduction: Information and Communications Technologies, Globalisation and Regulation' in C T Marsden (ed), *Regulating the Global Information Society* (London, Routledge, 2000) 1.

technologies in the specific context of global regulation, however, they become doubly significant, bearing on matters of both regulatory challenge and regulatory opportunity.

By 'regulatory challenge' (or 'regulability' as Lawrence Lessig would term it),[4] I mean the challenge of putting in place a regulatory framework for the development and use of these new technologies.[5] Judgments about the adequacy of such a framework, as about our success in rising to this regulatory challenge, will focus on at least three questions: namely, whether regulation is *effective*, whether it is *legitimate*, and whether its *design* is optimal. In general, I take it that our starting point is (i) that we want to derive whatever benefits we can from these new technologies (and their successors)[6] but (ii) that we must not permit such technologies to be developed or applied in ways that compromise fundamental values, especially human rights or human dignity.[7] By 'regulatory opportunity', I refer to the possible incorporation of new technologies within the regulatory apparatus employed in regulatory zones, whether global, regional, or local (whether directed at the development and use of ICT and biotechnology or, more generally, within the criminal and civil justice systems).[8] Here, again, I take it that we start in much the same place. If so, then, we accept that, for better or for worse, these technologies will insinuate themselves into our everyday lives;[9] and, whether we are thinking about the regulability of the new technologies or their regulatory power and potential, the essential challenge is to maximise their benefits consistent with respect for human rights and human dignity.

Francis Fukuyama's *Our Posthuman Future*[10] offers a helpful stage for the discussion in this chapter. For present purposes, Fukuyama poses

[4] L Lessig, *Code and Other Laws of Cyberspace* (New York, Basic Books, 1999).
[5] For reflections on the 'newness' of these technologies, see M E Price, 'The Newness of New Technology' (2001) 22 *Cardozo Law Review* 1885. For scepticism concerning the regulability of science, see eg, U Beck, *Risk Society* (trans M Ritter) (London, Sage Publications, 1992) (first published in German, 1986); and, against scepticism in relation to the regulability of the Internet, see eg, J Goldsmith, 'Against Cyberanarchy' (1998) 65 *University of Chicago Law Review* 1199.
[6] For speculation about the trajectory of these technologies, see J Garreau, 'The Next Generation' *Washington Post*, April 26, 2002, page C01. On the regulation of nanotechnology, see *Scientific Research: Innovation with Controls* (Better Regulation Task Force, London, 2003) 32–3.
[7] See eg the Preambles to the Convention for the Protection of Human Rights and Dignity of the Human Being with Regard to the Application of Biology and Medicine: Convention on Human Rights and Biomedicine, 1996, and to UNESCO's Universal Declaration on the Human Genome and Human Rights, 1997 (adopted by the UN General Assembly in 1998, see Resolution A/RES/53/152). See text below at 213.
[8] Cf, J Boyle, 'Foucault in Cyberspace: Surveillance, Sovereignty and Hardwired Censors' (1997–98) 66 *University of Cincinnati Law Review* 177.
[9] Cf, S H Cutliffe, *Ideas, Machines, and Values* (Lanham Maryland, Rowman and Littlefield, 2000) at viii: 'At the turn of the millennium, society is faced with both the promises and the dangers of scientific and technological endeavors (sic) such as the human genome project and electronic communication systems, developments that must surely change our lives, either for better or for worse, but most likely for both.'
[10] (London, Profile Books, 2002).

three important questions: first, whether we should regulate biotechnology; secondly, if so, why we should do so; and, thirdly, if we do try to do so, whether we have any prospect of regulating the technology effectively. In response to the first question, Fukuyama observes that, whereas some technologies are relatively benign (the development of the Internet, he suggests, falls into this category), others are dangerous. Further, in this latter category, whereas some technologies are obviously and transparently dangerous (for instance, nuclear technology), others are less obviously dangerous (but, *ex hypothesi*, dangerous nevertheless). Fukuyama places biotechnology in this latter division, from which it follows that he advocates a vigilant approach by the regulators. Turning to the second question (the answer to which is already implicated in the view that biotechnology is an insidiously dangerous development), Fukuyama suggests that the distinctive reason why we should regulate biotechnology is not that it is unsafe (otherwise it would be a transparently dangerous technology) but that it threatens to compromise human dignity. Finally, with regard to the third question, Fukuyama is well aware that doubts have been expressed about the capacity of regulators to hold biotechnology in check, especially when globalisation permits the technology to be developed in safe regulatory havens.[11] Nevertheless, he rejects a defeatist attitude and argues that the values at stake here are too important to be abandoned to the technology. Certainly, in a global setting, it would be irresponsible to deny that there is a significant regulatory challenge; and Fukuyama urges us to address it as best we can.

So stated, it seems to me that Fukuyama's position suppresses two important tensions, one arising from competing conceptions of human dignity, the other concerning the compatibility of human dignity with a technologically-driven regulatory strategy.

The first of these tensions speaks directly to the question of regulatory challenge, particularly to the question of legitimacy; for, it is relative to our particular conception of human dignity that we will judge whether the limits set by regulation are justified — whether we are over-regulating or under-regulating. There are, of course, many conceptions of human dignity but two in particular are focal for present purposes.[12] Whilst one conception ('human dignity as empowerment' as we may term it) captures much of our concern about information technology, especially about threats to privacy, the other conception ('human dignity as constraint' as we may term it) features prominently in many of the concerns expressed about biotechnology. Although these conceptions can

[11] L Silver, *Remaking Eden* (London, Weidenfeld, 1998).
[12] Much of this discussion, including the terminology, draws on D Beyleveld and R Brownsword, *Human Dignity in Bioethics and Biolaw* (Oxford, Oxford University Press, 2001).

sometimes operate alongside one another in registering their distinctive concerns, they are fundamentally incompatible with one another. In relation to the question of regulatory challenge, the import of this incompatibility is that there is a serious conflict written into our assumed starting point, namely that regulators should allow the benefits of the technology to be exploited while protecting human rights and *human dignity*. Are we presupposing human dignity as empowerment or human dignity as constraint? We need to know because there is a danger that we will argue past one another;[13] and, crucially, because we cannot regulate in a way that satisfies both conceptions of human dignity.

This first tension carries through to the expression of a second tension, one bearing on regulatory opportunity and effectiveness. The deep tension here is, quite simply, this: if we conceive of human dignity in terms of promoting and preserving the human capacity for autonomy, for making one's own choices, then does it follow that we must reject regulatory approaches that seek to achieve effectiveness by eliminating choice? If so, we may find that we must tolerate a degree of regulatory ineffectiveness for the sake of regulatory legitimacy.

Let us suppose that future global regulators (much like present local regulators) encounter compliance problems (compounded by complications arising from questions of jurisdiction, choice of law, extra-territoriality and the like) that diminish the effectiveness of their regulatory interventions.[14] As Fukuyama recognises, this may engender defeatism in some quarters. At least as likely, however, is the possibility that there will be a regulatory turn to technologies that promise to secure higher levels of compliance. As Matt Ridley has argued, technical fixes have been employed to make people healthier, wealthier, and wiser; and, by and large, what improves the quality of life is invention rather than legislation.[15] Regulators may well conclude, therefore, that what the world needs now is hi-tech social control (after hi-tech war comes hi-tech law). If so, where technology is deployed in support of traditional measures of prevention and enforcement, respect for human rights and human dignity continues to be relevant to the lines that we draw around the acceptable use of the technology (by the regulators). However, we can imagine an ideal-type, 'techno-regulation', in which the technology — whether by fixing the 'environment' or by fixing 'humans' — designs out the very possibility of

[13] For example, as in the Relaxin Opposition at the European Patent Office (HOWARD FLOREY/Relaxin [1995] EPOR 541). See R Brownsword, 'The Relaxin Opposition Revisited' (2001) 9 *Jahrbuch für Recht und Ethik* 3.

[14] Seminally, for electronic environments, see D R Johnson and D Post, 'Law and Borders: The Rise of Law in Cyberspace' (1996) 48 *Stanford Law Review* 1367; and, for more traditional environments, see eg H M Watt, *Choice of Law in Integrated and Interconnected Markets: A Matter of Political Economy*, 7 *Ius Commune*, Lectures on European Private Law (February 2003).

[15] M Ridley, 'We've Never Had it so Good — and it's all Thanks to Science' *Guardian Life*, 3 April 2003, 8.

non-compliance. With techno-regulation, we do more than improve the likelihood, or even certainty, of detection; we do more than improve the likelihood of prevention and compliance; with techno-regulation, we *guarantee* compliance by altogether eliminating any option for non-compliance. If information and biotechnologies are developed not merely to assist traditional forms of regulation but to operate as techno-regulatory solutions, and if we are committed to the conception of human dignity as empowerment, then we face the hard choice presented by our second tension: do we settle for less effective regulation (possibly permitting a degree of non-compliance that impinges on the rights and legitimate choices of 'victims') or, for the sake of effectiveness, do we adopt techno-regulation (seemingly abandoning the importance that we attach to the dignity of choice and, with that, much of the basis on which our thinking about responsibility, as well as rights, is premised)?

The chapter has four parts. In Part I, Fukuyama's discussion of new technology serves as a platform for the two principal tensions to be addressed in this chapter. In Parts II and III, we tackle the three dimensions of regulatory challenge — legitimacy (in Part II), and effectiveness and optimal design (in Part III). In Part IV, the focus shifts to regulatory opportunity and particularly the prospect of techno-regulation. The tension between rival conceptions of human dignity is introduced in Part II and, in Part IV, it develops into the tension between effective and legitimate regulation.

I FUKUYAMA, TWO TECHNOLOGIES, TWO DYSTOPIAS

For Fukuyama, the end of history (in the sense of the collapse of the communist bloc) marked the beginning of the present epoch of globalisation.[16] With communist polities no longer an option, the way was cleared for the spread of liberal democracies. As new markets were opened to trade and technology, global conditions became more congenial to respect for human dignity. The globalisation of individual autonomy and choice, of human rights and responsibilities, was underway. Yet, as Fukuyama reminds us, globalisation carries forward two dystopian visions that caution us as to the relationship between technology and human dignity. First, there is the Orwellian vision of the panoptican state and then there is Huxley's vision of a brave new world. Does information technology create a pathway to the former and biotechnology a pathway to the latter? According to Fukuyama, the answer to the first question is negative; but, to the latter, it is positive unless regulation succeeds in closing off the dystopian avenues.

[16] *Quaere*: is the present instantiation of globalisation (understood as the export and import of commerce and culture) distinctive? If so, is it the nature of modern technology that accounts for this difference?

According to Fukuyama, information technology is largely benign calling only for light regulation. Of personal computers and the Internet, he says:

> [T]hese new forms of information technology (IT) promised to create wealth, spread access to information and therefore power around more democratically, and foster community among their users. People had to look hard for downsides to the Information Revolution; what they have found to date are issues like the so-called digital divide (that is, inequality of access to IT) and threats to privacy, neither of which qualify as earth-shaking matters of justice or morality.[17]

This is not the place to open a debate about where equality of access (which is a major issue in the Third World) and respect for privacy (which is an obsession in the First World) stand on a scale of moral significance. Suffice it to say that, in a global context, because of inequality, IT is just one other thing to which the economically disadvantaged of the Third World do not have access; and, in the First World, violations of privacy would occur with or without IT. Most importantly, we have a pretty good idea of what we think the risks are with IT; and, if we think that respect for human dignity is an issue, we probably locate it in questions of privacy or, possibly, the Internet as a vehicle for pornography. We might also agree with Perri 6 that, for the most part, the regulatory challenges presented by the Internet are generic, already familiar, and susceptible to reasonably successful responses — despite predictions to the contrary, the Internet has not proved to be lawless.[18]

When we turn to biotechnology, however, Fukuyama sees a far more insidious and earth-shaking threat. What exactly is wrong with the biotechnologically engineered and pharmacologically controlled world depicted by Huxley?[19] According to Fukuyama, the A grade answer runs along the following lines:

> [T]he people in *Brave New World* may be healthy and happy, but they have ceased to be human beings. They no longer struggle, aspire, love, feel pain,

[17] n 10 above, at 182.

[18] Perri 6, 'Global Digital Communications and the Prospects for Transnational Regulation' in D Held and A McGrew (eds), *Governing Globalization* (Cambridge, Polity Press, 2002) 145. Nevertheless, we should note Lessig's insight (n 4 above) that so much of the 'law' of the Internet derives from the architecture of the technology, that it is a case of West Coast Code rather than East Code Code. And for development of Lessig's account of regulatory modalities, see A Murray and C Scott, 'Controlling the New Media: Hybrid Responses to New Forms of Power' (2002) 65 *MLR* 491.

[19] We might note, with Matt Ridley, that Huxley's dystopia actually 'owes nothing to nature and everything to nurture. It is an environmental, not a genetic, hell. Everybody's fate is determined, but by their controlled environment, not their genes. It is indeed biological determinism, but not genetic determinism. Aldous Huxley's genius was to recognise how hellish a world in which nurture prevailed would actually be.' See M Ridley, *Genome* (London, Fourth Estate, 1999) 304.

> make difficult moral choices, have families, or do any of the things that we traditionally associate with being human. They no longer have the characteristics that give us *human dignity*.[20]

This is not to say that biotechnology offers no benefits for human health and well-being. However, Fukuyama's point is that our deepest concerns about biotechnology cannot be captured by a utilitarian calculation. Thus:

> While it is legitimate to worry about unintended consequences and unforeseen costs, the deepest fear that people express about [bio]technology is not a utilitarian one at all. It is rather a fear that, in the end, biotechnology will cause us in some way to lose our humanity — that is, some essential quality that has always underpinned our sense of who we are and where we are going [ie, human dignity]...[21]

In short, we need the concept of human dignity to articulate our deepest concerns about the biotechnological revolution — and, sure enough, many would join with Fukuyama in contending that the reason why human reproductive cloning, germ-line gene therapy, genetic enhancement, embryonic stem cell research and the like must be regulated (meaning, by and large prohibited) is precisely that such practices compromise human dignity.[22]

At first blush, then, it seems that the difference between information technology and biotechnology is that, while the former presents a fairly transparent, but none too fundamental, threat to human dignity, the latter presents a less transparent and more fundamental threat — but, again, it is human dignity that is endangered. However, closer inspection of the idea of human dignity being appealed to in debates about the new technologies shows that we actually have two conceptions of dignity in play. What is more, these conceptions are not compatible with one another. Thus, the dignity concerns that we have about information technology

[20] n 10 above, at 6, emphasis supplied. To similar effect, see B McKibben, *Enough: Genetic Engineering and the End of Human Nature* (London, Bloomsbury, 2003). And, in his own distinctive way, J Habermas, *The Future of Human Nature* (Cambridge, Polity Press, 2003) at 73, has a similar view of what is at stake:

> Without the emotions raised by moral sentiments like obligation and guilt, reproach and forgiveness, without the liberating effect of moral respect, without the happiness felt through solidarity and without the depressing effect of moral failure, without the 'friendliness' of a civilized way of dealing with conflict and opposition, we would feel, or so we still think today, that the universe inhabited by men would be unbearable. Life in a moral void, in a form of life empty even of cynicism, would not be worth living. This judgment simply expresses the 'impulse' to prefer an existence of human dignity to the coldness of a form of life not informed by moral considerations.

[21] n 10 above, at 101.

[22] R Brownsword, 'Bioethics Today, Bioethics Tomorrow: Stem Cell Research and the "Dignitarian Alliance"' (2003) 17 *Notre Dame Journal of Law Ethics and Public Policy* 15.

and, concomitantly, about the Orwellian dystopia are quite different to the dignity concerns voiced against biotechnology and implicated in our discomfort at Huxley's dystopia. The sooner we understand what this difference amounts to, the sooner we can work out where we stand with regard to regulatory legitimacy; and the sooner we can begin to develop a strategy for regulatory effectiveness.

II REGULATORY CHALLENGE I: LEGITIMACY, AND TWO CONCEPTIONS OF HUMAN DIGNITY

By reference to which criteria should we judge a regulatory intervention to be appropriate and successful? Clearly, effectiveness is one criterion: whether the regulatory purpose is to facilitate or to prohibit and control, no intervention should be judged to be successful unless it is effective relative to the intended purpose. However, to judge success (or failure) solely in these terms would be to place no limits on acceptable regulatory purposes. Equally clearly, therefore, particular regulatory purposes must be legitimate; and, as we have said, in the context of regulating new technology, respect for human rights and human dignity is widely thought to be the acid test for legitimacy.

In this part of the paper, we can sharpen our thoughts about the rival conceptions of human dignity, human dignity as empowerment and human dignity as constraint, and begin to understand how they bear on the regulatory challenge. To do this, we can address the following five questions: (i) in what sense do we apprehend information technology as a threat to human dignity; (ii) in what sense do we apprehend biotechnology as a threat to human dignity; (iii) are there different reference points for the demand that human dignity should not be compromised; (iv) where does Fukuyama's conception of human dignity fit in the scheme of things; and (v) what is the bearing of the rival conceptions of human dignity on the regulatory challenge?

Information Technology and Human Dignity

In what sense might information technology be thought to compromise human dignity? Principally, if not exclusively, our concern is that modern technologies of information collection, communication and processing will jeopardise our interests in privacy and confidentiality. Jurisprudentially, at any rate in the common law world, the development of a privacy interest is closely connected with technologies that enable others to collect information about ourselves without our permission.[23] Ironically, state of the

[23] S D Warren and L D Brandeis, 'The Right of Privacy' (1890) 4 *Harvard Law Review* 193.

art information technology threatens to return citizens to a Gemeinschaft order in which others know all about us and the private realm is eroded.[24]

Such distinctive concerns about information technology — or, at any rate, the dignity interest on which we base our privacy interest[25] — draw on the foundational ideas of the Universal Declaration of Human Rights, 1948, and its partner Covenants on Economic, Social and Cultural Rights, 1966, and on Civil and Political Rights, 1966. In these historic instruments, we have the essential ingredients of human dignity as empowerment. For instance, each Preamble provides that 'recognition of the inherent dignity and of the equal and inalienable rights of all members of the human family is the foundation of freedom, justice and peace in the world'; and Article 1 of the Universal Declaration famously proclaims that 'All human beings are born free and equal in dignity and rights.' What this amounts to is the claim that each and every human being has inherent dignity; that it is this *inherent* dignity that grounds (or accounts for) the possession of *inalienable* human rights; and that, because all humans have dignity, they hold rights equally. So understood, it will be appreciated that the injunction to respect human dignity is much more than a demand that we commonly make in contexts where we detect demeaning or degrading treatment, or where we are trying to give weight to an interest in privacy, it is the infrastructure on which the entire superstructure of human rights is constructed.[26]

Whilst the strength of human dignity as a justificatory base for human rights has been assumed rather than clearly demonstrated, in practice, once it is accepted that human dignity should be respected, it tends to be accepted that we should also respect human rights. Indeed, human dignity as empowerment has its own version of the triple bottom line, namely: that one's capacity for making one's own choices should be recognised; that the choices one freely makes should be respected; and that the need for a supportive context for autonomous decision-making (and action) should be appreciated and acted upon. Human rights then translate these underlying demands into entitlements that are due to each human as of right — and the fundamental right, as proclaimed, for example, by the 'pro-choice' and 'death with dignity' slogans, is to make one's own choices and have those choices realised and respected. Insofar as information technology adversely interferes with the context for autonomous action, possibly by exerting some inhibitory influence, we have a prima facie violation of human dignity (as empowerment).[27]

[24] Cf Lessig, n 4 above, at 150.

[25] See, eg, EJ Bloustein, 'Privacy as an Aspect of Human Dignity: An Answer to Dean Prosser' (1964) 39 *New York University Law Review* 962.

[26] See A Clapham, *Human Rights in the Private Sphere* (Oxford, Clarendon Press, 1993) at 143, n 22, for examples of the recurrent use of human dignity in international human rights Declarations, Covenants, Conventions, and Resolutions.

[27] See, eg, C Fried, 'Privacy' (1968) 77 *Yale Law Journal* 475, esp 489–93 (re electonic monitoring).

There are, however, tensions in this paradigm. First, although the community of (human) rights is designed to promote individual autonomy, there are limits to the choices that individuals may be permitted to make. Most obviously, each individual is required to exercise his or her autonomy in a way that is compatible with respect for the entitlements of fellow humans. Less obviously, the way in which choice is exercised must not damage the context in which a community of rights-respecting humans is itself possible. If information technology may inhibit the exercise of autonomy, biotechnology may so alter the context that autonomy (and associated ideas that go to the heart of a community of rights and responsibilities) is itself threatened. In other words, even in a setting dedicated to individual empowerment, human dignity may be invoked as a reminder of the required restraints — constraint, as it were, for the sake of empowerment. Secondly, the more that we emphasise that human dignity relates to the capacity to make one's own decisions or one's own informed choices or the like, the less compelling it becomes to present the rights built on this base as *human* rights. If the paradigm within this approach is a human with the relevant capacities in a developed form, including the capacity to operate the rights constructed on the dignity base, then many born humans (young and old alike) will be excluded; and the unborn will also be excluded. This does not mean that human dignity as empowerment has no resource to protect the interests of such excluded humans but the protection cannot be in the form of a direct right. In other words, any protective argument will have to be constructed indirectly and any 'rights' held will be enjoyed only in a secondary sense.[28]

Biotechnology and Human Dignity

According to Fukuyama, biotechnology raises deep and difficult concerns with regard to respect for human dignity. At one level, these concerns are of the same order as those found in relation to information technology. Bioethics has become almost synonymous with an insistence that the biosciences and their associated technologies must respect human rights and, concomitantly, the importance of informed consent.[29] Indeed, in some cases, such as the circulation of genetic information, biotechnology gives rise to the very same privacy concerns that we find in relation to information technology.[30] It should not be thought, therefore, that the

[28] See further D Beyleveld and R Brownsword, n 12 above.

[29] For analysis of the necessity and sufficiency of consent as a justificatory reason within a human rights framework, see D Beyleveld and R Brownsword, *Consent in the Law* (Engle wood Cliffs NJ, Prentice Hall, forthcoming).

[30] Cf G Laurie, *Genetic Privacy* (Cambridge, Cambridge University Press, 2002).

conception of human dignity as empowerment has no purchase on biotechnology. Nevertheless, biotechnology invites another stream of dignitarian concern; and it is this strain of thought that we must isolate.

In the most recent bioethical instruments — reflecting the pressure for at least a semblance of consensus in what John Harris terms 'the globalisation of bioethics' [31] — we find human dignity increasingly articulated as a limiting principle. For instance, the Preamble to the Council of Europe's Convention on Human Rights and Biomedicine,[32] requires its signatories to resolve

> to take such measures as are necessary to safeguard human dignity and the fundamental rights and freedoms of the individual with regard to the application of biology and medicine.

Similarly, the Preamble to UNESCO's Universal Declaration on the Human Genome and Human Rights,[33] states that while

> research on the human genome and the resulting applications open up vast prospects for progress in improving the health of individuals and of humankind as a whole . . . [it is imperative] . . . that such research should fully respect human dignity, freedom and human rights.

Even in the relatively technical EC Directive on the Legal Protection of Biotechnological Inventions[34] (which deals *inter alia* with the vexed question of the patentability of biological material, including copies of human gene sequences), the need for patent law to respect dignity is emphasised.[35] Insofar as these ringing declarations in favour of human

[31] J Harris, 'Introduction: the Scope and Importance of Bioethics' in J Harris (ed), *Bioethics* (Oxford, Oxford University Press, 2001) 5–7.

[32] This Convention is sometimes referred to as 'the Bioethics Convention'. Its full title is Convention for the Protection of Human Rights and Dignity of the Human Being with Regard to the Application of Biology and Medicine: Convention on Human Rights and Biomedicine, 1996.

[33] This Declaration, adopted unanimously at the 29th Session of the General Conference on November 11, 1997, was the result of more than four years work carried out by the International Bioethics Committee of UNESCO. On 9 December, 1998, the United Nations General Assembly adopted Resolution A/RES/53/152 endorsing the Declaration.

[34] Directive 1998/44/EC; [1998] OJL 213/13.

[35] See, eg, Recital 16, according to which 'patent law must be applied so as to respect the fundamental principles safeguarding the dignity and integrity of the person.' See too, Recital 38, which provides:

> Whereas the operative part of this Directive should also include an illustrative list of inventions excluded from patentability so as to provide national courts and patent offices with a general guide to interpreting the reference to *ordre public* and morality; whereas this list obviously cannot presume to be exhaustive; whereas processes, the

dignity simply reinforce the demand that human rights should be respected, they say little that is new. However, the new turn here is the articulation of a rival conception of human dignity, namely 'human dignity as constraint'.

There is more than one pathway to this conception of human dignity; but, in practice, it appeals to a coalition (a dignitarian alliance so to speak) of Kantians, Catholics and communitarians.[36] Famously, for Kantians,

> Every human being has a legitimate claim to respect from his fellow human beings and is *in turn* bound to respect every other. Humanity itself is a dignity; for a human being cannot be used merely as a means by any human being…but must always be used at the same time as an end. It is just in this that his dignity (personality) consists, by which he raises himself above all other beings in the world that are not human beings and yet can be used, and so over all *things*. But just as he cannot give himself away for any price (this would conflict with his duty of self-esteem), so neither can he act contrary to the equally necessary self-esteem of others, as human beings, that is, he is under obligation to acknowledge, in a practical way, the dignity of humanity in every other human being. Hence there rests on him a duty regarding the respect that must be shown to every other human being.[37]

These remarks, if taken literally, are an open invitation to claim that commodification of the human body — whether in the form of commerce in human organs or tissue, prostitution, surrogacy for profit, or patenting human genes — compromises human dignity;[38] and the new dignitarians are happy to add to this list. Typically, then, human dignity as constraint also condemns sex selection and positive (eugenic) gene selection, germline gene therapy, embryo research and abortion, euthanasia and assisted suicide, genetic discrimination, and (perhaps top of its current list) human reproductive cloning. The list, though, is hardly closed; and there surely will be additions as technology opens up new bio-options and opportunities.

> uses of which offend against human dignity, such as processes to produce chimeras from germ cells or totipotent cells of humans and animals, are obviously also excluded from patentability.

Generally, on the Directive, see D Beyleveld, R Brownsword, and M Llewelyn, 'The Morality Clauses of the Directive on the Legal Protection of Biotechnological Inventions: Conflict, Compromise and the Patent Community' in R Goldberg and J Lonbay (eds), Pharmaceutical Medicine, Biotechnology, and European Law (Cambridge, Cambridge University Press, 2000) 157.

[36] Generally, see J Rendtorff and P Kemp, *Basic Ethical Principles in European Bioethics and Biolaw (Vol I: Autonomy, Dignity, Integrity and Vulnerability)* (Copenhagen, Centre for Ethics and Law, 1999).

[37] I Kant, *The Metaphysics of Morals* (translated and edited by M Gregor) (Cambridge, Cambridge University Press, 1996) (first published 1797) 209.

[38] Compare the assault on the proposition that informed consent is a sufficient justification in O O'Neill, *Autonomy and Trust in Bioethics* (Cambridge, Cambridge University Press, 2002), esp at 147–9.

Many commentators have little time for this conception of human dignity. The fact that its proponents can so readily target practices as compromising human dignity invites the accusation that some fancy rhetoric is being wrapped around some fairly primitive (and conservative) inclinations and intuitions — such appeals to human dignity, as Dieter Birnbacher has aptly observed, seem to be little more than a 'conversation stopper'.[39] If the new dignitarians are conversation stoppers, they are also conduct stoppers. However, when speaking to the regulatory agenda, they are more interested in the question of *what* should be prohibited rather than of *how* the prohibition should be made effective. If we think of human dignity as constraint as offering an account of *ordre public*, it tends to do so without the dimension of (procedural) due process that has been very much to the fore in the first generation of human rights supported by the empowerment conception of human dignity.[40] When we turn to matters of regulatory opportunity, this difference between the rival conceptions is of some significance.

In the larger picture, we might expect the globalisation of human rights to overcome the dignitarian conception, especially if the emergence of the latter owes something, as Gregory Stock puts it, to 'European sensitivities'.[41] And, in any event, so long as bioethics is a secular discipline, this particular articulation of human dignity might yet fall away as quickly as it has asserted itself. After all, it is a mere thirty years since philosophers could write that human dignity 'seems to have suffered the fate of notions such as virtue and honor (sic), by simply fading into the past'.[42] Nevertheless, there is some reason for thinking otherwise. In particular, neither utilitarian nor human rights perspectives give much support to the interests of conservatism, constancy and stability. And, as the pace of biotechnology accelerates, we should not underrate the felt need to find a way of registering our concern that we should at least have the opportunity to hang on to those parts of the human condition that are familiar. Admittedly, we might not think that constraint for the sake of constraint (or human dignity in service of conservative interests) has much to recommend it but, as we have remarked earlier, even those who support

[39] D Birnbacher, 'Do Modern Reproductive Technologies Violate Human Dignity?' in E Hildt and D Mieth (eds), *In Vitro Fertilisation in the 1990s* (Aldershot, Ashgate, 1998) 325. To similar effect, see, too, H Kuhse, 'Is There a Tension Between Autonomy and Dignity?' in P Kemp, J Rendtorff, and N Mattson Johansen (eds), *Bioethics and Biolaw Vol II: Four Ethical Principles* (Copenhagen, Rhodos International Science and Art Publishers and Centre for Ethics and Law, 2000) 61 at 74; and J Harris, *Clones, Genes, and Immortality* (Oxford, Oxford University Press, 1998) at 31.

[40] For an analysis of '*ordre public*' in the context of exclusion from patentability under Article 53(a) of the European Patent Convention, see D Beyleveld and R Brownsword, *Mice, Morality and Patents* (London, Common Law Institute of Intellectual Property, 1993). However, at that time (1993), the idea of compromising human dignity had not crystallised so clearly as is the case now.

[41] G Stock, *Redesigning Humans* (London, Profile Books, 2002) at 13.

[42] M Pritchard, 'Human Dignity and Justice' (1972) 82 *Ethics* 299, at 299.

the empowerment conception of dignity will do well to be sensitive to the need for self-restraint (and, possibly, regulatory constraint) for the sake of preserving a context in which autonomy can flourish. If this is so, a further alliance, between the conservative elements of dignity as constraint and the conserving elements of dignity as empowerment, may form to resist rapid application of new biotechnologies.

Are there Different Reference Points for the Idea that Human Dignity Should not be Compromised?

When we say that human dignity is compromised or not respected, we do so by reference to a particular conception of human dignity. Our judgments are, thus, relative to a particular critical standard. But, each conception (critical standard) itself operates with a distinctive point of reference.

One such reference point, as in the UDHR, is the idea that human dignity speaks to what is special or specific about humans, that is to say, what is intrinsically and universally distinctive about humans. As Fukuyama himself puts it, the demand made in the name of human dignity is one for equal recognition which implies 'that when we strip all of a person's contingent and accidental characteristics away, there remains some essential human quality underneath that is worthy of a certain minimum level of respect…'.[43] This reference point is to be contrasted with the idea that human dignity speaks less to what is special about humans *qua* humans and more to what is special about a particular community's idea of civilised life and the concomitant commitments of its members. Here, appeals to human dignity draw on what is distinctively valued concerning human social existence in a particular community — indeed, on the values and vision that distinguish the community as the particular community that it is and relative to which the community's members take their collective and individual identity.

Now, in principle, each reference point may be linked to both human dignity as empowerment as well as human dignity as constraint. In practice, though, whereas the former tends to be closely associated with human rights movements aimed at giving individuals the opportunity to flourish as self-determining authors of their own destinies, the latter (as expressed by the dignitarian alliance) combines a (Kantian) view of what is distinctive about humans (their dignity) with views about what defines life as civilised (and, thus, respectful of human dignity) in a particular community.

[43] n 10 above at 149. According to Fukuyama, although 'many would list human reason and human moral choice as the most important unique human characteristics that give our species dignity, I would argue that possession of the full human emotional gamut is at least as important, if not more so' (p 169).

Fukuyama's Conception of Human Dignity

Where does Fukuyama's version of human dignity fit into all this? Fukuyama rejects the idea that the essence of humanity (which grounds dignity) can be reduced to any one capacity, such as the ability to reason, or communicate, or make moral choices, or the like. Instead, he suggests that human dignity refers to a complex of such capacities including a range of characteristically human emotions.[44] Most importantly, it is the survival of this range of emotions, the human emotional gamut, that is put at risk by a utilitarian-inspired biotechnology. Thus:

> That aspect of our complex natures most under threat has to do with our emotional gamut. We will be constantly tempted to think that we understand what "good" and "bad" emotions are, and that we can do nature one better by suppressing the latter, by trying to make people less aggressive, more sociable, more compliant, less depressed. The utilitarian good of minimizing suffering is itself very problematic. No one can make a brief in favor (sic) of pain and suffering, but the fact of the matter is that what we consider to be the highest and most admirable human qualities...are often related to the way that we react to, confront, overcome, and frequently succumb to pain, suffering, and death. In the absence of these human evils there would be no sympathy, compassion, courage, heroism, solidarity, or strength of character. A person who has not confronted suffering or death has no depth. Our ability to experience these emotions is what connects us potentially to all other human beings, both living and dead.[45]

These remarks do not map straightforwardly onto either the empowerment or the constraint conception of human dignity. Without claiming that the following is indisputably the best interpretation of Fukuyama's position, it is at least a plausible reading.

At the time of the Enlightenment, two conceptions of human dignity were common. One was the universalist Kantian view that attributed dignity to each human intrinsically; the other was a hierarchical, rank-related, view, the so-called dignity of the nobles, against which Kant was reacting.[46] According to this latter view, dignity was not a quality possessed by all humans; it was only those of noble status who were so lucky. Giving this notion an interpretation that has some meaning for modern societies, we might distil from the dignity of the nobles a virtue ethics that values just the kind of attitude to which Fukuyama refers — that is, the development of a character that prepares one to deal with

[44] at 171–4.
[45] at 172–3. See, too, the concerns of the Nuffield Council on Bioethics, *Genetics and Human Behaviour* (London, October 2002) with regard to the medicalisation of conditions within the 'normal' range of behaviour.
[46] See M J Meyer, 'Introduction' in M J Meyer and W A Parent (eds), *The Constitution of Rights: Human Dignity and American Values* (Ithaca NY, Cornell University Press, 1992) 1, at 4.

adversity in such a way that the right balance is struck between seeking to overcome and succumbing.[47] Putting it in these terms, Fukuyama might ask whether the exemplars of this kind of dignity, Socrates and Mandela for instance, would be able to express these qualities in an environment where biotechnology has minimised adversity.

If we read Fukuyama in this way, it is not difficult then to relate such a virtue ethics to the general support that he gives to human rights (and by implication human dignity as empowerment). Under the empowerment conception, humans have a right to the kind of context in which they can operate as autonomous actors; and, importantly, as Joseph Raz has suggested, autonomy implies the provision of a context offering more rather than fewer options.[48] On this basis, we might oppose a technical fix for adversity, not because it suits a great many humans who now prefer the easy life, but because it removes an option for some who may prefer an environment that allows for the emotional gamut to operate. Biotechnology, in other words, should be available to fix things for those who so choose; but, so far as possible, we should permit those who do not so choose to do things their own way. For example, it would be consistent with autonomy to allow those couples who so wish to sex-select and screen their offspring, thereby avoiding disappointment; but those who prefer a riskier and less controlled engagement with reproduction should also be allowed to pursue such an option.[49]

If we interpret Fukuyama in the way sketched here, we can treat his position as a coupling of the empowerment conception with a virtue ethics that leaves some space for those who prefer not to join in the biotechnological revolution. And, this leaves the two principal conceptions of human dignity intact as the main contenders.

Competing Conceptions of Human Dignity and the Regulatory Challenge

What does this distinction between human dignity as empowerment and human dignity as constraint signify with regard to the regulatory challenge? Most immediately, it introduces serious uncertainty and conflict into the guiding regulatory principle that we should capture the benefits of new technologies unless they or their products violate respect for human dignity. The uncertainty in question is whether we should set our limits by reference to human dignity as empowerment or by reference to

[47] Cf, D Beyleveld and R Brownsword, n 12 above.
[48] J Raz, *The Morality of Freedom* (Oxford, Clarendon Press, 1986).
[49] Compare the preference stated by H Putnam in 'Cloning People' in J Burley (ed), *The Genetic Revolution and Human Rights* (Oxford, Oxford University Press, 1999) 1, and the overwhelming opposition to sex selection for non-medical social reasons revealed in the Human Fertilisation and Embryology Authority, *Sex Selection: Options for Regulation* (London, November 12, 2003).

human dignity as constraint. The conflict is that these conceptions of human dignity do not yield matching regulatory benchmarks: what appears to be a case of over-regulation from one dignity perspective may well seem to be a case of under-regulation from the other. Suppose, for example, that human reproductive cloning were thought to present no safety issues. Then, from the standpoint of human dignity as constraint, because human reproductive cloning is regarded as compromising human dignity, it should be prohibited; failure to do so would be a case of under-regulation. By contrast, from the standpoint of human dignity as empowerment, it is arguable that regulation should take a qualified permissive stance; outright prohibition would seem to be a case of over-regulation. Similarly, suppose that the question was whether or not to permit genetic testing or genetic information to be used by employers and insurers. Whereas proponents of human dignity as constraint might argue for an outright prohibition, proponents of human dignity as empowerment would almost certainly see this as an over-regulatory response — instead they would argue that such information (or testing) should be available for use provided that human rights were respected (and provided that abuses were compensated, possibly by the tort system).[50]

Without uncovering the problem of the rival conceptions of human dignity, we will misdirect ourselves into thinking that the limits of regulation are more straightforward than they are. Even if we can agree on the conception of human dignity towards which regulation should be orientated, we still have a very long way to go. In particular, we need to think about how interventions at any point within the 'regulatory range' (whether in the form of prohibition, permission, or facilitation)[51] might be rendered effective as well as about optimal regulatory design (because, even if we agree on our criteria of legitimacy, the processes by which we make our regulatory judgments are an issue in their own right). It is to these questions of effectiveness and design that we now turn.

III REGULATORY CHALLENGE II: EFFECTIVENESS AND OPTIMAL DESIGN

This part of the paper has a dual relevance, both completing our sketch of the regulatory challenge and initiating a sequence of ideas that brings us to matters of regulatory opportunity. Two claims are central here.

[50] R Brownsword, 'Human Dignity as the Basis of Genomic Torts' (2003) 42 *Washburn Law Review* 901; and D F Partlett, 'Misuse of Genetic Information: The Common Law and Professionals' Liability' (2003) 42 *Washburn Law Review* 489.

[51] As, rather obviously, with e-commerce; and, less obviously, with the granting of patents. On the 'regulatory range', see R Brownsword, 'Regulating Human Genetics: New Dilemmas for a New Millennium' (2004) 12 *Medical Law Review* 14.

First, given that regulation in local settings enjoys only limited success, we should not expect this to change significantly once we move from local to regional and global arenas. Secondly, some matters are easier to regulate than others.[52] On the face of it, new technology does not present itself as one of the simpler cases of regulability. For, there is not a natural culture of compliance in this field (indeed, one might believe that there is considerable regulatory resistance both on the part of those with commercial interests in the development of the technology as well as on the part of those wishing to access the technology); and fast-moving technology represents one of the most complex challenges at the level of regulatory design.[53]

Jumping ahead to matters of regulatory opportunity, the sequence of ideas continues with the thought that, if we judge that traditional forms of regulation largely do not work, we might think that our regulatory social engineering needs more technical assistance. If we take a decisive turn to technology (especially to techno-regulation), we will again confront the question of what it means to respect human dignity.

Before we get to this question, however, we must speak to the matters that concern us in this part of the chapter: namely, the limits to effective regulation in general and the difficulties of regulating the new technologies in particular.

The Limits of Effective Regulation

If we knew how to regulate effectively in local settings, then we might have a manual to guide us in larger regional and global arenas. Alas, regulation in local settings is hardly a story of runaway success.[54] Put crudely, where regulation runs with the grain, or a predisposition to comply, local law will enjoy a measure of success; but, where it runs across the grain, encountering economic or cultural resistance, it will do much less well.[55] Whether one explains this limitation in terms of systems theory

[52] Generally, see L Macgregor, T Prosser and C Villiers (eds), *Regulation and Markets Beyond 2000* (Aldershot, Ashgate, 2000).

[53] Compare M Feintuck, *Media Regulation, Public Interest and the Law* (Edinburgh, Edinburgh University Press, 1999) for the problems of regulating for the public interest in the context of powerful countervailing (and global) commercial interests, the importance attached to consumer choice, and a rapidly developing new media technology.

[54] See, eg, R Danzig, 'Towards the Creation of a Complementary Decentralized System of Criminal Justice' (1973) 26 *Stanford Law Review* 1 (for the view that criminal justice systems largely fail to control or to correct; and D Garland, *The Culture of Control* (Oxford, Oxford University Press, 2001)). Within the 'regulation literature', it is now a commonplace that 'command and control' hierarchical law does not work: see, eg, the very helpful overview in J Black, 'De-centring Regulation: Understanding the Role of Regulation and Self-Regulation in a "Post-Regulatory" World' (2001) 54 *Current Legal Problems* 103.

[55] See, eg, I Jenkins, *Social Order and the Limits of Law* (Princeton NJ, Princeton University Press, 1980).

and Teubner's regulatory trilemma, or in terms of gaps, counter-cultures, 'hearts and minds' or unintended effects, it is an all too familiar problem.[56] When local regulation attempts to go regional, these problems do not recede; and as regulation assumes global aspirations the limitations are exacerbated and, if anything, multiply. We might say, therefore, that global law is local regulatory limitation writ large.

Even where we might think that global regulation is reasonably effective, its architecture is not at all self-evident. We find mixes of vertically integrated nested regulation working alongside horizontal convergence and co-operation. We also find harbours, havens and holes in the regulatory network — all of which must give us pause in relation to any regulatory aspiration that moves beyond the local. However, where we are focusing on the regulation of rapidly developing technologies, things look even more challenging, even more complex.

Regulating Technology

In what sense does regulating technology, in a global regulatory context, represent a more complex challenge? Amongst the strands of difficulty, we can mention the following.

First, we cannot assume that there will be agreement in all regulatory zones (local, regional, and international) as to the benefits to be derived from the technologies (in some places, techno-optimism will prevail, in others the mood will be one of techno-pessimism).[57] In consequence, we are likely to find different regulatory thresholds in different societies. Michael Kirby has put this point in the following way:

> [T]he achievement of effective global regulation of a pervasive scientific development is extremely difficult to attain. Quite apart from the different interests of different societies, there are often different starting points for the very idea of regulation. In some societies, the view is adopted that science carries risks and should not be permitted unless scientists can demonstrate affirmatively that there is no risk, or that the risks are negligible. In other societies, there is a presumption that science should be free to advance and will ultimately benefit humanity, as it has generally done in the past.[58]

But, even if we agree that our regulatory mind-set towards science should be neutral (neither low benefit/high risk nor high benefit/low risk in its

[56] See G Teubner, 'After Legal Instrumentalism? Strategic Models of Post-Regulatory Law' in G Teubner (ed), *Dilemmas of Law in the Welfare State* (Berlin, Walter de Gruyter, 1986) 299.
[57] Cf, M Ridley, n 15 above. And, compare the contrasting assessments in, respectively, Europe (negative) and the United States (positive) as to the benefits of GM crops.
[58] The Hon Justice Michael Kirby, 'Human Freedom and the Human Genome: The Ten Rules of Valencia' (paper given at international workshop on Freedom and Risk Situations, Valencia, Spain, January 25, 1999) p 13.

predisposition), we still need to agree on the limits within which science and technology should be permitted to operate. This takes us to the second point of difficulty.

Secondly, following through on our discussion in Part II of this chapter, we cannot assume that there will be consensus as to the nature of human rights and human dignity, or the balance to be struck between facilitation and protection (the different attitudes towards data protection and privacy rights in the US and Europe is a case in point).[59] The fact that there are contested conceptions of human dignity is not just a philosophical puzzle; it bears on the politics and practice of regulation, on effectiveness as well as on legitimacy — witness, for example, the unprecedented (and, as events proved, unsuccessful) Franco-German attempt to secure full UN agreement to a worldwide ban on human reproductive cloning.[60]

Thirdly, if there is significant regulatory variation from one zone to another, compliance becomes problematic for the more restrictive regimes — not just in the sense that technology can be transferred from the more restrictive to the more permissive zones, but in the sense that the knowledge that this is so weakens the position of those regimes wishing to take a restrictive approach.[61]

Fourthly, where national economies need research and development in new technology, politicians will be nervous about regulation that discourages investment.[62] We have seen how much pressure was applied to pave the way, legally speaking, for e-commerce; and the economic agenda behind the UK's liberal regulatory framework for embryonic stem cell research is an open secret.[63] Local regulation, in other words, can operate only in the shadow of whatever local political will prevails; and the prospect of regulatory arbitrage between jurisdictions competing to host technology-based business militates against the adoption and enforcement of regional or international minimum standards.

Such considerations suggest that there will be a global patchwork of regulation, ranging from outright prohibition to unqualified permission, with various compromises forged along the way. However, in those parts of the world where the regulation of new technologies is treated as a

[59] See, eg, A Charlesworth, 'Data Privacy in Cyberspace: Not National vs International but Commercial vs Individual' in L Edwards and C Waelde (eds), *Law and the Internet* (2nd edn) (Oxford, Hart Publishing, 2000) 79.

[60] R Willing, 'UN Plan Would Ban Cloning to Create Human Baby', *USA Today*, September 23, 2002, at A3. And, for the contrasting positions taken in Europe with regard to embryonic stem cell research, see S Halliday, 'A Comparative Approach to the Regulation of Human Embryonic Stem Cell Research in Europe' (2004) 12 *Medical Law Review* 40.

[61] Cf M Radetzki, M Radetzki, and N Juth, *Genes and Insurance* (Cambridge, Cambridge University Press, 2003) (re offshore insurance).

[62] According to *Scientific Research: Innovation with Controls* (Better Regulation Task Force, London, 2003), at 8, by 2005, the biotechnology market in Europe will be worth $100 billion and will be responsible for employing some 3 million people.

[63] *Ibid*, at 26.

serious and ongoing business, there is a further dimension to be discussed, that concerning regulatory design.

Optimal Design

Where regulatory decisions are being made about new technologies, the form and style of the regulation and its institutional array needs very careful consideration.

There is a huge amount to be said about this and, once again, I can only begin to scratch the surface.[64]

Consider, for instance, the position taken by the Better Regulation Task Force. Here, we find a proposal for five principles of good regulation, namely, transparency, accountability, proportionality, consistency, and targeting.[65] Each of these head principles includes a set of sub-principles (transparency, for example, breaks down to include requirements for clarity of regulatory purpose and clear communication of that purpose, consultation, clear penalties for non-compliance, clear drafting of regulations, and information, support, and guidance for those subject to the regulation as well as time to comply); and proportionality and targeting (necessity) are geared to counteracting the tendency towards over-regulation in a risk averse society.[66] These principles already hint at the complexity (and, possibly, pro or ante-regulation disposition) in any attempt to develop guiding principles. However, these problems are dwarfed once it is appreciated that principles of good regulation tend to hunt in (oppositional) pairs.

This major difficulty is brilliantly sketched by Michael Trebilcock and Edward Iacobucci in a paper that focuses on the design of competition law institutions.[67] Although their focus is not on the regulation of technology as such, what they say is of general application. According to Trebilcock and Iacobucci, the five key pairs of opposition are between independence and accountability, expertise and detachment, transparency and confidentiality, efficiency and due process, and predictability and flexibility. In this light, three of the principles proposed by the Better Regulation Task Force look one-sided: transparency needs to be balanced with confidentiality, accountability with independence, and consistency

[64] See eg, A Murray and C Scott, n 18 above. And, for helpful regulatory 'maps', see Black n 54 above, esp at 134–5, and C Scott, 'Accountability in the Regulatory State' (2000) 27 *Journal of Law and Society* 38.

[65] See *Scientific Research: Innovation with Controls* (Better Regulation Task Force, London, 2003) Appendix C, p 36.

[66] *Ibid*, p 3: 'The UK has a proud history of scientific research and innovation, but in an increasingly risk averse society this is in danger of being undermined by excessive regulation.'

[67] M Trebilcock and E Iacobucci, 'Designing Competition Law Institutions' Cambridge Lectures, July 2001.

(or predictability) with flexibility. This, however, is not yet the end of the complexity because, as Trebilcock and Iacobucci point out, many of the values 'interact with each other in polycentric, mutually reinforcing or antithetical ways. For example, accountability may be antithetical to administrative efficiency by proliferating appeal or review processes, while expertise may enhance administrative efficiency. Confidentiality and flexibility may be antithetical to due process, but due process in turn may be in tension with expertise.'[68]

When we begin to apply these values specifically to the regulation of the new technologies, we can see why, even with the best will in the world, the challenge is so daunting. For example, it is commonly remarked that regulation needs to stay 'connected'; in other words, regulation will be ineffective or inappropriate if the frame of reference for the regulation has been left behind by the technology. This implies that regulation needs to incorporate a degree of flexibility or open-endedness; that regulation should, wherever possible, adopt 'technologically neutral' strategies;[69] that regulation should be interpreted purposively;[70] and that soft-law[71] or light regulation[72] might sometimes work better than hard or hard-wired confining law.[73] However, all these features geared for connection and flexibility militate against predictability and consistency. Equally, if connection is maintained by regular review of legislation,[74] the price to be

[68] at 9.
[69] As advocated, for instance, in relation to electronic signatures (see eg, P Samuelson, 'Five Challenges for Regulating the Global Information Society' in Marsden (ed), n 3 above, 316, at 320–1) and electronic money.
[70] As exemplified by the approach of the appeal courts in the Pro-Life Alliance case: see *R v Secretary of State for Health, ex parte Bruno Quintavalle (on behalf of Pro-Life Alliance)* 15 November, 2001 (Crane J); *R (Quintavalle) v Secretary of State for Health* [2002] EWCA, 18 January 2002; [2003] UKHL 13, 13 March, 2003. For discussion, see D Beyleveld and S Pattinson, 'Globalisation and Human Dignity: Some Effects and Implications for the Creation and Use of Embryos' (above, this volume chp12). Similarly, see the purposive approach of the Court of Appeal in *R (Quintavalle on behalf of Comment on Reproductive Ethics) v Human Fertilisation and Embryology Authority* [2003] EWCA Civ 667. For discussion of this interpretive approach, see R Brownsword, n 51 above; and for detailed analysis of the latter, see R Brownsword, 'Reproductive Opportunities and Regulatory Challenges' (2004) 67 *Modern Law Review* 304.
[71] On the soft law approach to the regulation of genetic testing, see P Gannon and C Villiers, 'Regulation of Genetic Testing' in L Macgregor, T Prosser and C Villiers (eds), n 52 above, 125 at 130.
[72] See, eg, J Huntley, P Carlyle, and J Caldwell, 'Competition in the Telecommunications Sector' in L Macgregor, T Prosser and C Villiers (eds), n 52 above, 99 at 119 (for the insight that the technology itself introduces an element of competition, driving out the need for *ex ante* regulation and encouraging a 'light touch at the tiller').
[73] See, eg, *Scientific Research: Innovation with Controls* (London, Better Regulation Task Force, 2003) at 5 on the 'mismatch' between the creative and exploratory nature of scientific research and regulation that tries to order the future but serves only to close off avenues of inquiry.
[74] See *ibid* at 31 where the Task Force recommends a three-yearly review for the legislation regulating research on embryonic stem cells.

paid is a period of regulatory uncertainty which, arguably, serves to chill investment and research initiatives.[75] Similarly, regulators charged with dealing with the latest technology must have expertise in their own right or, at least, access to expert advice[76] but without this impairing detachment; we also want regulators to be positioned to give quick decisions but without this opening them to the accusation of failing to give the matter full consideration. Again, as recent experience with the HFEA has highlighted, the demand for accountability can become insistent where an independent regulatory body moves ahead of popular opinion.[77]

Standing behind these particular design problems, there is a more general issue. In some parts of the world, it would be no exaggeration to say that there is now a crisis of confidence in both the practitioners and the custodians of new technology; scientists and regulators alike are no longer trusted. How is this breakdown in trust to be repaired? How are trusted institutions to be re-built? As Onora O'Neill has astutely observed, we can introduce processes that are designed to manifest trustworthiness (processes that are geared for transparency and accountability and the like) but this does not necessarily engender trust.[78] Paradoxically, procedures that are designed for trustworthiness might contribute even more to the breakdown of trust.

The lesson of all this is clear: if regulatory institutions are to enjoy the trust and confidence of the public (where there are concerns about the technology) as well as meeting the demands of their political and technological stakeholders, there are major design challenges ahead.[79]

[75] R Brownsword, 'Stems Cells, Superman, and the Report of the Select Committee' (2002) 65 *MLR* 568.

[76] As Justice Stephen Breyer has said, 'in this age of science we must build legal foundations that are sound in science as well as in law' (1998) 280 *Science* 537 at 558. However, experts all too easily become agents for regulatory capture or compromise: see eg, S Boseley, 'WHO "Infiltrated by Food Industry"' *The Guardian*, January 9, 2003, p 1 (remarking on the easy movement of toxicologists between private firms, universities, the tobacco and food industries and international agencies).

[77] See S Boseley, 'MPs Hit at Fertility Watchdog over Designer Baby' *The Guardian*, July 18, 2002.

[78] O O'Neill, *Autonomy and Trust in Bioethics* (Cambridge, Cambridge University Press, 2002), Ch. 6.

[79] Cf, Kirby, n 58 above at 18–19:

> Without global institutions, talk about prohibitions, regulations and moratoriums will be just that: talk. The absence of effective inhibitions amounts to a permit for science to go where any individual researcher chooses... Ultimately, we require effective institutions of regulation and lawmaking which render the genomic scientist and the technologist, like everyone else, answerable to the law.
>
> ... One of the biggest challenges to the freedom of humanity in the coming century will be to build more effective national and international institutions which can respond with appropriate speed and expertise to the challenges of science and technology.

IV REGULATORY OPPORTUNITY, TECHNO-REGULATION, AND HUMAN DIGNITY

In all dimensions, the regulatory challenge is a formidable one. However, the challenge of new technology is also an opportunity. The question that now presents itself is how we might respond to a situation in which, on the one side, there is a record of regulatory failure (regulatory ineffectiveness), but on the other side there is the prospect of employing new technologies to much greater regulatory effect. Is this an opportunity to be seized?

Regulatory Attitudes: From Defeatism to Perfectionism

Let us take stock with Fukuyama. Fukuyama contends that 'pessimism about the inevitability of technological advance is wrong, and it could become a self-fulfilling prophecy if believed by too many people. For it is simply not the case that the speed and scope of technological development cannot be controlled.'[80] To be sure, in the absence of regulatory intervention, technology can advance at its own pace — at any rate, it can do so subject to any popular resistance (such as we have seen in relation to GM crops and GM food). On the other hand, Fukuyama concedes that:

> [N]o regulatory regime is ever fully leak-proof, and if one selects a sufficiently long time frame, most technologies end up being developed eventually. But this misses the point of social regulation: no law is ever fully enforced. Every country makes murder a crime and attaches severe penalties to homicide, and yet murders nonetheless occur. The fact that they do has never been a reason for giving up on the law or on attempts to enforce it.[81]

So, we have pessimists and we have realists. However, whether we are pessimistic about traditional forms of regulation or realistic about their limitations in a global context, or in the face of new technologies, or both, the critical question is how we respond. One response is, in effect, to abandon regulation (resigning ourselves to a regulatory race to the bottom and the prospect of technological might dictating what is right). A second response is to try at least to hold the regulatory line, concentrating resources on the most serious violations.[82] However, the response that is particularly relevant to this discussion is one that might take a radically fresh look at traditional regulatory strategies — in particular involving a

[80] n 10 above, at 188. This is echoed by Kirby, n 58 above at 19: 'This is no time for despair, resignation or pessimism. It is an exciting time for science. But it is, equally, an exciting time for bioethics and law.'
[81] n 10 above, at 189.
[82] Cf Perri 6, at n 18 above, at 160, for a dispassionate analysis of what we can reasonably expect from our regulators.

turn to new technology to assist our regulatory projects. To respond in this way, regulators would not need to be perfectionists who aspire towards zero-tolerance and total compliance (although this might help). All that it would take would be the birth of a breed of regulators, willing to invest heavily in regulatory technologies, and to think creatively about how technology might improve regulatory effectiveness.[83] If there were such a birth, and if the spotlight were on compliance rather than detection, then we would need to think hard about where this new regulatory path might lead us.

The Regulatory Learning Curve: Towards Techno-Regulation

Regulators surely will learn from their experience of seeking to regulate the new technologies. They will understand more about the strengths and weaknesses of traditional forms of regulation as they will come to appreciate the potential of employing the new technology itself in a regulatory role — not merely to regulate the primary users of the technology (in the way, for example, that privacy enhancing technology might be deployed for the protection of Internet users, or filtering technology designed into mobile phones with Internet access so that children do not have access to chat rooms, pornography and gambling sites)[84] but far more broadly (in the way that genetic profiling, CCTV, computer mapping of crime, monitoring and tagging, and so on are already used in the criminal justice system). The speculation is that, alongside traditional forms of regulation, whether concerned with preventive channelling or dispute settlement, we will find new forms of technologically assisted regulation being piloted and adopted.[85] Once this happens, the technological revolution beyond the law will have initiated a technological revolution within the law.

[83] Cf Boyle n 8 above. At 204, Boyle remarks: '[T]he idea that the technological changes of the digital revolution are always outside the control of the state seems unproven. In fact, the state is working very hard to design its commands into the very technologies that, collectively, are supposed to spell its demise.'

[84] See D Batty and J McCurry, 'Children to be Shielded from Abuse via Mobiles' *The Guardian*, January 12, 2004, p 3. Which is likely to be more effective, a statute making the 'grooming' of children a criminal offence, or technology that denies children access to Internet sites where they are likely to fall prey to paedophiles? If we think the latter, we are already thinking like the new breed of regulator.

[85] Generally, see Black n 54 above at 137–8. Recent suggestions include the use of scannable microscopic computer chips embedded in high value bank notes (to combat forgery); vehicle number-plate recognition technology to enable cars to be matched against an insurance database (to combat driving without insurance); joined up information systems (following the murder of Victoria Climbié, to identify children at risk); and tagging paedophiles using global satellite positioning technology. On the first, see A Osborn, 'Computer Chip Plan to Fight Banknote Fraud' *The Guardian*, June 9, 2003, p 4; on the second, S Coughlan, 'Driving

This technological revolution within the law does not manifest itself at once as 'techno regulation' (in which compliance is technologically guaranteed). We can envisage three steps towards 'techno-regulation', the time frame for which is anybody's guess.

The first step is simply to employ technology within the framework of traditional 'obey or pay' forms of regulation. The technology might be designed to discourage non-compliance or to improve the chances of detection, or both; it may be pretty crude (for example, speed bumps or other traffic calming measures within restricted areas)[86] or it may be more sophisticated (for example, CCTV, smart cards, tracking devices, forensic data bases, and so on). No matter how sophisticated the technology, however, there is always the option of non-compliance and always some chance that one will not be detected. Nevertheless, there is reason to think that such technological assistance might make some areas relatively crime-free. For example, Richard Scase, in a report for the Office of Science and Technology's Foresight programme,[87] sketches a possible scenario for 2010 thus:

> City life is very different from twenty years ago. Government initiatives in the 1990s are now bearing fruit. Urban decline has been reversed and the fear of crime reduced due to technologies which enable citizens to call police response centres directly. The tagging of those with criminal records is now also taken for granted. Crime in London is almost non-existent in the wealthy, single-person, inner city areas.[88]

Of course, not all law-abiding citizens are expected to be quite so fortunate. For those who are socially excluded or who lack the skills to reap the benefits of the information economy, crime will be confronted on a daily basis; and, from the police perspective, containment may be accepted as the limit of what can be achieved.[89]

The second step is to improve the technology to the point where, although the regulatory form is traditional, non-compliance will be detected and the application of the designated sanction is guaranteed.

Home the Hot-Spot Danger Zone' *The Guardian* (Jobs and Money), September 13, 2003, p 6; on the third, M Cross, 'Eyes on the Child' *The Guardian* (Life), September 18, 2003, p 16; and, on the fourth, J Doward, '500 Paedophiles to be Tracked by Satellite Tags' *The Observer*, September 21, 2003, p 1. The introduction of 'smart' ID cards is another important indicator of this tendency: see A Travis and P Wintour, 'ID Cards are on the Way' *The Guardian*, November 12, 2003, p 1.

[86] For relatively straightforward design initiatives, see N K Katyal, 'Architecture as Crime Control' (2002) 111 *Yale Law Journal* 1039.

[87] R Scase, *Britain Towards 2010: The Changing Business Environment* (London, Department of Trade and Industry, 1999). <http://www.foresight.gov.uk> (Accessed 27 August 2004).

[88] *Ibid*, p 8.

[89] Compare *ibid*, at pp 8–9.

We can imagine an 'all-seeing' 24/7 surveillance technology that enables the regulators to monitor our every action. If we fail to comply, we will be seen—and, in conjunction with database and recognition technology, we will be identified. We can elect non-compliance but we do so in the certain knowledge that we will pay.[90]

Finally, there is the third step: traditional regulation gives way to 'techno-regulation'; rules and regulations give way to technologically secured results; in the ideal-typical case, compliance is guaranteed because non-compliance is not an option. How so? Possibly, this could be by a technical fix to the environment — for example, by taking cash as we know it out of the economy and replacing it with electronic money (which, admittedly, may simply replace one kind of crime with another) — or by a technical fix to human biology (employing programmes of genetic screening and selection) or by a combination of controlling interventions applied to human predisposition and our particular environment. With techno-regulation, there is no such thing as the perfect crime; criminality is no longer an option.[91]

Does The World Need Techno-Regulation?

What I have just said may be dismissed out of hand as pure science fiction.[92] If so, what follows should be treated as no more than a thought experiment. The question to be posed is whether, relative to the two conceptions of human dignity sketched already, such use by regulators of technology is acceptable.

In the lead up to techno-regulation, we can anticipate that concerns about human dignity will draw on the empowerment conception to challenge the regulators' invasions of privacy[93] — including, as Geoff Peck's

[90] See, eg, C Norris and G Armstrong, *The Maximum Surveillance Society: The Rise of CCTV* (Oxford, Berg, 1999) Ch 10.

[91] Cf L Lessig, *The Future of Ideas* (New York, Random House, 2001) at 249:

> Technology, tied to law, now promises almost perfect control over [artistic] content and its distribution. And it is this perfect control that threatens to undermine the potential for innovation that the Internet promises.
>
> To resist this threat, we need specific changes to re-establish a balance between control and creativity. Our aim should be a system of sufficient control to give artists enough incentive to produce, while leaving free as much as we can for others to build upon and create.

[92] But, in the context of information and communications technology, sceptics should read L Lessig, n 4 and 91 above. And, generally, on the importance of attending to regulatory modalities, including 'code' (ie, the architecture of a particular technology or combination thereof), see L Lessig, 'The New Chicago School' (1998) 27 *Journal of Legal Studies* 661.

[93] See, eg, D Whitfield, *Tackling the Tag: The Electronic Monitoring of Offenders* (Winchester, Waterside Press, 1997); C Norris and G Armstrong, n 90 above; C Gallagher, 'Nothing to Hide, Nothing to Fear?' *Liberty* (Autumn, 2003) 6; and A Gentleman, 'ID Cards may Cut Queues but Learn Lessons of History, Warn Europeans' *The Guardian*, November 15, 2003, p 21.

recent successful action before the European Court of Human Rights illustrates all too vividly,[94] their casual handling of personal data once collected and stored.[95] If the all-seeing all-knowing regulatory state is necessary for the protection of more compelling rights, some loss of privacy may be justified. However, serious questions about the limits of technological assistance will be raised for the context required by the conception of human dignity as empowerment can only take so much intrusion. Once we enter the realm of techno-regulation, however, the emphasis shifts to the elimination of choice, to the treatment of subjects as though they lack the capacity to choose. From the standpoint of the empowerment conception, this is surely the most fundamental kind of affront to human dignity. It throws doubt on the status of humans as bearers of both rights and responsibilities. Just as Castle, the sceptical philosopher in *Walden Two*, is uncertain whether the crime-free behaviourally engineered community is utopian or dystopian, the prospect of techno-regulation prompts the same equivocation and concern.[96]

Yet, this is such a blunt warning that it merits double-checking. Let us suppose that some action, X, is categorically contrary to human rights and a clear violation of the empowerment conception of human dignity. From the standpoint of human dignity as empowerment, there is no merit in X being permitted. Let us suppose that the only way of ensuring that X is not done is to techno-regulate it. On these premises, how can it be argued that for the sake of preserving human dignity as empowerment we should not take (techno-regulatory) steps to eliminate X, itself a clear failure to respect human dignity as empowerment? Three arguments may be advanced.

First, traditional regulation respects human dignity as empowerment by giving individuals the choice of compliance or non-compliance. Regulation is not neutral between, or indifferent towards, these options. Compliance is very definitely the preferred option. However, the final choice is left to individuals. Accordingly, it is implicit in this model that human dignity as empowerment values not only the right choice being made (to comply) but the process of choosing itself. Generalising this, human dignity as empowerment is committed to a framework for action in which humans may choose to do the right thing as they may choose to

[94] *Peck v United Kingdom* (2003) 36 EHRR 719. The Court held that the actions of a local authority in releasing CCTV footage that captured a suicide attempt by Peck engaged his Article 8 right under the Convention. And, whilst the local authority may have been well-intentioned in its desire to publicise the success of its CCTV scheme, its failure either to mask Peck's identity or to obtain his consent meant that its interference with his Convention right was disproportionate and unjustified.

[95] See too, O O'Neill, *Autonomy and Trust in Bioethics* (Cambridge, Cambridge University Press, 2002) at 109–110, for general cautionary remarks to this effect.

[96] BF Skinner, *Walden Two* (Upper Saddle River NJ, Prentice Hall, 1948, 1976) see, esp at 161 and 227.

do the wrong thing; to take away from humans their capacity to make wrong choices is an insult to their capacity for choice, the worst kind of affront to their dignity. Moreover, the sense in which the context for moral community is a seamless web might be added to this. Quite simply, if humans can no longer harm one another (rights are guaranteed), the need for morality disappears. Why should A remind B that X is categorically prohibited if B cannot do X anyway? In other words, moral community, inspired by the conception of human dignity as empowerment, presupposes a context populated by agents who can choose and agents who can be harmed (who are, in this respect, vulnerable).

Secondly, it may be objected that, even if techno-regulation could be justifiably used in the hypothesised case, it should be opposed as setting in motion a culture of diminishing respect for the importance of choice. The argument would run that, once it is accepted that it is legitimate to techno-regulate X where X is plainly wrong, it will not be long before it is accepted that it is legitimate to techno-regulate X where X is almost certainly, or probably, wrong; and so on down a slippery slope. The further we slide, the greater the risk that we mistakenly restrict options for action, and the greater damage that we do to the ideal of human dignity as empowerment. Moreover, if this is a plausible risk in a well-intentioned human-rights respecting liberal society, how much greater the risk of abuse in a society where the ruling class discovers the full potential of its techno-regulatory powers? In the face of such risks, the argument is that we would do better to steer well clear of techno-regulation — it is a temptation to be resisted.

Thirdly, it may conceded that techno-regulation would be justifiably used in the hypothesised case — or, at any rate, it would be justifiable as a measure of last resort. However, it would be argued that the premises underlying the hypothesised situation are implausible and atypical. The crucial premise is that X is categorically contrary to human rights. How many such Xs are there that would be applicable in a broad spectrum of contexts? If the answer is 'relatively few', then techno-regulation would be of little practical significance. Similarly, if many such (prima facie) Xs can be found but they are context-dependent, then the option for non-compliance might be too difficult to define and design out of existence — in which case, techno-regulation would be of little practical significance.

Of these three arguments, it seems to me that, although the third points to some difficulties in putting techno-regulation into practice, it is the first two that represent the real lines of resistance. Of these two, the second is weakened by its reliance on contingencies; essentially, it is an invitation to precaution that some subscribers to the empowerment conception may decline. The main line of defence, therefore, is the first argument which, in a further twist, echoes Fukuyama by insisting that (regulatory) failure and human misfeasance is part of the larger picture of respect for human dignity as empowerment.[97] And, pushing this thought yet a step further, we approach Jürgen Habermas' view that human dignity requires a context in which agents are what they are, and responsible for their actions, by virtue of genetic chance and individual choice.[98] In other words, human dignity as empowerment requires a particular balance of chance and choice which must be respected if instrumentally rational interventions (for more effective crime control, for more effective humans) are not to become self-destructive.[99]

What, though, of human dignity as constraint? Does it remain silent during the march towards techno-regulation? Although the new dignitarians have a conservative bias, it is difficult to see how they can oppose techno-regulation. It is true, they can arbitrarily oppose pretty much anything they choose, by insisting that it compromises human dignity. However, to oppose techno-regulation is to oppose the elimination of choice; and to argue that the elimination of choice, or the failure to respect choice, is what renders techno-regulation inconsistent with respect for human dignity is to play right into the hands of the empowerment conception. It follows, then, that even if there were no other reasons for rejecting human dignity as constraint (which, I should emphasise, is not at all the case),[100] we should anyway reject it if we reject the idea of techno-regulation.

CONCLUSION

Globalisation implies the spread of technology and its products, whether by accident or by design. Everything, including the law, is destined to

[97] Cf, L Lessig, n 4 above, on the relationship between efficiency and value. For example, at 208–9, he says:

> To identify a value that has been lost by efficiency is only to raise the question of whether in fact the 'efficiency' is efficient, or efficient to a particular end. The question is what the end should be. If the value that is lost is of value, then it may no longer be efficient to sacrifice it. Compare: driving on highways is a quicker way to get between two cities, but you lose a sense of the countryside when you drive only on interstate highways.

[98] J Habermas, *The Future of Human Nature* (Cambridge, Polity Press, 2003).

[99] As Habermas, n 98 above, puts it (at 92–3):

> The morality of egalitarian universalism stands in question as such. To be sure, this modern form of moral consciousness provides the only rationally acceptable basis for the normative regulation of action conflicts in pluralistic societies. But why shouldn't complex societies simply drop their normative foundations entirely, and switch over to systemic(!) (or, in the future, biogenetic) steering mechanisms?...Today, the relevant controversy is played out between a naturalistic futurism, committed to a technical self-optimization of human beings, and anthropological conceptions whose 'weak naturalism' has them accept the views of neo-Darwinism (and scientific views in general) without scientistically undermining or constructivistically outstripping the normative self-understanding of speakers and actors, for whom reasons still count.

[100] See the position defended in D Beyleveld and R Brownsword, above n 12.

become more 'hi-tech'. If we allow that these developments are capable of delivering benefits, there is also agreement that technology should not be promoted in ways that undermine respect for human dignity. However, what we make of this agreement depends on what we make of human dignity. If we operate with the conception of human dignity as empowerment, we will impose human rights limits on technology, especially privacy rights; but, if we operate with the conception of human dignity as constraint, we will take a much more restrictive view.

Globalisation also implies the spread of a common culture, of ideas like respect for human rights and human dignity. But, there is more than one conception of human dignity and, whilst human dignity as empowerment might seem to have better global prospects than its rival, human dignity as constraint has strong local roots. It cannot be assumed that regulators drawing on the empowerment conception will be pushing at open doors.

If regulators have less common cause than they assume (because of the competing conceptions of human dignity as a limiting principle), they anyway face a daunting task in bringing forward a strategy for effective regulation in local arenas — and *a fortiori* in regional or global arenas. To some extent they may be assisted by new technologies which present fresh regulatory options and opportunities. Some of these options will promise improved prospects for compliance and, provided that they do not unnecessarily or disproportionately impinge on privacy (or other interests protected by human dignity as empowerment), their greater effectiveness should be welcomed. However, if the regulatory opportunity leads to the adoption of 'techno-regulation' we have the ultimate challenge to human dignity as empowerment.

What can we say, then, about the credentials of the rival conceptions of human dignity? In the current climate, the new dignitarians stand out as not liking the choices that some would like to make, particularly choices that make use of the latest reproductive and bio-technologies.[101] This betrays not only conservative attitudes but a preoccupation with *what* should be regulated (with, so to speak, a black-list for regulators) rather than *how* it should be regulated. By contrast, because the jurisprudence of human dignity as empowerment is so closely associated with the modern human rights movement, its principal focus is on establishing an array of human rights (political and civil) that protects the citizen against the overbearing state. First generation human rights are largely directed at due process and the Rule of Law. This jurisprudence also serves to protect

[101] Recent examples include the Pro-Life Alliance litigation: *R v Secretary of State for Health, ex parte Bruno Quintavalle (on behalf of Pro-Life Alliance)* 15 November, 2001 (Crane J); *R (Quintavalle) v Secretary of State for Health* [2002] EWCA, 18 January 2002; [2003] UKHL 13, 13 March, 2003; and that involving the Hashmi family: See *R (Quintavalle on behalf of Comment on Reproductive Ethics) v Human Fertilisation and Embryology Authority* [2002] EWHC 2785 (Admin); [2003] EWCA Civ 667.

subjects against overbearing technologists who fail to take human rights seriously and, for example, co-opt persons into research projects without securing their informed consent. In the final analysis, however, it matters not whether the technology that abuses human rights is employed in the private sector or by public regulators — it needs to be checked by reference to human dignity as empowerment. It follows that, in the face of techno-regulation, it is only the empowerment conception of human dignity that already has the script of opposition written.

Finally, to return to Fukuyama, should we conclude that, once we take our lead from the empowerment conception of human dignity, we can see that the relevant concern about biotechnology, as about information technology, is that human rights are properly respected? Indeed, we should so conclude. Going beyond Fukuyama, however, what we should also conclude is that human dignity is liable to be threatened by the regulators (and their technological apparatus) as much as by the technologists whose activities they aspire to regulate.[102]

[102] This paper is not as explicit as it might be in relating the idea of 'techno-regulation' either to the literature on 'situational crime prevention' (particularly the kind of concerns raised in A von Hirsch, D Garland, and A Wakefield (eds), *Ethical and Social Perspectives on Situational Crime Prevention* (Oxford, Hart Publishing, 2000)) nor to that on 'smart' regulation (as elaborated in N Gunningham and P Grabosky, *Smart Regulation* (Oxford, Clarendon Press, 1998)). However, I have picked up these threads in a discussion of the fundamental importance (for both human dignity and our understanding of law) of regulatory pitch (in particular, whether or not regulators seek to channel conduct by engaging with the practical reason of regulatees); see, R Brownsword, 'Code, Control, and Choice: Why East is East and West is West' (2005) *Legal Studies* (forthcoming).

Index

Printed in the United Kingdom
by Lightning Source UK Ltd.
102872UKS00003B/61-153